15

An Intriguing Life

AN INTRIGUING LIFE

A Memoir of War, Washington, and Marriage to an American Spymaster

CYNTHIA HELMS,
with CHRIS BLACK

ROWMAN & LITTLEFIELD PUBLISHERS, INC.
Lanham • Boulder • New York • Toronto • Plymouth, UK

Published by Rowman & Littlefield Publishers, Inc.
A wholly owned subsidary of The Rowman & Littlefield Publishing Group, Inc.
4501 Forbes Boulevard, Suite 200, Lanham, Maryland 20706
www.rowman.com

10 Thornbury Road, Plymouth PL6 7PP, United Kingdom

Distributed by National Book Network

British Library Cataloguing in Publication Information Available

Library of Congress Cataloging-in-Publication Data
Helms, Cynthia.
   An intriguing life : a memoir of war, Washington, and marriage to an American spymaster / Cynthia Helms, with Chris Black.
       pages cm
   ISBN 978-1-4422-2131-4 (cloth : alkaline paper) — ISBN 978-1-4422-2132-1 (electronic) (print)
   1. Helms, Cynthia.   2. Washington (D.C.)—Biography.   3. Political culture—Washington (D.C.)—History—20th century.   4. Helms, Cynthia—Friends and associates.   5. Helms, Cynthia—Marriage.   6. Helms, Richard.   7. Great Britain. Royal Navy. Women's Royal Naval Service—Biography.   8. World War, 1939–1945—Participation, Female.   9. England—Biography.   10. Women immigrants—United States—Biography.   I. Black, Christine M.   II. Title.
   F200.3.H45A3 2013
   955'.05092—dc23
   [B]   2012033938

∞™ The paper used in this publication meets the minimum requirements of American National Standard for Information Sciences—Permanence of Paper for Printed Library Materials, ANSI/NISO Z39.48-1992.

Printed in the United States of America

To my family, who asked me to tell my story, with love and gratitude
and hope that their lives are as rich and rewarding as mine

CONTENTS

1

‒⟐‒

IN SEARCH OF A LIFE
OF MY OWN

In early April 1968, I drove my car into downtown Washington, DC. I had just returned from six weeks in Reno, Nevada, having secured a quickie divorce on March 25, ending a twenty-four-year marriage to Dr. Allan McKelvie. I had married a dashing Scottish navy doctor at the height of World War II while still a teenager. Much had changed since my days as a naïve young bride. On that day I had an appointment with my divorce lawyer, Edmund D. Campbell, whose office was near Fourteenth Street and New York Avenue, the heart of downtown, just two blocks from the White House.

For much of that year a thick psychic fog had enveloped me like a damp sheet, making even the most routine task seem awkward and clumsy. Ending a long marriage, upsetting my four children, and trying to seize control over and improve my own life clouded my thinking and at times overwhelmed me. It clearly never occurred to me that I might be in danger driving the few blocks from my room on Massachusetts Avenue to the lawyer's office. Had I been in my right mind, I would have realized that the city was quite literally on fire that day.

Just the night before, the Reverend Martin Luther King Jr., the inspiring civil rights leader, had been murdered in Memphis, Tennessee, as he stood on a motel balcony. In those days Washington was still very much a southern city in terms of style and custom. From a legal standpoint, one would call it de facto segregated. The laws did not separate blacks from whites, but practice most definitely did. The black residents lived in their own neighborhoods and were an almost invisible presence in the rest of the nation's capital. They were there but not there, if you know what I mean. Most African Americans held service jobs. They drove taxicabs, waited on tables, and mowed the beautiful green lawns in the largely white and affluent northwest quadrant of the city where I lived. While women were seen and not heard in those days, the black people were silent and barely seen. They were like the infrastructure of the city, like traffic signs or streetlights. Their presence was simply taken for granted. A few African American pioneers had broken through the social and cultural constraints of the time with tenacity and education to become doctors, lawyers, or even museum directors, like my good friend John Kinard. But black professionals were rare, and it was difficult to meet them in everyday life. As I came to understand later, the black community had its own hierarchy and social life, a life that was invisible to the white majority.

Dr. King's death broke the heart of a community that looked to him for inspiration and leadership. It also understandably enraged them. The rioting began within hours of his death on Thursday night, April 4. By the time I unwittingly drove to Ed Campbell's office the next day, the riots had spread to the core of downtown Washington. Teenagers raced through Woodward & Lothrop, screaming at the top of their lungs and scaring half to death every white person within earshot. As I hunted for a parking spot on New York Avenue, I came upon a mob of young African American men who had smashed the window of a clothing store. They literally clambered over the front of my car, their faces inches from my own. I sat transfixed in my locked car. While it was initially a bit frightening to see such ferocity and unleashed energy, I quickly realized the young men, the ages of my own children, were much more interested in the contents of the shop than in me. They seemed to be having a wonderful time, trying on the pilfered clothing in the middle of the city street. The exuberance was unmistakable. I rather enjoyed watching them trying on and discarding this jacket and that pair of shoes and having such a delightful time of it. I suppose it was a totally inappropriate response on my part. After all, they were looting, which is illegal.

The riots were costly in many ways for Washington. A dozen people died, and more than one thousand others were badly injured. More than twelve hundred buildings, including nine hundred businesses, burned to the ground. Sadly, the black community itself paid the highest price for the riots. Those businesses provided jobs to many black people, and many were owned by African American businessmen. The rubble remained untouched for decades, turning a once vibrant shopping area into a wasteland that only began to revive in the twenty-first century, a good forty-odd years later. The rioting also sparked more white flight from the city and a quicker exodus of the black middle class. Washington's ethnic breakdown flipped from two-thirds white and one-third black to three-fourths black and one-fourth white in twenty years. The true tragedy for the city was that the black middle class, the sturdy bedrock of the black community, effectively abandoned Washington, leaving behind the poorest, least educated, and least able to move up the economic ladder. The white people who remained tended to be the most affluent, best educated, and, not really surprisingly, most liberal. As a result, Washington, DC, became a polarized city of economic extremes over time, though still reliably Democratic in every national election.

It may seem a bit odd for an Anglo-Saxon woman raised in Great Britain to begin her memoir with this image of black rage, but the decade of the 1960s represented a turning point in my life. Just as the black people who had lived with so much unfairness and oppression for so long finally exploded and demanded the rights they were entitled to under the law, I made my own small step toward personal liberation. I certainly am not comparing myself to people who were systematic victims of overwhelming discrimination dating back to slavery. In many respects, I enjoyed a life of privilege as a white woman from a family with some means. But I did empathize with the black people's plight. I could hardly blame them for exploding in anger and frustration. I had some sense of what it felt like to be treated as less than an equal.

I did not burn my bra or make a dramatic political statement—I got a divorce. Nine months after asking for the divorce and effectively ending my first marriage, I married again, this time to a man who treated me as an equal partner. He happened to be a prominent public official, Richard Helms, the director of central intelligence (DCI) for the United States and a man both celebrated and denounced for keeping the nation's secrets. We were very happily married for thirty-four years, and during that marriage I came into my own as a separate and unique person.

Being born with a curious mind can be either a blessing or a curse. My nature made me an explorer of people, places, and things. I simply could not be any other way; some inextricable force impelled me to learn and seek and investigate and always keep moving forward. When I ended one marriage and began another after completing the most demanding years raising my children, I had the most wonderful time and some of the most rewarding experiences of my life. Moshe Dayan personally showed me his archeological artifacts at his home in Israel. King Hussein of Jordan carried my suitcase and took me water skiing. For four remarkable years as an ambassador's wife, I explored the treasures and culture of ancient Persia in Iran before the overthrow of Mohammad Reza Shah Pahlavi. I listened enrapt as Golda Meir delivered an impromptu geopolitical assessment of the world from the sofa in her living room while smoking a cigarette. The now famous society doyennes of Georgetown were some of my closest friends. I played cards with a Supreme Court chief justice, chatted with a Beatle, and cheered the first U.S. astronaut to circle the Earth.

I grew up on a farm in rural England and dodged bombs and steered boats through black seas as a young navy sea woman during World War II. Those experiences molded my character. But not until my middle years did I have the opportunity to satisfy the thirst of my mind. I dug through the treasures of the extraordinary richness of the Smithsonian Institution with a weekly interview radio show in what I view as the first "real" job of my life. Each week I interviewed another remarkable curator, scientist, or thinker from one of the obscure dusty cubicles of the United States' own national museum and learned about this specialty or that genre of art. A concern for the environment led me and a few friends to begin an environmental campaign to alert American housewives to the presence of toxic materials such as phosphates in soap and lead in paint many years before such environmental awareness became commonplace. In this way, I achieved a great deal of personal fulfillment.

An old proverb holds that history is written by the victors. Men were the victors. History was largely written by men and about male exploits and achievements. With a few exceptions, women were footnotes, playing a supporting role as wives, daughters, consorts, or muses. Women, from a historical perspective, were simply not that important, although, let's be honest, there would be no history without them. In the course of my lifetime, which has stretched over three-fourths of the twentieth century and a good part of the start of the twenty-first, the role and status of women in Western culture—indeed, in much of the civilized world—changed. It was a change for the better. In the twentieth century, women won or affirmed many rights, including the right to vote and to hold property, and the opportunity to express personal talent and pursue professions. Legal equality did not eliminate all discrimination, but the differences in the quality of lives of women between then and now are dramatic.

Opportunity for girls was far less expansive when I was born in 1923 between the two world wars. Victorian-era morality and mores lingered, limiting women to very specific roles as wives, mothers, and helpers. At the time, all those rules were characterized by submission to a male will. As I grew into adulthood and then middle age, women began chafing against the constraints of the traditional roles. I didn't just witness the changes that allowed women to become fully functioning and thinking members of society; I lived the changes. I quite desperately wanted a life of personal achievement independent of the accomplishments of my husbands and my children.

I spent fifty-eight years of my life married to two men. In many respects, the marriages defined my role in society. I was someone's wife. I was also the mother of four children who grew up to be excellent company as well as productive and caring and participating members of society. But I am more than a wife and mother, as are all women. I did not want marriage and my role as a wife and mother to be all that defined me.

In this book, I am going to tell stories from my life, stories my children and grandchildren are pressing me to tell. It feels very narcissistic to dwell on my life. I did not write a bestseller or invent a lifesaving medicine or achieve high position in government. Yet I have had an interesting life. Fate brought me into contact and proximity with the headliners and major events of my time. I knew Georgetown society matrons, presidents, kings, and ambassadors. My second husband, Dick Helms, one of the great spymasters of the twentieth century, had a wide circle of fascinating acquaintances and friends. I met many spies and much later learned the identities of the actual KGB spies assigned to spy on Director Helms's new wife in 1968.

At the same time, I came into my own as a person and must acknowledge I was helped along by the positive changes in the role and status of all women. My children, particularly my daughters, benefited from these same social and cultural changes and have had different choices and different opportunities. My daughters, Jill and Lindsay, both earned advanced academic degrees, just as my sons, Rod and Allan, did. I never lived through my children. I think parents who do that do a terrible injustice to their children. Yet I did find all of their achievements deeply satisfying. My grandchildren and great-grandchildren live in a world with almost unlimited opportunity, regardless of race or gender. It is human nature to take for granted that which is given. By understanding my history, perhaps they and others like them will more fully appreciate the wide, expansive opportunities they enjoy.

I begin this memoir in the 1960s, a decade of change and turmoil, which marked a great upheaval in my own life. With the benefit of hindsight, I see clearly that many forces helped me make the decision to end a less-than-fulfilling marriage and marry again. The cultural, political, and social order changed in the United States in the 1960s. The younger generation just coming of age, including my four children, questioned authority in a way that never would have been allowed, or even occurred to, their parents at their age. I was affected and influenced by the times in which I lived. The changes and liberation movements popping up all around me probably emboldened me to seek my own liberation. The 1960s, with all their messiness, came after a decade of extraordinary stability. Those of us who survived World War II yearned for calm, home, security, and peace after the trauma of war. An entire generation suffered from a kind of posttraumatic stress disorder. It was not a specific mental disorder, like the one that sadly afflicts so many combat veterans today, but the war did deeply affect almost every life at every level. I lost dear friends and a couple of beaus in combat. War made us hungry and cold and stressed. Nearly everyone was involved in fighting the Axis powers during World War II. Each person did his or her bit. The men fought or produced goods to support the war effort. Those on the front lines saw so much death and destruction that most of them would not speak of it for decades afterward. At home the women took over jobs once held by men to free up men for the front lines, testing and stretching themselves beyond what they could have imagined. Elderly women knitted and crocheted scarves and gloves and caps for those of us in the military service. For Europeans, the war was immediate and threatening, and the skittishness that comes from living with the fear of sudden death lingered even after the armistice.

World War II was a truly just war, one that absolutely had to be fought. The forces of oppression, hate, and true evil were simply compelling. No decent person could ignore the threat, and proudly, as a generation, we united and fought it. My generation has been called "The Greatest Generation," and I always felt that was a bit overdone. We did what we had to do. To ignore Adolf Hitler or the Japanese aggression was simply not conceivable. That we did not ignore it is, of course, a credit, but I still must say this task was thrust upon us, and I hope that every generation would aggressively fight that type of evil. Yes, we did step up to the challenge. But it was necessary. There truly was no other option.

World War II affected me more than I could have appreciated when I was an innocent teenager on the family farm in Essex, hanging on every stirring word Prime Minister Winston Churchill spoke on the radio each night. The radio was the Internet of our time, not nearly as comprehensive or responsive to whim but the primary source of news. The war made me grow up very quickly as I joined dozens of other young British women in the Women's Royal Naval Service (WRNS), known as the Wrens, doing the jobs that men had done manning the ships in British harbors. I grew from a protected eighteen-year-old girl into a more aware twenty-one-year-old woman, though I must say, as I look back, that when my military service ended because of my first pregnancy, I was still very naïve and unworldly and had so much yet to learn. Still, the war taught me a great deal about human nature, human frailty, and human strength.

Women like me got a taste of freedom during the war because they left home and hearth and worked in jobs once held by men. But the social order quickly righted itself afterward, and the war came to be seen as an aberration. The overwhelming desire for home led to an idealization of the nuclear family and the role of wife and mother. Fathers, of course, could still go out and slay dragons in the business and corporate world. But women went back to the traditional role of homemaker. The long-established patterns reasserted themselves more firmly than ever. I did not resist this impulse at the time. I, too, wanted to fit in and live a peaceful life.

As a result, the 1950s became a decade of remarkable conformity. The man in the gray flannel suit became an iconic image of middle-class striving in lockstep in corporate America. Men worked to build the postwar prosperity, and women stayed home to keep house and raise children. This was expected of us. And the needs of the baby boom generation, all those millions of children born after the war ended, kept most of us quite busy.

The 1950s passed in a blur for me, as they did for many women raising children. Caring for four small children consumed my life, but as they grew older and more independent, I began to wonder if this was all there was. The taste for freedom I experienced as a Wren never left me. I did not go to university because of my military service and marriage during the war. Despite an excellent boarding school education, I yearned to learn more and took classes from time to time when the children were still young. I was not alone. The yearning for more was building in others at the same time.

While racial minorities in the United States had been freed from slavery in the nineteenth century, equality before the law proved elusive, and opportunity remained severely limited. They had waited long enough and demanded their rights in a civil rights movement that culminated with major legislation in that decade. Young people were embracing their own music, clothing, and lifestyles and questioning every single symbol of authority in every possible way. At the same time, many women were also growing frustrated at not having an opportunity to do more than change diapers, drive carpools, and cook dinner. The women's movement did not explode as dramatically as the civil rights or antiwar movements. It was far subtler. Betty Friedan had published *The Feminine Mystique* in 1963. At the time I paid little attention to the fledgling women's movement, although her book described women just like me. The book grew out of a survey Betty Friedan conducted in 1957 for the fifteenth reunion of her Smith College class. She discovered that many of her classmates from the Class of 1942, mostly white, middle-class wives and mothers living in the suburbs, were unhappy despite the privilege and material comfort of their lives. She concluded that women needed meaningful work just as men do, and forcing women into limited roles as wives and mothers with no other outlets was "the problem that has no name." It was a powerful manifesto that acted as an ignition switch for many women living lives of quiet desperation in their split-level ranch houses in fashionable cul-de-sacs ringing the cities of the United States. My own source of inspiration was the pioneer women of America, not the frustrated suburban housewives who looked just like me; still, the fact that so many others were demanding rights and acting on their frustrations certainly affected the environment in which I lived. I clearly suffered from "the problem that has no name."

Sociologists have analyzed the postwar period more thoroughly than I ever can. I do remember that the Cold War, the battle for global dominance between the United States and the Soviet Union, was chillingly pervasive. We feared a nuclear war perhaps more than was realistic because we remembered so acutely the incendiary bombs of World War II. The Cold War mentality grew directly out of the experiences of World War II. Indeed, it effectively began, particularly for people like my husband Dick, who was involved in intelligence during the war, before the timbers cooled from the hot war of World War II. That the ideology of the enemy differed had little relevance.

Joseph Stalin morphed from an ally during the war into as fierce and feared an opponent as Hitler because of the manner in which he consolidated and kept power. He died in 1953, but the Communist threat became, if anything, more ominous as the decade wore on. Then, when the Soviets launched *Sputnik*, the first satellite to orbit the Earth in 1957, the entire Western world shuddered at the thought the Soviets would outpace the West in the technology of the future. Few people remember now, but the big issue between John F. Kennedy and Richard M. Nixon in the 1960 presidential campaign concerned the alleged missile gap with the Soviet Union.

I suspect that the postwar period of outward conformity and underlying anxiety temporarily tamped down a lot of deeper issues that could not be denied by the 1960s. The chemical mix of factors fermented over time and then exploded in a series of shocks. These seismic shocks were experienced throughout the entire country, but the impact was profound in the capital. Each affected me or people I knew well.

The Cuban Missile Crisis, which brought the United States to the brink of nuclear war during John F. Kennedy's term in office in 1962, terrified the entire country. Coming to the cusp of a nuclear war made everyone feel there was no time to waste. It was not so different from the carpe diem sentiment of World War II, but there was a different sense, too, of the pillars of establishment disintegrating. President Kennedy was assassinated on an early campaign trip in Dallas, Texas, in November 1963. I had attended teas held by the Kennedy women during the 1960 campaign at private homes in Washington. While I was not personally close to the Kennedy family, I knew many people who were very close to the Kennedys or held senior positions in the Kennedy administration, including the neighbors directly across from us on Forty-eighth Street, Charles and Martha Bartlett. The Bartletts introduced Jacqueline Bouvier to John F. Kennedy at a dinner party in their home in 1952. The president's death shocked everyone. John Kennedy was the first of his generation to win the White House, so his election signaled a coming of age for the World War II generation.

In 1968 both Martin Luther King Jr. and Robert F. Kennedy, the former attorney general and the assassinated president's younger brother, were killed. Middle-class children were getting high on hallucinogenic drugs and dropping out of school and society. Racial riots were taking place in nearly all the major cities, and antiwar demonstrations grew louder and larger by the month. Terrible riots disrupted the Democratic National Convention in Chicago in the summer of 1968. The world seemed a bit unhinged.

In the 1960s the young challenged the very premise of the war in Vietnam. I initially had a difficult time understanding how anyone could question the government on such a grave issue. The World War II experience had made me dutiful, patriotic, and ready to stand up and smartly salute the commander in chief, or, as it happened to be at the time, the queen. The universal draft put young male Americans at risk, however, and that draft contributed to the antiwar movement, which eventually succeeded in getting the United States out of Vietnam. I worried about the fate of my own oldest son, Rod, who graduated from Harvard in 1968. The draft did not end until 1973. Robert McNamara, the secretary of defense during the Kennedy and Johnson administrations, once said he had dropped off his own son at an antiwar demonstration as he went into a White House national security meeting. The war in Vietnam literally ripped apart families. It was all anyone talked about at dinner parties in Washington. You were for it or not; the arguments were incredibly intense.

My own neighborhood in the northwest quadrant of the District of Columbia, then as now, looked very much like a suburb. The real suburbs were just becoming established in the 1950s, thanks to Dwight D. Eisenhower's federal interstate highway initiative and the widespread desire to own a detached single-family house with a green lawn. The leafy streets of single-family homes in northwest Washington were populated by government officials, doctors, teachers, and other professionals. We led a comfortable life. By the 1960s, we belonged to a country club in northern Virginia. The children attended private schools. I played tennis with my friends. We went to cocktail parties and dinner parties at the homes of my husband's patients and friends.

Official Washington was still a relatively small community. There was a lot of cross-pollination between government, journalism, and the other professions. Service in the war, university education, and professional networks linked members of the community together. Many of my second husband's closest friends served with him in the Office of Strategic Services (OSS), the forerunner of the Central Intelligence Agency (CIA), during World War II. As a British native, I often came in contact with others from my homeland. The graduates of Harvard, Yale, Princeton, and other Ivy League universities kept in touch after leaving school. The old boys' network was very real. Moreover, government service brought together people from different parts of the country and different backgrounds. This was long before social networks like Facebook, but the social connections brought together disparate elements.

Of course, we were literally neighbors too. Our children attended the same schools. We worked on community issues together. My first husband's patients included government officials, and his charitable work overseas brought invitations to state dinners and embassy parties. I still have a photograph of me and my first husband taken with Alice Roosevelt Longworth, the headstrong and controversial daughter of President Theodore Roosevelt and wife of House Speaker Nicholas Longworth, who was considered one of the great wits of her time. She lived for ninety-six years until 1980. We watched Arabian horses with her in Maryland one day in 1960, and her wit was as sharp as ever. My second husband also knew Alice, and she liked Dick quite a lot, so we were regulars at her wonderful parties in the 1960s and 1970s. The interlocking circles of the different worlds in Washington at times gave my life a bit of a Zelig-like quality.

My first next-door neighbor in Washington was Major General Kester L. Hastings, the quartermaster general of the U.S. Army. He was responsible for providing food and clothing to the entire U.S. military and was intimately involved in construction of the Pentagon, then the world's largest office building, in a breathless seventeen months during World War II. He was a wonderful man, a career soldier, and a terrific neighbor. He mowed my lawn when he did his own. I appreciated it.

It often seemed as though the six-degrees-of-separation theory was at work in those years. I actually knew three of the women who were Jacqueline Kennedy's bridesmaids. Two of them told me they rarely saw her after the wedding. That made me wonder if the woman had any real friends. But I learned she did. Charles Whitehouse, a career Foreign Service officer who had worked in the early years of the CIA, kept an eye on Mrs. Kennedy's horse at Paul Mellon's farm in Virginia. Charlie had a solid friendship with her. I remember him telling me that she was an extraordinarily strong woman. She could handle any stallion.

When I first moved to Washington in 1951, I met the British ambassador, Sir Oliver Franks. A mutual friend arranged the introduction because we had small children who were close in age. That introduction made my husband Allan and me part of the expat list invited to the occasional embassy function. My first husband's charitable work in the developing world also opened the doors to embassy functions and an invitation to a state dinner at the White House for Jordan's King Hussein, whom I actually got to know far better when my second husband served as head of central intelligence and then ambassador to Iran.

My neighbor who lived just three doors away from the first house we owned in Washington, Kathleen Stans, often invited me to official government events in the 1950s. Her husband, Maurice Stans, served as director of the Bureau of the Budget, a forerunner of the Office of Management and Budget, during the Eisenhower years and later as commerce secretary during the Nixon administration. Her husband was pulled into the Watergate scandal when he served as treasurer for the Committee to Reelect the President (CRP, also known as CREEP), Richard Nixon's reelection campaign committee, in 1972. Maurice was indicted for perjury and obstruction of justice but cleared of any wrongdoing. I always thought Kathleen was quite lonely, but many women of that era were lonely because the men spent most of their time working or attending quasi-official social events to further their careers.

Work did not end at 5 p.m. It continued at cocktail parties and at private dinner parties throughout northwest Washington, in McLean, Virginia, just across the Potomac, and in Chevy Chase and Bethesda, Maryland. I do not think this happens today because senators and members of Congress tend to leave their families at home, so they are rarely in town on weekends. A great deal of information was exchanged over hors d'oeuvres and canapés. The socializing was a form of work; senators chatted with government officials in a relaxed, comfortable setting, a drink or two or three loosening their tongues and encouraging a level of human interaction that made it easier to find common ground.

Dick and I often joined the regular crowd in a Georgetown social scene that became emblematic of the era: we had dinner at the Georgetown homes of Polly Wisner Fritchey, Kay Graham, Pam Harriman, and Joseph and Stewart Alsop and elegant brunches with oysters at Evangeline Bruce's home. My second husband needed to make appearances at many official functions, particularly embassy events, and we got quite expert at the twenty-minute cameo and quick escape out the back door. Dick Helms knew the back exit to every embassy in Washington.

While a White House invitation is always a great privilege and honor, I became reluctant to attend White House functions during the Nixon administration, when my husband retained his job as director of central intelligence, because I got so depressed seeing Pat Nixon. I had an immediate and visceral reaction to her. I felt deeply sorry for her. She had the telltale pained, pinched look of a beleaguered spouse. During his early years as president, Richard Nixon invited us to a birthday party for Pat. She had been born on March 16, the day before St. Patrick's Day, always a great time for a celebration. Her husband, the president, never once mentioned her name in his remarks at the event even though it was her birthday and her party. He ignored her.

Years later, Dick called me after the opening of the Ronald Reagan Presidential Library on November 4, 1991. I was eating cold cuts in Florida with a group of African women and did not attend. The Reagan Library opening celebration featured five living presidents—Richard Nixon, Gerald Ford, Jimmy Carter, Ronald Reagan, and George H. W. Bush—and six First Ladies. After the event, my husband was standing among a small group of men outside. As Mrs. Nixon walked to the limousine, she fell to the ground. She was seventy-nine years old at the time and quite frail. She had suffered a stroke a few years earlier and would die of lung cancer two years later. Nixon refused to allow any of the men to help her to her feet. Dick could not believe what he was seeing. He said it was the most terrible scene. She literally could not stand up. Mike Deaver, the longtime Reagan aide, later told me the exact same story. It did not surprise me. I had an intuitive sense of their relationship when I met them. I thought he was mean to her. News reports said Nixon sobbed out loud at her funeral in 1993. It was taken as a sign of deep grief. I hope he realized what a good woman she had been. History did not treat her well. Poor Pat deserved better.

Washington, DC, offers opportunities to its residents that many take for granted. But as a British native, I never passed up the chance to expose my children to the wonders and opportunities in the city. I took my children to the grounds of the White House for a special reception for John Glenn on

February 26, 1962, after he became the first man to orbit the Earth in *Friendship 7* just six days earlier. The children found it very exciting to see this genuine American hero in person. I did too.

Two years later, I became the envy of every teenage girl in the neighborhood on the day the Beatles, the British singing sensation, played a concert in Washington on their first American tour. I was invited to a reception for them at the British embassy on February 11, 1964. The Beatles were running late, apparently because of mobs of screaming fans, and I grew tired of standing, so I found a chair in a room off to the side of the main salon. Quite unexpectedly, I found myself sitting next to Paul McCartney, the so-called cute Beatle, who had sought the quiet of that room for the very same reason. We had a lovely chat. He was great fun. My daughters and their friends were deeply impressed.

At times, my family pulled me into the circle of official Washington. My older daughter, Jill, was a good friend of Lynda Bird Johnson, the older daughter of President Lyndon B. Johnson and Lady Bird Johnson; they had been classmates at the same high school, the National Cathedral School, the female counterpart to St. Alban's School for Boys, a private Episcopal school in the shadow of the Washington National Cathedral. After her father become president, Lynda would call Jill and ask her to round up their friends and bring them to the White House to play bridge. I fretted endlessly about Jill wearing loafers to the White House and carrying bags of potato chips with her. It seemed one ought to dress better when going to the White House, and the snacks just seemed inappropriate somehow. Invariably, there were changes in the bridge foursome between the phone call from Lynda and the arrival at the White House. When the guards asked who was in the car, Jill would counter with her own question—Who is on the list?—and insist that the identities on the list matched exactly the girls who rode in the car with her. Needless to say, security at the White House has been appreciably beefed up since that time.

Much to my chagrin, Jill always brought bags and bags of potato chips and other snacks with her. Evidently, there was nothing to eat at the White House after the kitchen closed. And Lady Bird Johnson kept a hawk-like eye on the president's diet ever since his near-fatal heart attack at the age of forty-seven in 1955. The heart attack caused him to quit his heavy smoking and avoid things like potato chips, except when Jill and the girls were around. Jill said the president never failed to show up and carry off some treats.

The Sunday after John Kennedy was killed, Lady Bird Johnson called Jill and asked her to contact Lynda Bird, who was just coming home from the University of Texas. She wanted her daughters to be surrounded by familiar and reassuring friendly faces. It was so characteristic of Lady Bird to be sensitive to the needs of her daughters at a time of national trauma when she had to be utterly overwhelmed by the events of that tragic day and her husband's unexpected ascension to the presidency. Dick and I visited the Johnsons at the ranch after he left office, and she was always a gracious and kind hostess and an exceptionally nice woman.

My tennis pals included people who were considered members of the A list of Washington society. B. A. Bentsen, the wife of Lloyd Bentsen, the long-time senator from Texas who became treasury secretary during the Clinton administration, and I played tennis together for dozens of years. Sandra Day O'Connor, the first woman to sit on the Supreme Court, was another close friend and tennis partner. We became great friends because she said she wanted to have friends who were not lawyers. Sandra is a formidable woman with a tremendous career as a lawyer, legislator, and Supreme Court justice. But I would sometimes have to hold down Dick when she lectured him on how to play bridge. He did not always take well to her bossy ways. Sandra did not discriminate. She once tried to tell Sharon Osberg, a women's world champion bridge player who taught Warren Buffett and Bill Gates to play the game, how to make a move.

After my marriage to Richard Helms, Polly Wisner, then the widow of Frank Wisner, who had been Dick's boss at the CIA, acted as my guide to the Georgetown set. She later married Clayton Fritchey, a syndicated columnist who also had a long career in public service.

It is with some bemusement that I look back on my life and realize that people who were just dear friends to me became historically significant figures in the various dramas of the federal government. Katharine Graham, the publisher of the *Washington Post*, and Pamela Harriman, the Democratic Party doyenne and fund-raiser who became the U.S. ambassador to France at the end of her storied life, were women whose company I enjoyed. I did not quite realize it at the time, but my proximity to and engagement with these famous people also gave me an insight into the events of the time that few in the public can enjoy. I knew these people as individuals. And those human characteristics are often telling and revealing when one looks back on the decisions and actions of a different time.

I saw close up the deceit of Richard Nixon. I recognized his genius at foreign policy because Dick Helms, a discerning observer of the powerful, had a full appreciation of Nixon's deep knowledge and insight. But I was there the night Dick got a phone call from the CIA security officer informing him of a break-in at the Watergate Office Building at the headquarters of the

Democratic National Committee. And I listened to Dick worry out loud and try to figure out what Nixon and his senior White House aides were attempting to do as they strove, without success, to position Dick and the CIA as the responsible parties behind their own illegal activity.

I saw the physical toll that the war in Vietnam took on Lyndon Johnson. His anguish over the war was real and deep, and I'm certain it shortened his life. Later, it was difficult to see Dick Helms publicly humiliated when he followed the law and his own internal moral code and declined to tell an unauthorized Senate committee anything about a CIA covert operation in Chile. I took note of the deceptiveness of the U.S. senator who publicly asked my husband questions that he knew from his own private briefing could not be answered in that forum.

It was a curious time. The big events of the decade—the civil rights movement, the space race, the first man on the moon, the war in Vietnam—all played out live on television screens for the first time. At the same time, there were always hidden agendas at work. In an era when the public was actually seeing more events as they took place—or, in those days before live television, shortly after they occurred—I began to question appearances.

Dick Helms made a game of this inside/outside dichotomy. Leaking stories and information is a Washington pastime. It is intrinsic to the ways of governance in a system with three coequal branches. Members of the House whisper to reporters; senators counter by slipping an internal memo to another journalist; White House aides tell tales to congressional staff, who pass them onto their bosses, who drop the morsels of information during cocktail parties like so many delicacies. The bread crumbs of information litter the city.

While Dick always kept his counsel about the true secrets of the United States, he gave me an inside view of this game. Over breakfast each morning we worked our way through a stack of newspapers, including the *New York Times*, the *Washington Post*, and the *Wall Street Journal*. Dick playfully guessed at the sources of the various leaks that made up the headlines of the newspapers. Of course, it was often sheer speculation, but I venture he was rarely wrong. He was the quintessential insider.

The journey that brought me to that point had begun on a lovely English farm forty-five years before.

2

⚜

MALDON

I was born on a summer day, August 21, 1923, in what may well have been the coldest house in England. In those days, a cold Essex farmhouse was really cold. A bitter east wind whipped from the North Sea across the flat low land of Essex with single-minded, chilling effect. I was a teenager before I realized all eastward winds are not bone-cracking cold. At that time, central heating was not only rare but considered "unhealthy." It seems that being chilly was inextricably tied to building character. Too much comfort and warmth could coddle a child and make her incapable of survival in the cruel, cold world. I may have joined the Ratcliff family at the warmest time of year, but in my earliest memories, I am steeling myself for the brutal assault of chill air as I leave the warmth of a fireplace to dash to another room.

I was born at Brick House, the main house on our family farm in Maldon, a beautiful, rural, and ancient town located on a hill overlooking the estuary of the Blackwater River. The town is Saxon. The name Maldon comes from *dun*, or "hill," and *mael*, or "place of meeting." In ancient times, Saxon armies conferred on the high hill overlooking the waters below before doing battle with the Danes, who made a habit of raiding the eastern coastal area, a prime spot for those on the European continent looking for a convenient place to pillage.

Brick House is the house where my own mother was raised. My mother was forty-two years of age and my father forty-six at the time of my birth, and by the standards of the time, they were considered quite emphatically middle aged. As the youngest of six children, I always viewed myself as an afterthought and likely a vague source of embarrassment, given that middle-aged

yeoman farmers like my parents were supposed to be well beyond issues related to reproduction at that point in their lives. Queen Victoria died in 1901,
but her legacy, the rigid customs and strict social mores that governed behavior and manners during the Victorian era, lingered for decades in England.

Although my parents were fortunate to live into their eighties, the life expectancy for citizens of the United Kingdom in the 1920s was the late fifties.
In other words, most people my parents' age were on the last lap of their lives
and a decade or so away from dying. Moreover, I was born in the midst of
a severe economic depression. The Great Depression took place in Europe
and the United Kingdom a full ten years before the 1929 stock market crash
in the United States. Money was tight. My parents considered themselves
"poor" when they married in 1907 because they had only five servants and
two gardeners. By the 1920s and the time of my birth, they owned a lot of
land but had little cash because the depression reduced the cost of agricultural
commodities. They were land rich but cash poor.

So it was a difficult time and little surprise that people seemed to grow older
faster then. Having older parents affected my life as much as growing up on a
farm. I always assumed that they were depleted after raising my older siblings
or perhaps just more relaxed about child rearing by the time I came on the
scene. They were loving parents and firm about discipline but left me largely
to my own devices and allowed me the run of the farm. The old proverb about
children being seen and not heard applied to me and was often stated. My
brother Leonard and I played in the day nursery during the day and slept in
the night nursery at night. A servant brought me down from the day nursery
each afternoon for the ritual English tea of scones, cucumber sandwiches, and
cakes and—the highlight of my day—reading with my father. He would read
to me from children's books and act out the parts of the characters in Aesop's
time-treasured fables. Many of the fables feature animals, which seemed particularly relevant to me in the rural setting. I still remember the tales about
the lion and the mouse, the hare and the tortoise, the mouse, the frog and
the hawk, and recall the implicit lessons of patience, constancy, humility, and
courage. My father insisted each of us be able to read and write by the age
of six. As a result of these influences, I became a voracious reader, an avid
student of the physical environment of the farm, and a child with a healthy,
active imagination.

Nothing fired my imagination more than the view of the Blackwater estuary from my second-floor bedroom window. At low tide, I could see the
ancient Roman causeway leading to Northey Island where the great Battle of
Maldon took place in AD 991. The causeway was four hundred yards long,

about the length of four American football fields. During my childhood, the area was still rural and unscathed by development, and the causeway at low tide looked much as it had nearly a thousand years earlier. In my fevered imagination, 991 might have been the previous year. Essex County contains the oldest settlements in England, dating to well before the Roman conquest. Maldon received its first royal charter from Henry II in 1171, but the town is actually far, far older. It was settled as early as the Middle Bronze Age some fifteen hundred years before the time of Christ.

However, Maldon's location on the Dengie Peninsula on the east coast left the area exposed to hordes of invaders who arrived from the Continent by sea, particularly the Vikings. One of the greatest epic poems in English literature tells of the Battle of Maldon, when Byrhtnoth, an Anglo-Saxon leader during the reign of Ethelred the Unready, led a fearsome two-week battle against Vikings who invaded in a massive force of ninety-three longboats. The Vikings sailed up the river Blackwater heading to Northey Isle, near the location of a mint. They intended to plunder the horde of silver coins that were a component of the country's first system of taxation. The mint exchanged each taxpayer's small hoard of silver pieces each year for fewer pieces, and so you were taxed.

I read and reread the poem so many times that I could recite entire sections from memory. I imagined the fierce battle taking place beneath my window on the causeway. Byrhtnoth cut a distinctive figure according to the poem. He stood more than six feet tall with a mane of long white hair that, in my mind's eye, made him visible to his men as they confronted the invaders. He was a revered older statesman in his time and, at the time of the battle, was in his sixties, a remarkable age to be leading a fighting force when the average life expectancy was likely a third that age. His army was made up of his retainers and about five hundred tenant farmers, some on horseback, all armed with heavy wooden shields, bows and arrows, and long spears. Three Saxon swordsmen managed to keep the Vikings at bay until the Vikings made an appeal to Byrhtnoth and the legendary British sense of fair play and asked to be allowed to pass onto firm ground so they could have a fair fight. Byrhtnoth agreed and called off his trio of fearless swordsmen. It was a huge strategic error. There was a wild battle, and Byrhtnoth and his men fought bravely, but the horde of three thousand Vikings crushed the Anglo-Saxons, and the noble Byrhtnoth literally lost his head. His sarcophagus is in Ely Cathedral, the magnificent Norman cathedral in Cambridgeshire.

The great unanswered question of the battle is why Byrhtnoth allowed the Vikings to cross the causeway when he would have had a tactical advantage keeping them on the other side. As a child, I re-created the battle many times, flourishing my spear and shield and flushing my falcons in defense of my homeland, hearing in my mind the clash of metal spears, the grunts and cries of the warriors, and seeing a flash of the white mane of the brave leader at the head of the charge. In my play I would shout to Byrhtnoth, "Were you proud or foolish to let them cross to your side of the river?" I never did get an answer to that question.

Maldon is also, coincidently, where George Washington's great-great-grandfather is buried. Given that I later became an American citizen and lived for years in the nation's capital that bears his name, I always found that interesting. This great-great-grandfather, Laurence Washington, was a scholar at Oxford University and then rector of Purleigh near Maldon. He was charged with absenteeism and being a malignant minister in 1643, a charge almost certainly related to his loyalty to King Charles I, who was beheaded in 1649. Two of his six children immigrated to Virginia. The first president of the United States was the direct descendent of one of them. Laurence Washington was banished to a poor, miserable parish, Purleigh, after his disgrace and, after his death, buried in the churchyard of All Saints Church in Maldon. Many years later, in 1928, the town of Malden, Massachusetts, named by Joseph Hills, a native of the English Maldon, donated a beautiful stained glass window to the church in his memory.

There was far less drama in my daily life. My father, Stanley Oldfield Ratcliff, was well established by the time of my birth. He was a farmer by occupation and avocation who farmed not only the land on which we lived but twelve other farms covering three thousand acres throughout the county of Essex. He was a founder of the National Farmers Union (NFU) in 1908, the most prestigious farmers' association in the United Kingdom, and when I was ten, he was elected its president. He also served for many years on the town council in Maldon. One of my most vivid childhood memories is running down the long driveway to greet him on his return from the city after his daily labors at the NFU in his Rolls Royce driven by his chauffeur, Punchard. It took about an hour to get back to Maldon from London, and he invariably had Punchard pause to watch a local cricket game on the way back.

Father was born on September 15, 1877, at Woodlands, an Elizabethan moated country house and farm, in the village of Woodham Walter, just four miles from Maldon. His mother died when he was an infant, and his father remarried. My father did not like his stepmother and never spoke of his childhood home to me. In fact, I never saw it until many years after his death. He bought his own farm in 1898 at Great Beeleigh with a £100 loan and was the first to build a modern Danish pig-rearing unit in the county, displaying early evidence of a talent for the cutting edge in farming. He became well known as a pioneer in chemical weed and pest control.

He was an innovative and visionary farmer who recognized the threat to England's sugar beet crop far before others, when Adolf Hitler first came to power in Germany. Virtually all of England's sugar beet seeds came from Germany. Before World War II began, he helped develop a new strain of sugar beet seed with a Polish partner. After the war broke out in 1939 and England came close to starving, those seeds supplied the entire UK sugar beet crop. In other words, Stanley O. Ratcliff sweetened England's tea during the difficult war years when there was no other source of sugar. I remember in September 1939 taxis came to the farm sent by the Polish government to pick up all the Polish workers and administrators to bring them home to fight for their country against the Nazi menace. I often wonder what became of those hardworking men.

My mother, Constance Matilda Fitch, could trace her family back to the turn of the thirteenth century. Old records show Richard Fitch owned land in Steeple Bumpstead in Essex as early as 1407. The Fitches had been farmers, millers, and landowners for hundreds of years in Essex. One ancestor, Thomas Fitch, was governor of the Tower of London in 1659 and on duty presumably when Charles II reclaimed the throne for the Stuarts the following year in 1660. According to the history of the tower, Charles II broke with tradition and declined to stay overnight at the Tower of London the night before his coronation because the place was in such disrepair. The Stuart kings oversaw extensive renovations, and the tower today is one of London's most beloved and popular tourist attractions.

My mother's father, Edward Arthur Fitch, was a highly regarded local leader. A local newspaper described him as the Victorian equivalent of a superman. He was a scientist, writer, sportsman, farmer, and politician. He won election as mayor of Maldon six times and had a wide-ranging and eclectic intellect. He belonged to the Entomological Society and had an early interest in the biological control of farm pests. When he died in 1912 of gastritis at the age of fifty-eight, there was a huge funeral that contemporary reports say drew nearly the entire town to mourn his passing. My parents moved into his house, Brick House, after his death.

Mother was the third of thirteen children. Eleven of those children survived. When her mother, Fanny Belcham Fitch, died in 1917, four younger siblings were still unmarried at that time, and my mother assumed the role of family matriarch and family switchboard, maintaining the traditional family home and an active correspondence with her far-flung siblings. She named my brother Leonard after her own brother, Leonard Belcham Fitch, who died in July 1918 at the age of twenty-two from wounds suffered in World War I. Mother was an active woman and a great athlete. She played hockey, tennis, and golf. She would ride to the golf course, Maldon Links, on a bicycle, play a round, and cycle home again. She played golf with her best friend and always carried a slim little bag with about four clubs. I remember one day her girlfriend and golfing companion arrived at Brick House in tears. She was pregnant and clearly did not want to be. My mother instructed her to clamber up and jump off the kitchen table, repeatedly, to no avail.

Mother was a hardy soul. She skated to Chelmsford one bitterly cold winter on ice skates, played hockey for the county, and then skated home after the game. And she did it wearing the long skirts of the day. She was very much a woman of her time. She always wore a hat and gloves when venturing into the village, and I remember her querulously asking, "Why did that woman smile at me? We have not been introduced!" It was simply not acceptable to interact with anyone before being properly introduced. She always made certain there were fresh flowers in the house, particularly bowls of sweet peas, which stood up well in the chill air.

My four oldest siblings, Edward (Ted), Constance (Nance), Thomas (Tom), and Beryl, were appreciably older than I was. I idolized them. To my young eyes, they were glamorous figures. Edward was sixteen years older, and he watched over me in a calm, caring, and reassuring way. My sister Nance rode sidesaddle beautifully and always portrayed Queen Elizabeth I in local village pageants. My sister Beryl would get into trouble by riding ahead of the hounds, a serious violation of hunt protocol, and would routinely get tossed out of meets.

In those days before television and computers and video games, we lived a classic English country life of hunting, shooting, and riding with the hounds. We also played card games avidly. I learned every game early and developed a lifelong enjoyment of bridge, which I continue to play competitively and with friends on a regular basis. We were introduced early to gambling in a measured and controlled way. Father would give us money to lay bets at the horse races. We were allowed to keep our winnings, but if we lost, we did not get any more. When we played cards, we always played for money. During World War II, father installed a huge steel table in the kitchen as a type of ad hoc bomb shelter. We would huddle under that table during air raids and play poker for hours. If my ever-cautious mother placed a bet, we all threw our cards in because she never bet with less than four aces.

We had a loyal staff. By modern standards, they were almost indentured servants. Len remembers overhearing my parents discussing whether they would increase the cook's pay from £20 to £25 a year. Of course, she lived in our house and got two new uniforms a year, and she and the other staff members were treated like family, but still, the pay was pitiful. People who were "in service" in those years, however, did not seem to be resentful. The class structure was such that having a place to live, enough food to eat, and relatively benevolent employers was considered a big plus for the working poor. It was a very different time. If anyone had suggested that shabby chic and claw-foot bathtubs would one day be considered the height of fashion, we would have collapsed in howls of laughter.

Gertrude was our cook, and two housemaids helped her. Lily carried the meals from the kitchen and waited on the table. The other girl cleaned the house. We had gardeners who grew and canned the vegetables and kept the beautiful flower garden. Len and I once had a nanny named Ivy, whom we rather cruelly nicknamed "Foghorn Ivy" because of her distinctive voice, which Len always maintained could cut through the thickest pea soup. We proved to be too much for her, and she was dismissed, after which we were allowed to fend for ourselves. Our mother kept a wary eye on us.

Dinner was an adult affair. No child could attend the adult dinner until he or she was twelve years old. But breakfast was mandatory for everyone. My mother would open the windows by the time we all sat down to eat either to chill us into submission or because the cold outside air was warmer than the air inside the house. As the temperature dropped, the cold settled into the bones of the old house and created an icebox effect. She believed the medically correct way to cure our chilblains was to walk barefoot in the snow. Heat actually does make the symptoms of itching and pain worse, but no doctor would suggest a barefoot trek through snow as a cure today. We ate well because we lived on a farm: boiled beef, trifle, steamed ginger pudding, pheasant, partridge, and plover's eggs. My father was very particular about vegetables. If they had not been picked the very same day, he ordered them back to the kitchen. He could be a bit imperious about those vegetables and would check their progress and ripeness in the garden and greenhouse himself. My mother always acceded without comment to his demands for the freshest produce. During my lone re-creations of the Battle of Maldon by the ancient causeway, I would hunt winkles or periwinkles, the delicious edible sea snails from the salty riverbed. I would later boil them and eat them with a pin.

A room behind the kitchen contained cured hams hanging from enormous hooks, a keg of beer, and an entire Stilton cheese doused with port wine and kept until it matured to the exact right consistency. The wine cellar was full of sloe gin and dandelion wine made by my brothers and racks of bottles with old labels that I liked to examine, imagining the origin of the contents in exotic grape orchards in sunny faraway lands. My parents entertained a lot, so the alcohol was put to good and frequent use.

Father received a report each morning at breakfast from his farm manager. The primary topic was always the weather. In farming, nothing is more important. If the weather was right for the wheat, it was wrong for the fruit. My father believed anyone more than a generation away from the land was lost. I absorbed that ethos and developed an early appreciation for nature, the natural state, the purity of nature, and the benefits of outdoor living.

My four oldest brothers and sisters moved away to their own homes when I was still very small, and as a result I became closest to my brother Leonard Fitch Ratcliff, who was only four years older than I. We have remained close our entire lives, talking at least once a week on the telephone. Len claims that our mother asked him, when he was about three years old, to identify the one thing he would like most in the world. He said he wanted a baby sister. He got his baby sister a year later. With the benefit of hindsight, and having been the mother of two sons of my own, I seriously doubt Leonard wanted a baby sister at the age of three. I suspect it was a tale mother told him to soften the blow of another younger sibling who booted him out of his position as the much-adored baby of the family.

I became his acolyte, trailing after him like a duckling following the mother duck. My brother hated schoolwork but loved the outdoors and nature. He was an avid and enthusiastic collector of bugs, butterflies, moths, and birds' eggs. I was his loyal deputy, following his lead with the bottle of chloroform used to numb the bugs senseless and the box to hold the corpses. We mixed up vats of beer and honey and pasted the concoction on trees at night to catch moths. I was never allowed to use the butterfly net, however, because that was a boy's job. We played the gender roles expected of us even as children. We would walk the fields and search the riverbeds and gather hens' eggs, which we ate for breakfast, and birds' eggs, which were highly prized to eat with tea. Leonard sewed little white cotton muslin bags with string ties and sent me up into the tall trees to gather the eggs and ever so gently lower the bags to him, leaving me to get myself out of the tree as best I could. I was so utterly in his thrall that I remember once being confounded that my big brother could not get a bus to stop for us. I was about ten and he was fourteen when we decided to take a bus to a spot where we could gather mushrooms. We went to the end of the long driveway connecting the country road to our house, and Len signaled the bus to stop. It did not. I was completely amazed that a bus driver could ignore my brother.

During his school vacations back on the farm, Leonard bossed me around endlessly and routinely ordered me to strip off my clothes to fetch some prized object hanging over the water. One day our mother came across me stark naked, inching my way down a tree limb, my clothes in a heap on the dry ground, and told my brother she thought it was past time for me to be stripping off my clothing in public. I still laugh remembering that edict. We were utterly innocent as children. Our only concern was avoiding the wrath of my mother if I should tumble into the river and get wet knickers. But after that day I kept my clothes on. Mother's orders were to be obeyed.

The British Empire had become the world's dominant superpower during Victoria's long reign, and the Union Jack flew in every corner of the world. By the time of my birth, the British Empire governed one-fifth of the world's total population living on one-fourth of the Earth's landmass. As the saying went, the sun never set on the British Empire. Of course, the empire was already in decline by the time of my childhood. Restive colonials wanted independence, and the world was changing. But there was little sign of it in Maldon. We had uncles and aunts, my mother's many siblings, who lived all over the planet: China, Japan, India, and the Middle East. Between the civil service, military service, and commerce, English people of a certain class had the opportunity to travel and experience many cultures in those years. In fact, younger sons who did not inherit land were encouraged to go to the colonies. I still remember hearing about foreign cultures and politics when the aunts and uncles visited. We lived an isolated, quiet life on the farm, and our far-flung relatives brought the outside world to us and broadened our world outlook during their regular visits. It doubtless triggered my lifelong interest in travel and foreign peoples and cultures.

There were lots of shooting parties. My brother Len received his first gun at the age of eleven. My father owned a shooting syndicate and was very particular about maintenance of guns, and he taught my brother how to clean and store the weapons. They shot pheasants by the dozens. It was very much a part of the country life. Membership in the syndicate was a subject of great debate and concern. I had no interest in hunting, so I was responsible for preparing strawberries and cream for the weekly tennis parties and cleaning the tennis balls by rubbing them on a sisal mat. We maintained a beautiful grass tennis court, and the balls were supposed to last for many sets. No one opened a new can of balls for a new game. Even as an adult, I always felt a twinge of guilt opening a new can of balls. I loved to swim, and after extensive negotiations, my mother allowed me to swim in the springtime once the water reached fifty-five degrees at the local promenade. To this day, I love to swim in cold water.

We grew up wanting for nothing despite the lack of cash. Like my parents, I did not view the family as wealthy. Indeed, we never discussed money, our own or anyone else's. If I wanted an increase in my allowance, I needed to make a formal appointment to see my father in his study, a frightening and formidable challenge to get a few more pence a week.

The butcher and baker from the town would call the house each morning and take our orders for the day. A milkman delivered fresh milk twice a day. Our parents would sometimes pay for services in trade. I cannot recall the family ever receiving a dentist's bill. Father would send the dentist a brace of pheasants from time to time. Father had three hundred milk cows and eight hundred breeding ewes at the time of his death. Our parents somehow managed to find the money to send each of us to private school. There was little free education at that time, and Len and I wonder to this day how they managed to find the money each year for tuition and board for six children.

My father was the king of his domain. He smoked a pipe, which gave him an even more authoritative air, and was seldom without it. He and my mother enjoyed each other's company. I can remember them playing cards together in the evening after dinner in a corner of the room, a little island of privacy for the two of them. For some reason, he always called her Susan. My brother always called her Katie, as in "Cautious Katie," while playing cards. I never quite understood these nicknames. My father was quite definitely the man in charge. He had a favorite yellow plum tree, and one day I picked a few plums and ate them. I was soundly whacked and to this day hesitate to buy yellow plums.

One day I was accompanying my parents to London, probably to shop for school clothes. Father and his *London Times* went into the first-class car, and mother and I traveled third class. A penny dropped that day. For the first time, I questioned the discrepancy. My parents had a good relationship and loving marriage, but mother was just not equal to father. If he raged about the freshness of the vegetables at dinner, the less-than-flawless food was her fault, and she accepted the responsibility without comment. It was an early consciousness-raising moment for me. I did not speak of it, but it stuck in my mind like a little irritation, and as I grew up, other pennies dropped at different moments in my life that caused me to question certain assumptions and expectations for the girls and women of my time.

When Len went off to boarding school at the age of eight, as our older brothers had, he was miserable about it. My brothers went to the Felsted

School, which was founded by Sir Richard Rich, the first Baron Rich, one of the great villains of his time. He was a power broker in the court of King Henry VIII and an executor of his will, which always fell in something of a shadow. His misleading testimony contributed to the perjury conviction of Sir Thomas More. My brothers hated going off to school and became progressively "sicker" the closer we got to the school. They always packed large silk handkerchiefs to line their trousers in the event they were strapped for academic or social infractions. The handkerchiefs were supposed to provide some padding. They were always desperately unhappy when they were dropped off but quickly adjusted and rarely wrote home until they ran out of pocket money. They took large trunks off to school, and each included a tuck box stuffed full of edible goodies prepared by our cook.

When Len left for school, I was only four years old and left behind, the last child home alone. Living on a farm can be a somewhat isolated existence. The farm on which we lived was sizeable, and father owned much of the surrounding farmland. While this created a zone of safety that allowed me to roam at will, it was also quite solitary.

I attended a private day school in the village for my first six years of schooling and made friends there. Someone drove me into town in the morning, and I walked home. I would walk through the village vegetable garden and every day see a funny little old lady who sat there with a huge rhubarb leaf on her head to protect her face from the sun. She was clearly not quite right in the head, and that rhubarb leaf looked rather strange, but I would stop and chat with her every day.

Except for my parents, the household help, and Len on school vacations, I had few playmates. I found a world of entertainment and companionship in books. I am convinced I read every book in Brick House. I read constantly. I had red hair, and an old wives' tale contended that red hair like mine came with weak eyes and that redheads were susceptible to blindness. The old wives' tale proved wrong in my case. I never needed eyeglasses even as I grew quite old. Despite the dire threat of imminent blindness, I spent hours perched in a favorite spot on the stairs reading adventure stories, reliving past glorious battles and tales; later, I curled under my bedclothes with a flashlight many nights to continue to read long after the official lights out, not able to put down the book even to sleep. I never felt lonely because I had never really experienced anything else, so I did not miss the companionship of other children, and I vicariously lived the adventures of the protagonists in my books. Throughout my life, I have found entertainment, knowledge, and escape in literature. I highly recommend it.

I was quite taken with the tale of Artemisia I of Caria, then a part of Asia Minor. She became an admiral after the death of her husband and is famed for her bravery and strategic brilliance during the Battle of Salamis in 480 BC. At one point, while leading a fleet of five ships, she rammed her ship into one of the invading Greek ships. The Greeks were startled enough to think she was surrendering. She was not. She was allied with the Persians, who rewarded her handsomely for her performance for many years. Little did I know then, when enthralled by Artemisia's adventures, what a role Persia would play in my later life.

I never lost my appetite for adventure stories. When I began to learn about American history, I was fascinated by the stories of pioneer women, many European, who followed their spouses in an ever-westward push in America. They would arrive in Kansas or Minnesota or some other lonely, godforsaken place, having been lured by tales of fertile land and a new life. Instead, they found endless plains with no water, no trees, no other people, and cruel, relentless challenges from Native Americans, wild animals, hideous weather, and a hostile, untamed environment. Yet they survived and prevailed. I found them so inspiring. Feisty, independent, and indomitable women from history, women like Artemisia I and Harriet Tubman, the remarkable African American abolitionist who led dozens of slaves to freedom through the Underground Railroad that ran from the slave states of the South to the free states of the North, showed me that women could be powerful and distinctive and make a difference.

I was thrilled to be sent off to boarding school at the age of twelve. Unlike my brothers, I welcomed the escape. Leaving the farm was a chance for me to become a person in my own right. On the farm, I was the baby, the last of six children, and, to me, very much the footnote of the family. At school, I had the opportunity to become a person in my own right. And I did.

Manor House was a typical boarding school for young ladies located in Limpsfield Surrey. We were taught to eat asparagus with our fingers (the only proper way to eat asparagus), never to cut a roll of bread with a knife (one breaks it with one's hands), to ride bareback, and to play lacrosse. Hockey was deemed inappropriate because of the conviction that it would make us round shouldered. Every morning, the maid in cap and apron would wake me by announcing, "Miss Cynthia, your bath is ready." The bath was always ice cold. I'm not quite sure why. I suspect the school saved a great deal of money on heating bills. And physical discomfort was always associated with the British tradition of maintaining a stiff upper lip and not complaining. But a cold bath came to be associated in my mind with security. For the rest of my life, I would take a cold bath in times of emotional crisis to ease my stress and gather myself.

The school was small, with only nine girls in each class, so we all knew one another quite well. One of my schoolmates was Winston Churchill's youngest daughter, Mary Spencer-Churchill. She was a year older than I. Mary later married Christopher Soames and became a baroness. She was also an author of some note. She wrote a well-regarded biography of her mother, Clementine, in 1979 and edited a collection of her parents' letters. Many of the other students traveled there from all over the globe.

I loved school even though the food was terrible. The school regularly served a pudding we called "roof" because it stuck to the roof of the mouth and was impossible to get off. Once a month we were obliged to dine with the headmistress "on high" for a very formal meal. No one was ever allowed to ask for anything, including the salt and pepper; you were expected to pass it as a matter of course, and we learned to speak politely to the people on either side of us. It was a remarkable training in formal manners that stood me in good stead as an adult. For the rest of my life, I never had to worry about the proper way to behave, regardless of the setting or country, thanks to that early boarding school training.

I remember the headmistress quite vividly. She was an aging spinster with little tolerance for the self-important. She never passed on the chance to remind us that "the graveyard is full of indispensables." I came close to expulsion from school once for using a word, "bugger," that I had heard on the farm. I had no idea what it meant (it was a vulgar term for what was then called a "sodomite") and was bewildered by the furor my faux pas created. Victorian morality governed our behavior. We were taught to work hard, to be honest, chaste, and thrifty, and to exhibit a sense of duty. Saying something like "bugger" out loud was simply not done. We were taught a classical curriculum and studied hard, but we also had many athletic and cultural outlets. We performed plays and dance programs beneath the boughs of a huge ilex tree, an evergreen oak introduced to the United Kingdom in the seventeenth century. And a small bus carried us to many performances at the Glynbourne Opera, outdoor theaters, and, notably, the Old Vic Theater in London. Alec Guinness, Michael Redgrave, and Laurence Olivier, three of the greatest British actors of the twentieth century, joined the company of the Old Vic in 1936, a year after I went to boarding school. So I had the rare opportunity to see some of the truly great artists of my time tread the boards and perform Shakespeare. Guinness played the lead in Hamlet in the 1938 season. Those performances gave me a great love of live theater.

The rare times when I left the farm remain vivid memories. My father was able to secure two tickets to the coronation of King George VI on May 12, 1937, and my parents decided Len and I should use them. We were sent off to London on the train with our names and addresses and money securely pinned to our underclothes. I remember the extraordinary crowds and how exhilarating it was to be at such a festive occasion without supervision. Parents today are unlikely to send young teens into the city on their own, but in those days there was less fear and perhaps fewer threats.

I had long planned to study at Cambridge University after finishing at the Manor House. I settled on Cambridge because my uncle Edward had studied there and rowed in the crew. He brought the oars home to Brick House, and they hung high, like a permanent trophy, in the front hall and inspired in me fanciful notions of university life. I told my father that I would like to study the law.

But the war intervened. We were intensely aware of developments in Europe. Great Britain was extremely vulnerable in those years. The country was totally unprepared for another war, and Prime Minister Neville Chamberlain did his best to avoid World War II. He got a great deal of criticism for his policy of appeasement toward Nazi Germany and made strategic and moral errors, but many, including U.S. Ambassador Joseph P. Kennedy, agreed with his approach. He agreed to allow Germany to seize part of Czechoslovakia in hopes of maintaining an uneasy peace with Hitler in a deal struck on September 29, 1938. But Hitler continued his aggression and invaded Poland on September 1, 1939, just as I was ending my last year of boarding school. Two days later, Britain declared war on Germany.

Even after Chamberlain returned from Munich after striking the deal with Hitler, the nation still distrusted the German führer. My own father always assumed there would be another war. The country was on a war footing long before war was declared. We were organized at school in 1938 to dig trenches in case of surprise air attacks. We were so close to the Continent and air bases that it was an ongoing and realistic fear. It is hard for Americans who live in a nation surrounded by two enormous oceans to appreciate how threatened we felt by possible invasion by the Nazis. At the time, we viewed the trench digging as a lark, in part because the butler who was digging alongside us kept tumbling into the trench. We found his stumbles hilarious. I did not realize the cause until later. He was the first alcoholic I had ever met in my sheltered life.

The declaration of war changed everything. I remember when the first air raid siren sounded. It was a false alarm, but I came to dread that piercing shriek in the night. My education became a secondary concern, and I went home to Maldon. All the servants left for war-related jobs. My father put that huge iron table in the kitchen to protect us from bombs.

Our lives were changing, but at that point it seemed like a play at the theater, a bit unreal. Farmers became enormously important because the food supply for the country was so low. Food was rationed. Each person was allowed one quarter pound of butter, one quarter pound of meat, a few ounces of sugar, and occasionally one banana each month. The banana usually rotted away because it was such a treat that there was a tendency to postpone the pleasure of eating it until tomorrow. Those families living on farms were allowed to kill one animal, usually a pig or a lamb, every three months. My mother bought a commercial-sized refrigerator and a large freezer to preserve food but rarely used them because she said they made things taste different. Many years later, the freezer was used to freeze a single tray of ice cubes to greet me on my visits from America.

Very soon, home was deemed too dangerous for me because Maldon's location on the east coast made it vulnerable to a Nazi attack, just as it had been vulnerable to Viking attacks in another millennium. I was sent to Devonshire on the west coast to live with my mother's older brother, Edward William Fitch, who was a captain in the Royal Navy and a professor of navigation at the Royal Naval College at Greenwich. His son and namesake, Edward Basil Hollis Fitch, died in action on the Belgium border during the war. Uncle Edward's first wife, the mother of Basil, had died in 1927. He remarried the following year, and Aunt Nancy became one of my favorite relatives. She was extremely enlightened for the times. She supported a home for unwed mothers in Middlesex, which was quite controversial. She was a wonderful woman. Their son, Admiral Sir Richard Fitch, became second sea lord.

My uncle rode his bicycle through the surrounding villages to search for food items. Each expedition was a reconnaissance mission for him; a victory was represented by a jar of marmalade or another unexpected treat. He rationed our butter for the month with military precision. I usually enjoyed it at breakfast, though I did have to agonize about whether to spread it out in an extended "bread and scrape," with toast getting the barest hint of butter, or to have more and really enjoy it in a few days. I developed an intense dislike for margarine and dried eggs, a steady and nauseating part of our diet. My uncle was strict with me, and when I complained to my mother about my early curfew, my mother explained that my uncle had been a playboy and knew the pitfalls awaiting laxity in young ladies. Both of his wives were wealthy. I clearly remember him making his first wife account for literally every single penny of her own money and berating her when she came up short. She once wept at our house in frustration over not being able to account for one penny. We were eager to ease her pain and suggested maybe she had forgotten paying a penny for the use of a public ladies room.

Women were certainly not widely viewed as equal to men in those years. When I was born in 1923, adult women did not yet have the right to vote. Women over the age of thirty who owned property won the right to vote in 1918, but the age and property limit was not eliminated until 1928. Married women had no property rights at all until 1882. Women were viewed as under the care of their fathers and then husbands and incapable of bothering their pretty little heads with business or financial matters. Women were expected to stay at home, make babies, and care for their husbands and children. Although the law changed with regard to married women and property in the nineteenth century, the assumptions and practices of the past lingered, as my uncle's behavior demonstrated.

I experienced my first bomb attack while staying at my uncle's. The eastern section of England was largely spared the bombardment that hit the west and London, but the German bombers would often dump their extra bombs to lighten their load on their way back to the Continent after a bombing run over military targets. One of those stray bombs hit Torquay, very near my uncle's home. We were up all night, terrified there would be more bombs. My first beau, a handsome blond man named Tony, walked five miles to my uncle's house to make sure I was all right. He was a lovely young man of about eighteen. He later enlisted in the navy. He survived the war.

While under my uncle's care in the west of England, I was asked to help entertain servicemen who were undergoing rehabilitation at a magnificent hotel, a Mediterranean-style building built in 1866 overlooking the bay, in nearby Torquay. The hotel had been taken over and turned into a rehabilitation center for Royal Air Force (RAF) personnel who were injured during the Battle of Britain. The Battle of Britain, waged during the summer and autumn of 1940, was the first major campaign fought entirely by air forces. Hitler hoped to crush the Royal Air Force. He did not succeed, but the casualties were tremendous. Most of the young airmen and crews sustained horrible burns that left them tragically disfigured. Burn treatment and plastic surgery were rudimentary in those days. Indeed, the war helped to improve treatment, and later, when I was serving as a Wren, I met a remarkable plastic surgeon who transformed the treatment of burn victims.

I was just seventeen, and it was almost impossible for me to see the terrible disfigured faces and hands of these brave men without my eyes fluttering and my stomach roiling. I remember a young man approaching me to ask for a dance. His eyes looked directly and deeply into mine, and I could tell he was begging me not to flinch. It was a moment I will never forget. He had blue eyes, and the burns had left him horribly damaged, with hideous scars, looking almost like a monster. I found the will somewhere deep inside myself and met his direct gaze, and, I am proud to say, I did not flinch. But in that moment, I grew up. All of a sudden, I was no longer a carefree young girl. I understood, deeply and profoundly and in a way that had never really occurred to me before, that there were consequences in life. War was not a lark. Life was not a game. This brave young man, who only wanted to dance with a pretty girl and experience some semblance of normalcy after surviving a horrific plane fire, found the courage to approach me and wordlessly ask for acceptance. I felt the weight of the times, a sense of the stakes and my personal responsibility, a responsibility shared by all English men and women. I can still hear Winston Churchill's sonorous voice coming from the radio, telling me and all citizens of England that we each had to do our bit and pull together to fight and defeat this menace. The call to arms stirred sentiments buried in my psyche since my childish re-creations of the Battle of Maldon and appealed to my heritage as a daughter of England. My plans to attend the university at Cambridge were shelved. England needed me.

3

WORLD WAR II AND THE BOAT CREW WRENS

Few believed Prime Minister Chamberlain's claim that war would be averted by the deal he negotiated with Adolf Hitler in 1938. We were convinced war was inevitable. My older brothers, Ted and Tom Ratcliff, worked in food production, so they were exempt from military service and required to keep producing food. My older sisters were married. But my brother Len and I could serve our country, and we did. Len joined the Royal Air Force Volunteer Reserve at the beginning of 1939. In his telling, he was terrified of bayonets and trench warfare, and so did not want to be in the infantry. He hated the idea of drowning, which ruled out the navy, so he went into the air force. My brother had long been an avid fan of the aviation war stories from World War I, particularly the exploits of Baron Manfred von Richthofen, the so-called Red Baron. The Red Baron was a highly publicized and romanticized German flying ace who was considered the ace of aces. Len fancied himself following in that daring, chivalrous tradition as an aviator.

Len's service brought great distinction and pride to our family. But we did not learn the extent and importance of his wartime service until after the war. He was the wing commander and a pilot in the secret Squadron 161 of the Royal Air Force. He flew more than seventy missions in Lysanders and Hudson aircraft. It was his job to drop Special Operations Executive (SOE) agents into enemy territory, sometimes guided only by moonlight. He landed in farm fields to drop and pick up agents and equipment illuminated by the flashlights of resistance fighters. It was extraordinarily dangerous work involving long, lonely flights at low altitude in the dark of night over hostile territory. It is amazing he survived. In fact, his entire squadron was wiped out three times.

Len did not talk much about his service for many years. Many World War II veterans were similarly reticent to relive those traumatic days. But he does tell one tale. At the end of the war in the spring of 1945, one of the crews under his command flew into a remote section of Norway to drop leaflets and let the populace know the war had ended. When the pilot experienced engine difficulty and was forced to land at a German-controlled airport near Trondheim in Norway, Len set out on a rescue mission with a crew and a new engine. The crew included a Norwegian pilot and resistance fighter, Per Hysing-Dahl, who had become a member of his squadron after escaping from German-occupied Norway by rowing in an open boat across the North Sea. When they arrived in Trondheim, a German officer wanted to surrender with his force of sixty thousand personnel. Len ordered them to surrender to Captain Per Hysing-Dahl, who many years later became a distinguished Norwegian parliamentarian and president of the Storting. A plaque at a Trondheim airport memorializes this surrender. A British warship was radioed to come to Norway to handle the formalities.

With the war over, Per was anxious to see his longtime sweetheart, Dagny, so he called her, and she managed to get to Trondheim to join him. They were hurriedly married by the captain of a British cruiser, who had arrived to take over the official surrender of the German forces. The captain was very accommodating. He even lent the newlyweds his cabin for a honeymoon. The return of the newlyweds to England, however, became problematic. Reports of a strange woman in the returning plane caused great consternation back home. The Secret Intelligence Service (SIS) threatened to arrest Captain Hysing-Dahl as well as Dagny, whom they speculated might be a spy. Len was horrified and went to the SIS headquarters to roar, "You will arrest them over my dead body!" Disaster and arrest were averted. They listened to Len.

Len's service was acknowledged by many British honors, including a Distinguished Service Order signed by King George VI and the Distinguished Flying Cross, as well as the Croix de Guerre and the Legion D'Honneur from the French government. All were well deserved. By the time of the sixty-fifth anniversary of VE Day in 2010, Len was the sole surviving squadron leader in England from World War II. He did quite a few interviews with BBC and French television and drew many accolades. I was enormously proud of my big brother.

One day many years after the war, my phone rang in Washington. It was Per. He had come to Washington to visit President George H. W. Bush. He asked if he could come and call on me because he was so devoted to my brother. Dick and I were thrilled to see him and hear of his wartime exploits.

My service was probably less predictable and less spectacular than that of my older brother. But World War II was the first modern war to call upon the direct participation of women as well as men. Great Britain needed every able-bodied adult to fight the Nazi menace. J. B. Priestley, the noted novelist and playwright, wrote a book called *British Women Go to War* and explained that Hitler could draw upon a population of between eighty and ninety million people. But Britain contained only forty-five million people. To win this fight, Great Britain needed the help of all its adult citizens, including its women.

"Our survival as a free people depended upon our adequate use of manpower. Unless we made the very most of what we had, we could not hope to survive," wrote Priestley. "We had seventeen million adult women in this island. It was urgently necessary that women should play their part in the war effort." Priestley's own nineteen-year-old daughter, Sylvia, was a Wren dispatch rider. Women went into the factories to manufacture the supplies needed for the war effort and took over many jobs formerly held by men in the military. Women drove trucks and rode motorcycles. They repaired motor vehicles, packed and repacked parachutes, and inspected and maintained gun equipment and ammunition. Women ferried planes, including huge bombers, to airfields. Some of the girls were so small they had to put wooden blocks on the pedals so they could reach them to fly the aircraft. The war showed that women were necessary and important.

I was just one young girl, but I fully intended to do my part. Prime Minister Winston Churchill said, in his radio addresses, every citizen was needed to help with the war effort, and victory was impossible without the participation of everyone. He was very persuasive. I absolutely believed him and was determined to respond to his call. In fact, it was inconceivable to me that I would not serve. But I could not enlist until I turned eighteen in August 1941.

Meanwhile, the war was spilling over into our backyard. We could see the glint of sunlight off the silver fuselages of the fighter planes overhead from our home in Maldon, and we feared Hitler would invade our island. So my parents understandably worried about the safety of a young teenage girl and wanted me well out of harm's way and far from the Nazi hordes. The fear of invasion was almost imprinted on their DNA, given the experiences of their forebears. So they sent me to my uncle's home in western England.

Although I was out of the direct path of the bombers at my uncle's home, I was not unaware of the war. The signs of war were all around me, particularly the terribly wounded airmen from the Battle of Britain. I learned there of a remarkable plastic surgeon, Archibald McIndoe, a New Zealand physician who introduced many innovations in the treatment of burn victims at Queen Victoria Hospital in East Grinstead. He discovered the benefits of saline solution for promotion of healing by accident when the pilots and crewmen of planes downed over the ocean seemed to heal quicker after being soaked in seawater. And he developed new skin-grafting techniques. He also cared passionately about his patients' sense of well-being and mental health and actively promoted ways to normalize the lives of these horribly disfigured, brave men. The patients started something called "The Guinea Pig Club" in a self-mocking acknowledgment that they were being used as experiments in new treatment modalities. He encouraged local families in Grinstead to host the burn victims, and Grinstead came to be known as "the town that did not stare." The burned pilots we danced with in Torquay were among his patients. The Imperial Hotel in Torquay was being used as a rehabilitation center. I had such admiration for those courageous warriors and for that remarkable doctor who cared so deeply for them.

Not long after I arrived in Torquay, I noticed dozens and dozens of boats of all sorts, including sailboats, small yachts, and fishing boats, gathered in the harbor. It was an odd mix of vessels. Then one morning, I awoke and sensed something strange had happened overnight. When I looked at the harbor, every single boat was gone. The harbor was completely empty. This was my small window into what became known as the Miracle of Dunkirk.

The government had quietly mobilized every floating vessel in Great Britain to rescue the Allied troops stranded across the English Channel in Dunkirk, France. It was early in the war, and the Allied forces were struggling against a ruthless, better-organized, and better-equipped enemy. The Allied troops were trapped between the sea and the enemy. The small vessels could get closer to the beaches than the enormous aircraft carriers and larger vessels, so they acted as a kind of shuttle between the beach and shallow water, where thousands of soldiers waited in water up to their necks, and then carried the soaked soldiers to the bigger ships. Some of the little boats carried troops all the way home to England. Between May 26 and June 3, 1940, more than 338,000 British and French soldiers were rescued by the fleet of 850 boats. It was a remarkable achievement that boosted the morale of the British people at a particularly low point in the war. It showed that a united Great Britain could prevail against the Nazi menace. It also left me more resolved than ever to be part of the war effort.

As I approached my eighteenth birthday, I left the relative safety of my uncle's home in western England and went home to talk to my parents about my plans to enlist as soon as I reached the eligible age. I remember the strangeness of the train ride back to Maldon. The train was packed full of troops, and every single place sign at each station had been removed. This was an effort to confound any spy who might have snuck into our midst. Indeed, the street signs in towns near the coast were removed for the same reason. Fortunately, I recognized the stations.

I told my father that my education paled in importance next to the need to fight in this war, and I wanted to go to London to join the Women's Royal Naval Service (WRNS), known as the Wrens. The Wrens, the women's arm of the Royal Navy, had been created during World War I and reactivated in 1939. My parents were concerned for my safety but accepted my choice. Once I joined, I became part of an experiment to use the Wrens to perform tasks on harbor boats and free up sailors to serve on the front lines of the war.

The Boat Crew Wrens experiment almost did not take place. Wren superintendent Euphemia Violet Welby, the widow of a Royal Navy captain, Richard Martin Welby, felt very strongly that girls could replace sailor crews on harbor craft, but when she asked the Admiralty if she could try this, the naval powers were initially dismissive. She persisted, however, and eventually it was agreed she could try it out with sixty girls. I was one of them.

My father was worried about how I would survive in the military. I had always enjoyed the luxury of my own room and had become accustomed to my privacy and the quiet solitude of country life as well as the support of household help. He counseled me that I would only be able to survive living in close quarters with a large number of other women if I could learn to concentrate so totally that I could read a book in a crowded room. I learned how to do that and can do it to this day. As it happened, his counsel proved to be enormously helpful when I became a mother and had young children crawling all over me. It was some of the best advice he ever gave me.

I enlisted right after my birthday in August, even before the National Service Act became law in December 1941 and allowed the government to conscript young single women. I could not have anticipated the effect my military service would have on my life. It opened my eyes in many ways and gave me an education in life that I could not have received in a university classroom.

I reported for duty in London and asked to serve in the Fleet Air Arm in Scotland, but the military has its own way of doing things, and I was assigned to Malvern, Worcestershire, in the west of England where Malvern College, a boys' school, had been turned into a naval establishment. I worked for

Richard Miles, an attractive young naval officer, who became a great friend. He later was befriended by First Lady Eleanor Roosevelt when he went to America to drum up public support for the United States joining the Allies in fighting the Fascists. It is hard to remember that the United States did not automatically rush to the aid of the Allies. Indeed, isolationist Americans argued that the United States should stay out of "Europe's war." President John F. Kennedy's father, Joseph P. Kennedy, then ambassador to the Court of St. James, was firmly in this camp. Franklin Roosevelt had to deal with the political realities in the United States, but he quietly helped Great Britain in the years leading up to full U.S. involvement. Of course, everything changed after the Japanese bombed Pearl Harbor in Hawaii on December 7, 1941. The United States declared war on Japan on December 8, and three days later Nazi Germany and its Axis partners declared war on the United States. For those of us in Britain who were exhausted from two years of war, this was welcome news. We needed the Yanks. Mrs. Roosevelt met Richard Miles as a goodwill gesture when his travels brought him to Washington. She telephoned him when he was posted to the British embassy and invited him to spend Christmas with the Roosevelt family at the White House. He subsequently became a frequent guest there. In a letter to me during the war, he wrote, "I can testify how she would dump a newspaper clipping on the Presidential breakfast tray about an eviction perhaps or some injustice to a black family or unemployed steel worker. 'Franklin,' she would say, 'you must do something about that.'"

He recounted to me how he was summoned to dinner at 1600 Pennsylvania Avenue once and told that another "naval person" would be present. It was the eve of the Quebec Conference called in August 1943 to discuss the Allied invasion of Italy and France. The "naval person" turned out to be Winston Churchill, who was staying at the White House with his private secretary and doctor. After the dinner, Richard said that FDR and Churchill recited all of the verses of John Greenleaf Whittier's "Barbara Frietchie," the poem about the courageous elderly patriot during the Civil War who famously defied the rebels to defend the American flag:

"Shoot, if you must, this old gray head,
  But spare your country's flag," she said.

Although I treasured Richard's friendship, I felt I was not a very efficient assistant, and I yearned for a more active role. Fortuitously, a Wren officer came to see me. She wanted volunteers for the new Boat Crew department.

I was thrilled; I signed up immediately and became one of the original Boat Crew Wrens in Plymouth.

Plymouth is a historic port in Devon that had been a Roman trading post and one of the earliest settled parts of the island. The port has a rich history. Sir Francis Drake sailed on his adventures for Queen Elizabeth I from Plymouth in the sixteenth century. The Pilgrims who settled Plymouth, Massachusetts, in the colonies sailed from Plymouth in 1620. Charles Darwin left Plymouth for the Galapagos Islands, where he formulated his theory of natural selection in 1831. The city remained an important shipping and naval center in the nineteenth and twentieth centuries and was crucial to the UK war effort. No surprise that it became a favored target of the Luftwaffe. The city was bombed fifty-nine times between 1940 and 1944. Although the dockyards were the primary target, more than thirty-eight hundred houses and most of the city center were also destroyed. We could not miss the suffering of the civilian population in Plymouth. After bombing raids, we would return to the docks and see families wandering about with their household goods in tow. The dockyards continued to operate despite the barrage.

The Wrens manned most of the naval harbor craft at Plymouth at all hours and in all weather conditions. Because the navy had never used women in this way, it had no idea how to train us. So we got the exact same six weeks of training that the male sailors received: we learned to tie knots, to navigate by the stars and instruments, to handle boats. We swabbed the decks and polished the brass, just as the men did. I initially served on a hospital boat and was then assigned to the crew of the admiral's barge. We had a female engineer on the boat who had been an artist before the war, and she always carried her paints with her. As the crew of the admiral's barge, we took on board members of the royal family when they came to tour the naval vessels, and we worked with ships and submarines when they returned from combat as a kind of water taxi shuttle between the enormous vessels and the shore.

It was exciting and exhausting. We rarely got a good night's sleep because of the intermittent bombing. We slept with our warmest clothes and a few treasured keepsakes at the bottom of our bunk beds at the Wrenery. We lived together and shared the hardships of wartime, which included lots of rules and regulations. Lights were out at 10:30 p.m.; baths were limited to two inches of lukewarm water and no more than ten minutes' duration. We shared chores, neatly made up our bunks with the blue-and-white bedspreads with an anchor in the center, and religiously kept black paper over all windows to avoid alerting bombers to any signs of life below.

When the air raid siren sliced through the night air, we leapt into our clothes. Those of us with firefighting duty headed to the roof to toss water on any stray embers that might alight on any wooden surface from the incendiary bombs. I never went underground. I had an enormous fear of being trapped in a shelter. I would just huddle in a corner with the other girls. We never knew if we would survive those raids, but we came to accept them because we could not control what happened. It made me very self-reliant. I learned no one could rescue me under such dire conditions. One night I watched two of the girls solemnly shake hands before they climbed up to the roof to watch for incendiaries. I have never forgotten the poignancy of that handshake.

We felt endlessly sleep deprived. I realized afterward it was great training for caring for infants. I most remember being famished with hunger. Being out on the often very cold water for hours on end and doing physical labor made us all hungry all the time. But the food supply was limited and often unpalatable. The wonderful, plentiful, and wholesome food I enjoyed at home in Maldon was unavailable in Plymouth because of wartime shortages. Getting a loaf of freshly baked bread was impossible. We ate a lot of powdered eggs and suet puddings and mystery meat and potatoes. We would beg extra food from the officers' mess.

Plymouth harbor was loaded with boats of all sorts: battleships, cruisers, torpedo boats, minesweepers, and frigates. In addition to the British vessels, there were ships of the Free French, the Poles, and the Canadians, as well as oil tankers from all over. It was also a submarine base. And in the evenings we would go out to sea and watch the motor torpedo boats (MTBs) leaving for patrol and daring raids on the enemy coast. Many of the MTB crewmen were our friends. We saw the occasional aircraft carrier as well. We made so many great friends. The mail bags would be dropped at the flag-staff area each morning; we would look at the labels to find out which ship had come in overnight, and we would know which friends were returning on that day. Sadly, many friends, particularly the submariners, never came back.

I remember one time my father was quite disgruntled because a beau sheared off the top of a chestnut tree at Brick House when he dropped a bottle containing a message for me from his airplane. He was a wonderful young man. He had terrible eyesight and managed to trick the military into letting him join the RAF despite his poor vision. He died in combat.

I arrived in Plymouth months after the Plymouth Blitz, a reign of terror lasting from March 20 to April 29, 1941, that killed more than twelve hundred people. The bombing had left Plymouth a shadow of its former self. By the time I arrived, all of the children had been evacuated to safer areas in the country, and the population had fallen to about half the prewar level of 250,000. The Germans understood the importance of armaments and infrastructure and did all they could to cripple oil supplies with a fleet of U-boats. The U-boats relentlessly cruised the seas, taking out boats that ferried desperately needed supplies to Great Britain as well as the brave soldiers and sailors heading to the war front. The Germans aimed for the docks but hit the center city, leaving in rubble thousands of private homes as well as churches and other public buildings. The precision bombing so dazzling a half century later during the U.S. wars in Iraq and Afghanistan was nonexistent at that time. An estimated one hundred Luftwaffe bombers dropped one thousand bombs and twenty thousand incendiary devices in that five-week period. The damaged city felt like a ghost town.

History shows that the Allies were woefully unprepared for another war and needed to be creative in fighting the Germans, particularly in the first years of the conflict. I remember watching crews loading thousands of pounds of explosives into the bow of the HMS *Campbeltown* in Plymouth harbor. The ship was a vintage World War I U.S. destroyer and part of a transfer of obsolete ships from the United States to Great Britain at the start of the war. That old battle-scarred destroyer was loaded with dynamite and then cruised directly into the dry dock at Saint-Nazaire, the only German-held dry dock between the Continent and the Atlantic Ocean. By blowing up the destroyer and damaging the dry dock, the Allies effectively blocked passage of the German battleship *Tirpitz* into the Atlantic, where it posed a grave threat to convoys in 1942. The mission was successful.

The man who would become my first husband, Allan McKelvie, was in Plymouth during the Blitz. His parents in Glasgow, Scotland, tried to call him on the phone to make certain he was safe. Glasgow had also been bombed, and Allan was trying without success to call his parents to make certain they were unharmed. The trunk lines for long-distance phone calls were overwhelmed during the war, so these frantic efforts to call one another were unsuccessful. Allan wrote to his father and stepmother and suggested they go to the Isle of Arran, a beautiful rugged island off the coast of Scotland where the family had spent summer holidays, because it would be safer. In his response, William McKelvie, a former sea captain who was in his mid-sixties and considered himself an old man, wrote a poignant letter to his son.

"My dear Allie," he wrote. "You were writing Allie about us clearing out to Arran. But in the meantime, no. It would only be playing into Hitler's hand. . . . I have faith that all will turn out well yet. . . . Although you have all grown to manhood and womanhood, I still feel yet that that at any cry, I must rush to your aid and protection. And as far as I am concerned myself, I have had my day and now laid down my armour. It is you young ones on the threshold of your careers that I worry about." He signed off, "With love and may God keep and protect you, to the prayer of your loving father. William McKelvie." His sentiments were so typical of the British at that time. Regardless of age or station, the people of Great Britain refused to shirk duty or even consider anything short of victory.

The navy issued us dress blue uniforms with wool serge skirts and jackets and bell-bottom trousers for work. Nothing fit properly, and we spent hours trying to tailor our clothes to a better fit. We learned how to fold the trousers horizontally to get the seven perfect creases representing the seven seas sported by every well-turned-out sailor, and like our male counterparts, we put the trousers under our mattresses while we slept to press the creases into place. We received regulation women's underwear that was extraordinary in its volume. The bras were simply huge, and none of us, all skinny young girls, could ever hope to fill them. We used to laugh and speculate about the matrons who decided what would constitute standard-issue undergarments for young females. We all hated the standard issue Wren hat, which my colleague Paddy O'Brien Gregson described as a cross between a fisherman's sou'wester and child's sun hat in her memoir *Ten Degrees below Seaweed*. We folded the brims up as tightly as possible and wore them far back on our heads to achieve a jaunty look that was not really regulation style but, as time wore on, was tolerated by our superiors.

The old salts still serving on some of our larger boats, such as the hospital boats, were shattered by the intrusion of women into their sacred domain. They wondered what in the world had happened to their navy. But they understood that extraordinary times called for extraordinary measures. These grizzled old sailors—considered, much to their annoyance, too old to go to sea—tried to clean up their language and teased us by tying slip knots into the holding ropes of our hammocks, where we slept when we had overnight duty, so the hammocks fell down as soon as you put any weight in them. This never failed to trigger considerable hilarity. They also shared their rum ration with us, the ultimate compliment. It was the coarsest of rum, sheer rotgut. We tried to appreciate the gesture, but most of it went over the side. They used to make us tea with condensed milk and brown sugar. It was ghastly stuff, so thick a spoon would stand up straight in it.

Great Britain had been a very class-conscious country before the war, but universal service tended to eliminate class distinctions. For me, it was exhilarating and intensely interesting to meet young people from all sorts of backgrounds. The differences that had seemed so important to people of my mother's generation melted away in the heat of war. We were all fighting the same enemy. We would survive, but only by working together. Military service and universal conscription acted as a great big melting pot of humanity, mixing all sorts of people into a wonderful stew in both the United Kingdom and the United States. That type of shared experience builds understanding of differences and love of country and encourages shared sacrifice. I always thought it made an effective argument for mandatory national service.

I experienced a rare camaraderie in living and working with men and women of all shapes, sizes, beliefs, and classes. We were dependent upon one another for our very lives as bombs fell in the night. Although we were filled with the bravado and optimism of youth, the war and its threats had a deep psychological impact on us and created an urgency about living. The young men I spoke with at night in the bustle of the seaport taverns wondered aloud if there would be a tomorrow for them. They all wanted to get married. I am convinced they did not want marriage so much as they wanted to know they would survive the war; they wanted the security and the home that marriage represented. These young men sometimes poignantly admitted to being fearful that they would die and never experience the joys of parenthood or even the simple joy of living without fear of bombs. We were all away from our families and homes and desperate for the warmth and comfort of simple companionship.

After the United States entered the war, it was just a question of time before I saw my first ship bearing the American flag, a submarine called the *Blackfish*, a Gato-class submarine built in Groton, Connecticut, by Electric Boat. The sub had been badly shaken by depth charges and arrived in Plymouth for needed repairs. We were sent out to fetch the captain. We created quite a stir. The crew was stunned by the sight of girls coming alongside, and word spread quickly. The submarine tipped dangerously to port side as the sailors all rushed over to have a look. I was the coxswain of the admiral's barge and had the grand rank of leading seaman, or leading Wren. I never became an officer because I never reached the mandatory minimum age of twenty-one for officers while serving. The sailors invited us on board, and it was our turn to be stunned when they offered us the most amazing quantity of delicious food we had seen in years. I still remember that food, great slabs of salmon and huge buckets of ice cream in many flavors. The American troops always had enormous amounts of provisions and supplies and were always generous with food and knitted hats and gloves. The Americans introduced me to Jergens hand lotion, a most welcome balm for my sadly chapped hands. They were so generous.

I must note that there was a twinge of resentment against the Americans too. Despite our desperate need and gratitude, it did grate that these unseasoned sailors and soldiers behaved as though they were rescuing us. We not only experienced a far greater threat from the Fascist menace than America ever did because of our location, but we had also been fighting this war, doing without basics, and truly suffering for years. It was annoying that they criticized our unpasteurized milk and other things unfamiliar to them. To be fair to the American troops, we were also unaccustomed to their bold, forthright style. In the course of the war, however, I made great friends with many Americans and came to enjoy and appreciate our cultural differences.

We had the honor of hosting Queen Elizabeth one day. She accompanied her husband, King George VI, on a visit to Plymouth. I believe it was their first visit since March 20, 1941, the day the Plymouth Blitz began. No sooner had the royal train left the station on that day than the bombing began. This trip was mercifully more peaceful. The woman who became known years later as the queen mother (she was the mother of then princesses Elizabeth and Margaret; after George VI died, Princess Elizabeth became Elizabeth II) wore a pale blue dress and coat, a straw hat with net trimming, and high-heel shoes, according to the recollection of Paddy O'Brien Gregson, a fellow Wren. After she inspected the Wrens on the docks, she stepped into our Vosper motorboat. This was the first time the queen's royal standard had been struck on a boat manned by Wrens. My best friend, Pauline Davidson, and I executed our boat-hook drill, and we carried the queen from the naval barracks to have tea aboard the HMS *Drake*. I was a bit nervous. It was an important moment for the Wrens. We had no official designation from the Royal Navy, and the queen's visit gave some recognition of the role we were playing in support of the war effort. Her brief trip on our boat passed without incident. I was a very experienced sea woman by then.

Of course, we were all young and eager to have fun, and we did. My dear friend Pauline and I went to a local pub most nights. It was like a social club more than a nightclub. We ate lobster sandwiches and listened with rapt attention to the stories of the wartime adventures of the young sailors and soldiers. Lobster is regarded as a luxury food now, but in the 1940s lobster was the workingman's fish at seaports in both the United Kingdom and the United States, and you could buy a lobster sandwich for a shilling. We lived very much in the moment. Friendships were made quickly but felt profound, and many have lasted for my entire life. The bonds of friendship were solidified by the chaotic, dangerous times. It was a very different era, so these relationships were very proper and chaste. There was no effective birth control, and most brides were virgins on their wedding day. We were up at 5:30 a.m. and had a curfew of 9:30 or 10 p.m., so there was no real opportunity for wild living even if we had been so inclined.

Alcohol fueled much of the social life despite the best efforts of Lady Astor, an ardent advocate of temperance and the member of Parliament who represented Plymouth. Lady Astor was an American, Nancy Langhorne of Charlottesville, Virginia, who married Viscount Waldorf Astor and became the first woman to sit in Parliament. (She was not the first one elected. That honor was held by an Irish woman who went to prison for her Sinn Fein political beliefs and never formally assumed the office.) Lady Astor's political sway had declined by the time the war broke out, in part because she was as antiwar as she was anti-alcohol, but she managed to keep the official naval facilities, including the officer's club, dry. She is famously said to have explained, "One reason I don't drink is because I wish to know when I am having a good time."

Despite her best efforts, alcohol is very much part of the sailor tradition. I remember watching inebriated sailors who, after long duty at sea, had drunk as much as they could (probably just beer) in the brief two-hour liberty on shore before returning to their ships. Then as now, there is a rule that each sailor must reboard under his own steam. The drunken sailors would be positioned at the top of the gangplank, having been more or less carried up by their buddies, then stagger across the transom on their own, which was mandatory, and be caught on the other side by a friend on board. We had great fun watching them but could sympathize with the headaches they were going to have the next day.

I never drank very much. I did not share Lady Astor's sense of moral outrage; I just did not develop much of a taste for it, and alcohol made me feel sick, so I avoided it. For much of my life, I held a cocktail glass for show. But I had as much fun as anyone. We looked forward to weekly dances at the Moorland Links Hotel at Yelverton, about eight miles away from Plymouth. We went by bus or on the back of motorbikes. Alan Miller, a dear friend, used to pick me up and take me to these dances on the back of his battered old motorbike. I would carry a lantern because the bike had no lights. Alan tracked me down many years later and escorted me to the sixtieth anniversary of the end of World War II at Westminster Abbey. In his book *Over the Horizon, 1939–1945*, he tells how my long, green evening dress once got caught in the chain of the bike and was nearly ripped off my back.

I ran into him in the airport in New York many years later and was a little disappointed because I thought he had become a rather dull if successful businessman. But the next morning I was sitting in the chapel at my sons' school when he suddenly sat down beside me and whispered that he had finally sold the motorbike for £5, then he left just as suddenly. He had come to the United States to sail in the Newport-to-Bermuda race on his yacht, so he was not as stodgy as he appeared.

We Wrens shared everything, including our evening dresses. We did not get civilian clothing coupons, so we each donated one evening dress from our civilian days to a joint collection. In this way, we could wear a different dress at the dance each Saturday night. The men never noticed what we wore, but we enjoyed the variety. And when we had time, we took the train up to London to dance the night away and then sleep in the overhead hammock storage compartments on the last train home, dodging the knapsacks and luggage of other travelers. When we arrived back in Plymouth, we changed into our working clothes and went off to the docks again. Only the young can do that.

I loved my fellow Wrens. They were wonderful young women. There was a lovely girl who came from Argentina, where her parents had moved. Her ship was torpedoed as she made her way back to England to help fight the war, and she survived days in an open boat. Another woman had left her children with a nanny to join us. I listened to their life stories and learned a great deal from them. Although I had many siblings, I grew up somewhat alone because I was the youngest child. The Wrens gave me sibling-like relationships, which enriched my life and eased the loneliness of being away from Maldon.

There were many life lessons to be learned in the military. One day I pulled up to a ship to pick up a German prisoner of war, a tall, handsome, but bedraggled general, and his escort. There were no buttons left on his great coat. The German officer looked so utterly defeated. I'm sure he felt humiliated to be fetched by a bunch of girls. I felt a wave of sadness when he looked at me as I steered the boat into the dock. It reminded me always to be aware of the humanity of the enemy.

The war also had a major impact on my life when I met Dr. Allan M. McKelvie, a good-looking navy doctor from Glasgow, Scotland, during my first week in the Wrens. I was doing office work for Richard Miles in Malvern in the West Midlands. Dr. McKelvie was the medical doctor in residence. He was a classic Scot: a fun-loving and adventurous man who loved his whiskey and played the bagpipes rather badly. We dated for about two months before he left for an assignment on the HMS *Gambia*, a Crown Colony light cruiser assigned to trade-protection duties in the Indian Ocean. At about the same time, I went to Plymouth.

We wrote to each other every few months, and his letters were full of his adventures. He was extremely enterprising. He had a group of friends nicknamed "The Drones." One was assigned to another naval ship in the Indian Ocean. Another was a colonial officer in Nairobi, Kenya, then the capital of British East Africa and a great center of big-game hunting. He somehow, in the midst of a war, managed to go on safari, socialize with his friends, and have a grand time.

We had never discussed our relationship, but he returned eighteen months later in June 1943 with a beautiful diamond engagement ring. I barely knew him and had never met his family. The HMS *Gambia* was supposed to pull into Plymouth but had to go to Liverpool instead because of a bombing raid. We met in London and then went to Maldon to tell my parents of our imminent marriage, which loomed because his leave only lasted for a few weeks. He just assumed he was going to marry me, and I allowed myself to be carried along by his enthusiasm. Just weeks later, we were married at Trinity Church Brompton in London on July 10, 1943. The church was near the Rembrandt Hotel in Knightsbridge, the only place where my parents could arrange to provide enough food for a wedding reception in the midst of the war shortages. It is a popular wedding venue to this day. There was literally no place in Maldon that could supply food for a wedding reception, and London was also an easier place for guests to gather. I borrowed a wedding dress from the sister of Len's wife, Betty. It was not a very good dress, but it fit and it was white. A young naval officer who had given me an annotated copy of the poems of Rupert Brooke, which seventy years later still sits on the table beside my bed, stood outside the church and hoped I would change my mind. I never saw him again. Allan's brother Donald sent us a telegram on our wedding day to apologize for his absence and explain he was otherwise occupied. In fact, he was serving with the Seaforth Highlanders battalion of the Fifty-first Highland Infantry Division. The battalion was invading Sicily as part of Operation Husky, which began on July 9 and 10. The operation was wildly successful. The Allied forces drove the Axis forces off the island and opened up the Mediterranean sea lanes. This led directly to the fall of Mussolini and the Allied invasion of Italy. My marriage proved to have a more mixed record.

After the wedding, I returned to my Wren duties in Plymouth, and Allan went to his new assignment at a military hospital in Sherborne, Dorset, where Allied forces were preparing for D-Day casualties. A month before my twentieth birthday, I was a married lady, but did I really know the man I had married?

There were a few disquieting moments before the wedding. Allan's letters to me from the Indian Ocean were filled with his adventures and experiences, but he never once asked me what I was doing in Plymouth or about my work and experiences as a Wren. I subsequently realized that I was no longer the carefree teenage girl he had met in 1941 at the beginning of my enlistment. My experiences in Plymouth made me grow up quickly. I did not pay attention to my own misgivings. I considered myself quite grown up at that point, and I had been working hard and been independent for two years as a Wren. I never once expressed a whisper of doubt to my parents or anyone else. In hindsight, it was false pride that kept me from admitting to my parents that I really did not know Allan well enough to marry him.

I see now that I got caught up in the romance of the war. I was also very young, and Richard Miles and Allan McKelvie looked out for me when I first enlisted. I think they were almost surrogate parents for a young girl who was on her own away from her family for the first time. There had been other factors as well. Several of the young men who had been beaus while I was in Plymouth died in combat; one piloted a plane that went down over the English Channel when it ran out of petrol as he tried to get home. The pilot, a young man named Lance, had loved Brick House and the life there and wanted to be part of it. He sent many beautiful bouquets of roses to me at the Wrenery in Plymouth. The news of his plane going down was shocking and a real trauma for me. Many of the dashing submariners whom Pauline and I befriended simply disappeared beneath the sea and never returned. Young people typically share a sense of immortality, but war changed that for us. We all had an acute sense of our own mortality, and the old Latin phrase "carpe diem" ("seize the day") ruled the day. There was no thought of what we would do after the war. I assumed my navy doctor would be a country doctor somewhere, but I really did not think much about it. Marriage represented stability in the midst of chaos. It seemed everyone was rushing off and getting married. I grabbed for that anchor just like everyone else.

Allan also seemed like the sort of man a woman should marry. I had been raised with the assumption I would marry and become a wife and mother. Women did not aspire to the professions. The gender roles were quite specific and limited for women. He was also a medical doctor and eight years older than I. It was a very significant age difference at that point in my life. I looked up to him as a more mature, more experienced, and solid person. Doctors were revered in those days. He was also great fun, a true romantic and brimming with plans and dreams for the future. He was a wild Scot who played the bagpipes, partied hard, and relished the company of his buddies. I was a rather naïve teenager, and the fact he was great fun carried a lot of weight.

We did not get to know each other much better during our first married months because I was in Plymouth and he was at the Royal Naval hospital in Sherborne, Dorset. I would see him on occasional weekends. I requested a transfer to Weymouth to be closer to my new husband and secured my transfer on December 6, 1943.

My time in Weymouth was a dark and stressful one. The buildup to D-Day, the day of the Allied invasion of the Continent, was an intense period of preparation. No one knew exactly when it would take place, but everyone knew it was coming. The war had been under way for four long years. In Great Britain, everyone was exhausted and stretched to the limit. The Allied forces transformed the port of Weymouth into a massive depot for all sorts of ships and landing craft. The invasion entailed moving not only more than three hundred thousand men but thousands of tons of heavy equipment and thousands of vehicles. I saw Dwight D. Eisenhower, the U.S. Army general who was the supreme commander of the Allied forces in Europe, when he came to inspect the troops. The enlisted men were just raw with fear. The young sailors and soldiers knew that they might be going to their deaths when the invasion took place, and their anxiety and trepidation could be seen in the excessive drinking and almost manic behavior. Everyone was on edge. The fear was realistic and understandable. More than fifty-eight thousand Allied troops died during the invasion and subsequent battle at Normandy.

The Wrens had very difficult job manning the Liberty boats before the invasion, and we often felt overwhelmed. The Liberty boats were large whalers that ferried sailors to and from their ships and landing craft for their few hours of shore leave. At that time there were only British troops in Weymouth. When I look back, I feel it was too much for young girls. We took our boats out into the wide-open, often rough sea. There was no breakwater there. We could not use any lights at all on either sea or land; we had to navigate by the stars. On a cloudy night, when it was pitch black, I felt blinded. I could only make out the dimmest outline of ships and landing craft. The troops were almost all very young and very apprehensive. My heart would be in my throat as I eased my boat through the darkness and the roiling ocean waters. There would be just two of us on board as crew. Mercifully, it did not last too long for me because I became pregnant with my first child, and I was not allowed to continue to work on the boats. In April 1944, I received an honorable discharge on compassionate grounds from the Wrens, and my service ended.

In many ways it was heart-wrenching to leave those young men. So many of them just wanted to talk about their mothers. Many, boys still, were hauntingly bewildered. We would deliver them back to their ships or landing craft, but sometimes there would be a body left in the boat, a young man who had drunk himself into a stupor, and we didn't know where he belonged. So we would have to plough our way back and find where he belonged. It did not happen often. There was an informal buddy system in the military, and the young service members looked after one another as the Wrens did.

Plymouth had been hard but glamorous. There was no glamor in Weymouth. It was just hard. And I hated leaving those young men to their unknown fates as D-Day loomed just weeks away. I look back on that period of my life as a liberating experience. I learned a lot about myself and my ability to handle my own life. I learned a lot about humanity and the essential equality of all people. Class and background did not matter in war. My service changed me from a naïve young girl into a more grown-up woman with a deeper sense of compassion and duty.

I left Weymouth and the Wrens behind and for the first time lived as a wife with my husband in a centuries-old stone house in the charming medieval town of Sherborne, waiting for the birth of my first daughter, Jill. We had wonderful picnics with the American nurses and doctors based at the American hospital near there. As usual, the Americans had ready access to fabulous food. We supplied the bicycles; they brought the food. It was a pleasant interlude and a time of great anticipation, waiting for the end of the war as well as a new baby. Allan was not terribly busy yet. Both the British and U.S. hospitals were preparing for casualties, and we were weeks away from D-Day. I lived in town so I could walk to the baker and butcher and meet friends for coffee. I remember always scrounging for food. It was impossible to get a chicken. We ate a lot of canned Spam, a form of luncheon meat made mostly from pork, and the Americans were often our only source of butter. We sent Allan's brother a bottle of whiskey in a hollowed-out loaf of bread—it arrived for him on Christmas Day in Europe.

The war still felt very close. I went to London one day while I was in an advanced stage of pregnancy. The Germans had moved from bombing infrastructure to bombing people in a terror campaign and developed an early version of the guided missile, the V1 and V2 buzz bombs, which sounded like dustbins rattling. When the noise stopped, it was a signal the bomb was coming down, and it was time to run. I was at a railway station and enormous with child when I heard the familiar dustbins rattling. When the noise stopped, I ran for my life. It was terrifying.

I was in Sherborne when the D-Day invasion began on June 6, 1944. I remember seeing the enormous gliders carrying thousands of soldiers to the front. The entire sky was filled with aircraft, and the combination produced a buzz as if millions of bees were heading east through the sky at the same moment. The gliders were flimsy, engineless devices that were intended to be disposable. The only function of the gliders was to carry troops and equipment into war. They were towed by military transport planes and then released to glide to earth. The planes towing them flew very low. Many of the gliders cracked like eggs upon impact, causing terrible injuries and deaths even before a single shot was fired. Having known so many soldiers and being so sensitive to their youth, I was pained to see those gliders fill the blue sky, literally blotting out the sun, knowing many would not come home. A lot of bad things happen during war.

My first child, Jill, was born on November 14, 1944, at the local hospital in Sherborne. Allan and I had a disagreement over her name. I liked the name Prudence, and he did not. We lived near the hospital, and when my labor began, we walked over together. I remember clinging to a lamppost to argue for the name Pru. We compromised on Patricia Jill. I now think he may have been right about that. Jill was a much better name for a young girl growing up in the United States.

I had become very interested in natural childbirth. A notable physician, Dr. Grantly Dick-Read, created a stir with his arguments for natural childbirth. He said that the heavy use of drugs and excessive manhandling of the baby with forceps robbed the mother of the important positive experience of giving birth and led to unnecessary trauma for the baby. I met with him in London, and we had a wonderful talk. He was an extremely good-looking man. He would have been fifty-four years old at that time, and he kept admiring my hat, a little straw boater with a tiny feather in the hatband. Unfortunately, there were no doctors in Sherborne who followed his teachings, although I did like and admire the doctor who cared for me. Dr. Dick-Read was a man far, far ahead of his time, and it took another generation for the medical establishment to recognize the value of his views. Today he is regarded by medical authorities as one of the most historically significant figures in obstetrics. In one of those strange coincidences in life, it is interesting that the use of forceps in childbirth was introduced by the Chamberlen family of surgeons who lived at Woodham Mortimer Hall on one of my father's farms. The front gate carries a plaque commemorating the innovation. The Chamberlens were French Huguenots who fled religious persecution in France in the mid-sixteenth century and settled in England. The surgeons kept the instruments a secret for 150 years, and the mothers were blindfolded or kept behind a sheet to avoid seeing them.

D-Day in June 1944 set off a cascade of events that led to the end of the war in Europe in just eleven months and the end of war in the Pacific three months after that. Two months after D-Day, the Allies liberated Paris. In December, the Allies defeated the Germans in the Battle of the Bulge. Benito Mussolini was killed in Italy on April 28, and two days later Adolf Hitler committed suicide in his Berlin bunker. President Harry Truman, who had become president upon the death of Franklin D. Roosevelt in April, declared victory in Europe on May 8. The Japanese surrendered in September.

The end of the war in Europe lifted a huge weight off Great Britain. For the first time in five years, we all felt as though we could exhale. The relief was palpable. But the war left the country in terrible shape. There were still tremendous shortages of basic goods, with little food, few clothes, and no consumer goods to speak of. The first winter after the war was not a lot better than wartime from a lifestyle perspective. The infrastructure of the nation was damaged, nonexistent, or severely overextended. The transition to peacetime did not happen with the flick of a switch. It took time.

Allan wanted to be a surgeon, so we decided I should return to Maldon with Baby Jill and Allan would go by himself to Edinburgh to study for the Fellow Royal College of Surgeons certification. This would take about three months, and once he passed the exams, he could practice anywhere in England or Scotland.

As we packed up in Sherborne, Allan's much-loved brother, Donald, was getting married that September in Hamburg, Germany. Allan figured out a way to get to Hamburg to attend the wedding. Without a word to me, he hitched a ride to Germany, much to his brother's delight because it was wonderful to have a member of the family with him at his nuptials. But it was not so good for me. Allan could not get home again, and was stranded in Germany for two full weeks. I had no idea where he was. He hadn't told me he was going to the wedding. He never called. That two-week period with no knowledge of his whereabouts was disquieting. I felt I could not tell anyone that I had no idea where my husband was. I always had the feeling that if he did not want to be with me, it was somehow my fault. Young women always think it is their fault. I was twenty-one. My mother was a stickler for courtesy, but I began to realize the operative word in my life was "adjust."

Once Allan mustered out of the military and headed to Edinburgh, I returned to my parents and Maldon with Jill and was delighted to be home. The wartime shortages of food and goods were never felt as acutely on the farm, where we had access to fresh food and all the basic necessities of life. Brick House survived the war intact. A bomb had landed near the house, blowing out some windows, but the family home and my parents were safe. My parents were happy to have me and their grandchild in residence. While the regular household staff had all left for wartime duties, my parents always had someone helping out at the house, so I had plenty of help with my baby. By now I was pregnant with my second child.

I visited Allan a few times in Scotland. He soon announced that he was off again. He had been awarded a Commonwealth Scholarship in 1939 to study medicine in the United States at Massachusetts General Hospital, the famous teaching hospital in Boston affiliated with Harvard University. The war had caused a suspension of the program. With the war over, he received notification in the spring of 1946 that he had to use his scholarship right away or else forfeit it. He decided he would rather study at the Mayo Clinic in Rochester, Minnesota, then as now one of the world's best medical research and treatment facilities, and convinced the program to allow him to transfer the scholarship.

Transportation after the war was either inadequate or overwhelmed. Allan left in July for the United States. Our plan was for me to follow. But many months passed before my father could arrange for my passage. There were no planes and no ships yet in service or scheduled after the war. Allan had hitched a ride on a merchant vessel.

Finally, my father scheduled my trip in the fall. By that time, I had two babies: Jill, who was two years old, and five-month-old Rod. Allan somehow missed Rod's birth in May. But I got excellent care from the town midwife. She made her rounds in a long skirt and starched cap on an old upright bicycle and brought generations of Maldon children into the world. Rod was born in her house in a room she kept for just such occasions. The family doctor, Dr. Pirrie, who always wore striped pants and a vest and coat, helped her. He would call at Brick House each Saturday morning for a glass of sherry. His visits and inquiries after their health constituted my parents' medical checkup. They lived into their late eighties, never having heard the term "cholesterol." A modern doctor would lecture them on their fat-laden farm diet. My first son, Rod, arrived without incident, and I had a second beautiful baby.

My husband's absence did not bother me very much. But it did worry my parents. They never said a word to me, but I overheard them talking quietly at night in their bedroom, which was next to mine. My mother would hiss, "Where is he?" to my father, who clearly was not happy that Allan was away from me and the children for so long. I had come home for three months, which turned into eleven months. I can understand their anxiety to get me passage to America; having a daughter with two children in residence for so long asked a lot of them, and they obviously thought a married woman should be with her husband.

At that time, I assumed I would return to England upon the conclusion of Allan's studies, but my father must have had some prescience that I would not. He sternly warned me to resist the American impulse to buy on credit and cautioned me only to use cash and only to buy what I could afford. He handed me a few hundred dollars, which I later used to purchase a car. On November 14, Jill's second birthday, he took me to the airport. I held Jill's hand and carried Rod in a basket. My father tried to hide his tears by fumbling with his reading glasses. He was not a demonstrative man. He pulled a small bottle of brandy from his coat pocket and handed it to me. I was too overwhelmed by his display of emotion to ask about the brandy. Afterward, I wondered if he knew something about Rochester that I did not.

I was on my way to America, to Rochester, Minnesota, which might as well have been on the moon. I had no idea where it was and no idea of what to expect.

4

⚜

COMING TO AMERICA

The flight from London to New York stretched over seventeen interminable hours. Poor Jill experienced a very strange second birthday. The government had lifted wartime restrictions on overseas flights for civilians the previous January, and the first transatlantic civilian flights from London had begun in July. But there was a lengthy waiting list, so it took four months to secure our passage. In those days before jet travel, the propeller planes needed to stop at Reykjavík in Iceland to refuel. The U.S. military built the Reykjavík airfield during World War II to serve heavy bombers for the European war, and after the war it became the favored refueling spot for transatlantic flights. Of course, from my frazzled standpoint, the refueling stop just made the trip even longer.

I still remember that the female airline attendants, then called stewardesses, were not very nice to me. They much preferred waiting on the male business travelers or those men still in uniform to dealing with a harried young woman with a two-year-old toddler and a five-month-old infant. Fortunately, my own Sir Galahad, my dear friend Richard H. Miles, who had been my first boss when I enlisted in the Wrens, rescued us at the airport in New York City. He took us to the elegant Fifth Avenue house in Manhattan of Marion Wasserman, the wife of a prominent investment banker, William S. Wasserman. Richard was then a guest at the Wasserman home, and he prevailed upon their hospitality to take us in as well. One of Marion's children, Marie, and I later became friends in Washington. Marie Wasserman became a journalist and married Walter T. Ridder, a member of the famous newspaper family.

Marion Wasserman could not have been kinder to me. More than sixty years later, I remember with the same great relief and gratitude I felt at that time the hospitality she extended to the bedraggled young mother and two small children. She got us cleaned up, fed, and rested that night, and we caught a second flight to Rochester, Minnesota, the very next day. Marie Ridder says her mother talked about our brief visit for years. We must have seemed rather exotic, a variation of the European refugees still making their way to America!

Richard seemed to know everyone. He was part of a British intelligence and propaganda operation in the United States during World War II to promote the British cause and fight the isolationism that threatened to undermine full U.S. involvement in the war. This diverse and colorful crew included Roald Dahl, the famous children's author who was married for thirty years to the great actress Patricia Neal; Ian Fleming, author of the popular James Bond novels; and David Ogilvy, the legendary advertising executive. Jennet Conant wrote a book about them called *The Irregulars.* I thought she overstated the influence of Dahl and understated the role of Richard in her book, but Dahl was better known to the public because of his children's books, so the emphasis was understandable from a commercial standpoint.

The brief respite in New York was welcome. I had no idea of what awaited me in Minnesota, and the small break gave me a chance to pull myself together because I felt as though I had landed on Mars upon touching down in Rochester. We were greeted by a winter snowstorm. The temperature fell below zero degrees Fahrenheit. It was an unusually severe winter that year and a true shock to the body after the more moderate climate back home. Minnesota hugs the Canadian border, and Rochester is located on the south fork of the Zumbro River. Rochester had been a stagecoach stop between St. Paul, Minnesota, and Dubuque, Iowa, in the nineteenth century. By 1946, it had grown larger, but it was still a somewhat isolated rural community. The Mayo Clinic, then as now, was the largest employer in the area. The town population was about 28,500 by the end of the war. Many years later, IBM, the business conglomerate, was located in Rochester. I asked Tom Watson, IBM's CEO, why Rochester? He laughed and explained the company needed a Midwestern location, and his board squabbled about precisely where that should be. To end the argument, he smacked his gavel and decreed Rochester was the place. He said Rochester was literally the only place he knew because his airplane had once stopped there to refuel. So much for careful demographic analysis by corporate America!

My husband had made a shrewd choice in asking to be reassigned to Mayo. The clinic enjoyed an international reputation for excellence in patient care and research. The world-famous clinic had grown to international renown from modest beginnings. Dr. William Worrall Mayo came to Rochester in 1863 as an examining surgeon for draftees during the Civil War. He stayed and settled in what was then a genuine frontier community. His two sons, William James Mayo and Charles Horace Mayo, joined his medical practice in the 1880s. They helped establish the first hospital in Rochester after a devastating tornado in 1883 destroyed much of the community, killing twenty and injuring more than two hundred.

Charles Mayo's son, Charles W. Mayo, was carrying on the family tradition and working as a surgeon at the clinic when we were there. Chuck Mayo was a wonderful man. He lived in a huge house but had very little money. The nonprofit foundation that ran the clinic took most of the revenues from the practice of medicine. His financial constraints were compounded by the fact that he was raising six children plus the children of his brother, Joseph G. Mayo, who had died young. His children babysat for me. Chuck died on July 28, 1968, his seventieth birthday, in an automobile accident near Rochester.

Allan and I moved into prefab housing that the clinic set up to house the families of the fellows, as the doctors who were studying there were called. The houses were small but very snug, and the tiny space was easy to keep clean. Unlike in Maldon, where there was always a staff, I was on my own in Minnesota. Allan worked extremely long hours, from 8 a.m. until at least 8 p.m., and in the beginning he hated the hospital food, so he often called and asked me to bring him dinner. I would dress the children, put them in the car, install the chains on the car tires in the winter (a necessity to get through the snow and ice), and drive over the meal. I had remarkable energy when I was young. The first night in the prefab, I opened all the windows despite the low temperature. Allan advised me not to, but I had never slept with a window closed in my life, and I was not about to start. An airtight, hermetically sealed house just seemed unhealthy. In the morning, sheets of icicles covered the inside walls around the windows. I had no idea how very cold it could get in Minnesota. Maintenance men from the clinic had to come out and chip away the ice. I also had been accustomed to putting Rod outside in the fresh air in his pram to nap; when I did this in Rochester and he sucked his thumb, the mitten froze stiff. I had much to learn. My father apparently had a vague idea of the climate when he handed me that bottle of brandy at the London airport. I had packed my riding clothes and my squash racquet, but there was nowhere in Rochester for a woman to play squash, and no horses were available to me.

The postwar period at Mayo was exciting and stimulating. The war had interrupted the careers of many other medical students, doctors, and researchers, so many of the students and fellows were, like Allan, experienced older men and women who had served in the military and arrived with spouses and children. While we lived there, there were three other couples from Great Britain, including Doctors Reginald and Joy Bickford, whom we had met in London when we went to get our visas for the United States. Joy became a lifelong friend. She was a pediatrician but was not allowed to practice medicine at Mayo because her husband was a research fellow. Because the clinic rules forbade husbands and wives working together, she returned to school and earned another advanced degree in psychiatry. Another seven years passed before she could resume her practice, but once she started, she practiced psychiatry for more than fifty years in Minnesota and California. Reg became an esteemed professor at the University of California noted for his brain research. He was a brilliant man and always engaged in interesting, but to me slightly bizarre, research. When you went to their house, strange gadgets on the floor trailed after visitors. He was a trifle forgetful. He would do things like take the toilet apart and then neglect to put it back together again.

The clinic attracted patients from all over the world. The Mayo's reputation for excellence was so well established that Saudi princes would fly into Rochester on private planes to avail themselves of treatment. Although the city was a bit remote, the world quite literally came to Rochester, and the atmosphere replicated to some degree the international camaraderie I had experienced in Plymouth during the war. Sitting in a waiting room to see a doctor was quite an experience because you were surrounded by people from everywhere.

The Mayo brothers created the first integrated practice of medicine in which all the medical specialties collaborate in the care of a single patient. This seems so sensible now, but it was revelatory when they introduced the concept. The model attracted the best and the brightest. Sir Alexander Fleming, the Scottish physician and researcher who discovered penicillin, visited Mayo after winning the Nobel Peace Prize in 1945. Allan brought Sir Alexander's wife, Lady Sarah Marion McElroy Fleming, home for tea. I had put a kettle on the stove to heat water and was reading a letter from my mother when the flimsy curtains right next to the kitchen stove blew in and caught fire. As Lady Fleming entered the tiny house, I dashed past her with the flaming curtains and apologies.

Dr. Benjamin Spock, the world-famous pediatrician, worked at the Mayo Clinic in those years. He told me rather breezily one day that if there was trouble with a child, it was the parents he wanted to see. This was a bit disconcerting for a young mother to hear from the best-known pediatrician in the United States. He cut quite a distinctive figure on the dance floor at the Rochester Country Club. The doctors worked very hard and for very long hours, and the Saturday night dances were the time to cut loose and have some fun. We danced the night away, the men drank too much, and the wives had to get them home.

I was a bit shaken by the differences between the United States and Great Britain. It had not been easy leaving England, and often I truly felt as though I had landed in an alien world. Even the geography seemed strange, and I felt unmoored being so far away from my family and the familiar. Although long-distance and particularly transatlantic phone calls were very difficult in those days, for the first few weeks I repeatedly telephoned my mother in tears. I didn't just cry; I bawled. I never anticipated the cultural differences and the utter strangeness of Rochester. I had met many American servicemen and assumed that we were similar. After all, we all spoke English, the same language, or at least I thought we did. My mother was never one to coddle. She kept saying, "You must hang up now, dear," in her kind but firm way and conveyed to me without saying it explicitly that I needed to pull myself together. She was sympathetic but never enabled weakness.

My assumption that we all spoke the same language was also wrong. Each time I telephoned England, the long-distance operator in England would ask, "Are you through?" meaning, was I connected to my party. When I replied, "Yes," the American operator would disconnect the call, assuming I was finished. Operators listened in on all the long-distance calls back then. Instead of reciting poetry, my daughter Jill could repeat verbatim the most hilarious conversations between an American and an Englishman using the difference in meaning of phrases. One time, a doctor and colleague of Allan's kindly offered to take me fishing. He wanted to leave early in the morning when the fish are more likely to bite, so I asked him, using a British phrase, to "knock me up early." My new American friends laughed about that for months. There were many such misunderstandings.

Americans were far less formal than the British. I was taken aback when not only a neighbor but in fact everyone I met, young and old, addressed me as Cynthia immediately upon meeting me. My mother would have been shocked into silence by that sort of familiarity. I was surprised but quickly adjusted, although I found it hard to call older people by their first names when we first met; it seemed disrespectful.

After the wartime shortages of food in Great Britain and the paucity imposed by rationing, I was not prepared for the plenty of an American supermarket. The Piggly Wiggly supermarket simply overwhelmed me. I could not make a single decision when confronted with so much food wrapped in such different ways. The cans and bags and wrapped meats and bread were utterly unfamiliar. When I returned home empty-handed after my first supermarket excursion, Allan was quite rightly impatient with me.

The climate and living conditions also required some adjustment. The washing machine and vacuum cleaner were two houses away, so I had to put the children in their snowsuits and walk outside in that bitterly cold weather to do the laundry. With young children and babies, laundry was a daily chore. I remember the ringer on the clothes washer crushed all the buttons on the children's clothes. There were no clothes dryers then, so I hung the clothes on an outdoor clothesline, and they would literally freeze in place and stand up on their own. When it was snowing, I'd drape the laundry throughout the inside of the house. All the baby diapers were cloth and needed to be soaked in Borax, then washed. There were no disposable diapers in those days and no prepared baby foods. But there were magical moments. I loved the fireflies that came every evening, sparkling like tiny little diamonds in the darkness. I had never seen them before and was quite entranced. They were like the faeries of English legend flickering outside my door.

I learned some things the hard way. I did not always sort the clothing properly. One day a red child's sock got mixed in with the white clothes and turned all of Allan's underwear an anemic shade of pale pink. He complained bitterly that he was acutely embarrassed by his pink underwear in the doctors' changing room before surgery. I suggested he should be proud and consider himself a trendsetter. I have to confess that this happened more than once.

I used my father's cash gift to purchase a Nash, an American automobile made in a neighboring state, Wisconsin. I learned how to drive in the snow, an essential skill for much of the year. The automobile had no turn signals, and when it was too cold to open the car windows, I copied local practice and opened the car door each time I was going to take a left turn to signal my intent. It did seem like the thing to do at the time. Of course, we had no seat belts. Winter driving was made easier by the extraordinary road-maintenance crews who cleared the main roads of snow and ice on a daily basis in time for everyone to head off to work in the morning. There was something quite exhilarating about that American can-do competence, but I suppose people adjust to their environments.

No one in Rochester seemed the least bit interested in anything political outside the United States. That insularity is very American and doubtless reflects the size and geographic position of the country. We never had the luxury of ignoring the outside world in Great Britain. At the time it just seemed very odd to me. Country music, which I ultimately learned to love, seemed to be the only type of music available on the radio. BBC broadcasts seemed like part of a very distant past.

I had been accustomed to a classic farm diet of mostly meat and potatoes, treacle tart, and bugs in a bolster (our favorite name for suet pudding that was shaped like a bolster and loaded with raisins). I was introduced to an utterly different type of Midwestern cuisine in Rochester. When I asked my neighbor how to cook a hamburger, she collapsed in laughter at the notion that anyone would not have mastered such a basic skill. The wives in the prefab housing brought me an endless procession of tuna noodle casseroles and green Jell-O and banana molds to welcome me to the community. I had never seen or even heard of canned tuna fish or a casserole. But I eventually developed a taste for this classic Midwestern fare and became quite fond of the green Jell-O. People were so kind.

Although the war had ended, it took me a while to adjust to peacetime. We lived near a fire station, and I dove under the bed every time the siren sounded. It took many months to get over the instinct honed during the war to seek cover. Eventually, a sense of adventure and excitement displaced my homesickness. I couldn't wait to see the famous steamboats on the Mississippi River. To me, those steamboats represented America, with the evocation of Mark Twain's novels and the Longfellow poem about Hiawatha, one of my very favorite poems while I was growing up. I also discovered the wonder of the Sears Catalog in those years. I ordered pretty white curtains for the windows of the pea green prefab, and I delighted in many other household goods from Sears. The catalog was called the "Wish Book," and I thought it was just marvelous. I rarely went into town to shop. I just ordered from Sears, and the item appeared almost magically via the postal service on my doorstep. The Sears Catalog was the answer to almost everything. I found creative ways of furnishing our little house. I built bookcases with bricks and slats of wood—you have to have bookcases wherever you live. Some of the other wives sponsored Stanley Home Products tea parties, so I could purchase cleaning goods and supplies while visiting with them. The Stanley Home Products company had been created by a couple in Massachusetts during the Depression as a way for housewives to sell everyday products at home-based house parties. The parties were wildly popular because they gave the wives an outlet for socializing with one another and a chance to buy brushes, mops, and household cleaners. I found that sort of entertaining quite exotic and endlessly amusing. The Jewel Tea Company was also part of this trend after the war.

I always entertained. My parents had always hosted parties and dinners, and I did the same, even though we did not have much money and the house was tiny. Allan received a small stipend with his scholarship. I learned how to sew some of my own clothes and those adorable smocked dresses for little girls, which I sold. I also sold my blood to the clinic at $25 a pop. I loved getting that $25. I would window-shop and imagine buying shoes and other personal items with it, but the money invariably went for food. My mother marveled that I could do any entertaining at all without the support of a staff. She would say that when I was growing up, all she needed to do for guests was to ring the bell and ask the help to set another plate.

The children loved Rochester. They had lots of playmates, and the families were enterprising in finding fun activities. We used the hand hose to create an ice rink for the children, so they learned to skate. The families also got together and created a small ski area. I still remember their snowsuits. Those bulky insulated suits turned little children into small, colorful tubs of puffy fabric. It took enormous amounts of time to get them on and off squirming little ones, but the snowsuits provided a layer of protection from the bitter chill. The adults had fun too. The four British couples remained close friends and would get together for dinner once a month. Allan and I had driven to New York to pick up one of the couples—they had brought a huge dog with them, hoping to make money breeding him, but I think he just slept all the time and failed to generate much income or progeny.

The war had taken many lives, caused great damage, and interrupted the careers of millions for years. Everyone felt tremendous pressure to make up for lost time at every level. Entire nations were rebuilding after the destruction and loss of the war years. All of us were expected to play our role in this postwar drama, just as we had done our bit during the war. For the women who had been called to serve in factories and the military during World War II, the independence and opportunities changed when the men returned home. The clock rolled back, and women returned to their traditional roles as wives and mothers and left the factory floors for the kitchen. Even the popular culture reflected this new ideal. The families portrayed on television were perfect: a perfectly coiffed mother in pearls and a dress who maintained an immaculate, perfectly run home; a handsome father who went out to work in his business suit; the perky daughter with a pony tail; a charming, well-behaved son; a mischievous and very cute little brother. The popular television shows *Leave It to Beaver*, *Father Knows Best*, and *The Adventures of Ozzie & Harriet* reinforced the social expectations of the time. The postwar period put enormous emphasis on family stability and conformity. Despite my taste of freedom during the war, I fell in with the other wives and did not question my life. I was busy and kept having children, who filled my days and nights. It is safe to say that the children dominated my life during those years.

I had a strong sense of responsibility to my children. We had brought them to America, where they did not have a single relative. I also felt that if anything happened to me, I could not imagine anyone in England to whom I would entrust them. It was utterly unfair to burden my aging parents with young children. I felt that I was all they had to look after them, even though they had a father who loved them and provided for them. I suspect the long separations from Allan during the early years of our marriage fostered this sense of independence and personal responsibility. And the men of his generation focused intensely and almost exclusively on their careers. Most men did not participate in child rearing in the way they do today. That was considered a mother's job. So my job entailed being the chief decision-maker for the children, arranging for their schooling and monitoring their progress, attending their sporting events, and driving carpools. Raising four children is an all-consuming job, but I never questioned my responsibility or regretted it for a second. I actually had a lot of fun with them. I was young too and enthusiastically threw myself into my maternal role as chief champion, director, and manager of the McKelvie children.

The Commonwealth scholarship required Allan to return to a British territory after two years. So we moved to Vancouver in British Columbia, where he worked at the Children's Hospital for one year. Vancouver is located near the Pacific Ocean and surrounded by mountains. It is one of the most physically beautiful places in Canada. My son Allan Jr., whom we call "Bones," was born there in November 1949. Rod came up with that nickname because Allan Jr. was a chubby little boy. It is counterintuitive to name a chubby boy Bones, but it struck us as terribly funny and it stuck. We call him Bones to this day. The extra year allowed my husband to work in private practice and earn some money for our growing family. After the year, we moved back to Mayo for almost two more years.

Our youngest daughter, Lindsay, was born at the Mayo Clinic in July 1951. I had cooked six weeks of meals for the family before I went into the hospital to give birth, and I stored them in a freezer in the basement. The night Lindsay was born, a historic flood hit Rochester. Our house, like the other prefab units, was completely flooded when the Zumbro River overflowed its banks. The floodwaters tipped over the freezer, and I lost all the packed food. In addition to the food, we lost photographs and family papers, and I lost my precious record collection, including the Artie Shaw version of Cole Porter's

"Begin the Beguine," one of the best-selling records of the prewar period. Allan was in surgery at the clinic, so the neighbors stepped up to help because I was still in bed recovering from the birth at the hospital. Our friend Dr. Reg Bickford found a boat and rowed it to the house to rescue the children and their babysitter. Allan was at that time in the operating room, and the hospital would not let me speak to him. I left Baby Lindsay in the hospital and went home to a destroyed house with mud everywhere. In the midst of the cleanup, a neighbor offered me lunch, and I complained that I was not feeling too well. Fortunately, he was a doctor and he immediately diagnosed puerperal fever, a potentially fatal condition caused by contraction of an infection immediately after giving birth. I became infected cleaning up all that mud. I was back in the hospital for two weeks for treatment. Puerperal fever, also called childbirth fever, killed millions of women before doctors made the connection between bacteria and infection and the disease. It is almost unheard of in developed countries these days, but it is still a deadly fever for women in the developing world.

I adjusted to America fairly quickly. After the initial sadness of missing England, a sense of freedom and anticipation grew within me. I was still in my twenties and viewed America as one big glorious adventure. The expansive fields of wheat and corn acted as a kind of metaphor for a country with almost unlimited space and promise. In England, houses had been surrounded by hedges or fences for hundreds of years, demarking property lines. In the United States, I felt that there really were no restrictions. Anything was possible in America. I adored my children, and as I played with them and watched them grow, I became very thoughtful about their future. My instinct was that it was important to raise them as Americans so they would be full, unquestioned citizens of this land of opportunity and not to divide their loyalties between America and Britain.

Our time in Rochester eventually drew to a close. Allan entertained many job offers because of his experience at Mayo, but he had set his heart on moving to Washington, DC. So we moved there in the autumn of 1951. When we arrived, I was a twenty-eight-year-old mother of four children under the age of seven. Allan immediately dove into his practice of medicine, working long hours at the office and hospital, and I went about creating a new home in a very different place from Rochester.

The population of Washington, DC, peaked at an all-time high of 802,178 in 1950 after years of government growth, which began with Franklin Delano Roosevelt's New Deal in the 1930s and World War II defense-related spending in the 1940s. Thousands of Americans moved to the city to work for the federal government. At the time, Washington's racial mix was 65 percent white and 35 percent African American. That would flip the other way over the course of the next twenty years as construction of a federal system of interstate highways drew many people to the suburbs and terrible riots in the 1960s caused significant white flight. "Official" Washington was still quite small, however. The children of the middle-class families went to the same schools, and there was a fair amount of socialization in people's homes. Virtually no one entertained in restaurants in those days. Within months of our arrival, one of Allan's patients invited us to attend Dwight D. Eisenhower's inaugural ball at the Mayflower Hotel on Connecticut Avenue, just a few blocks from the White House. I was utterly dazzled. It was fun to get dressed up for a black-tie event. I wore a long, strapless white gown with a green stole and long white gloves. I felt quite glamorous. At the ball, I saw President Eisenhower for the first time since catching sight of him inspecting the troops in Weymouth during the war. I felt we had both come quite a long way. When I went home, my father would hold me personally responsible for the policies of John Foster Dulles, Eisenhower's secretary of state. He would lecture me about the shortcomings of Dulles's foreign policy in a modification of the "topics-of-the-day" discussions he insisted upon when we were growing up.

My life in those years revolved around our children. The girls went to National Cathedral School, and the boys were enrolled in public schools. We gave many class parties. I drove the carpool to National Cathedral so many times over the course of fourteen years that I'm quite certain the car could make the trip on its own. I went one day to an event at Rod's public school, and the teacher had no idea who he was. The public schools were not very good in the District then, so I withdrew the boys and enrolled them in a wonderful Catholic school, Our Lady of Victory, in the Palisades neighborhood not far from us. That lasted until the morning Bones asked his father for a quarter so he could buy a new set of rosary beads. Allan had not focused on the fact that the boys were enrolled in Catholic school. I'm quite sure I told him, but he really had little interest in that sort of thing. Neither Allan nor I was particularly religious, but Allan came from a defiantly Protestant Scottish heritage, and Catholic nuns educating his children simply would not do. So Rod was enrolled in Longfellow School and Bones in Landon.

Allan had a medical meeting in Los Angeles in 1957, and I proposed that I drive to Los Angeles with Jill and Rod, the two older children who were twelve and ten at the time, and he fly to the West Coast with the two younger children and meet us there. We would all then drive home on the northern route across the country to Washington. We had the most wonderful trip. I had found an excellent map from the Department of the Interior that showed all the national parks and their facilities. National parks were an inexpensive way to see America. We put a little pup tent on the top of the car and set off on the southern route to the West Coast. The first stop was Elvis Presley's house, Graceland, in Memphis, Tennessee. Elvis Presley was only twenty-two and had just emerged as the first rock-and-roll superstar. We camped at national parks all the way. I refused to deal with the pup tent and told the children it was their job to figure out how to set it up. On our first night camping, I washed the plastic dishes in hot water, and they melted, much to the hilarity of the children, so we had strangely warped bowls and plates for the rest of our journey.

We visited the Petrified Forest, the Hoover Dam, and the Grand Canyon and picked up mandatory water bottles before crossing the desert. When we called home, Allan told me a woman had forgotten to put the brakes on at the Grand Canyon, and her car holding her children had gone over the edge. It made me so nervous that I kept a foot on the brake the whole time. When we got to Las Vegas, I decided to teach the children a lesson about the evils of gambling and rather pompously announced that I would show them how easy it is to lose money. I took four quarters and put three into the slot machine and hit the jackpot. Money just poured out of the machine and spilled over the floor. This was not the lesson I expected to teach. To celebrate this unexpected bit of good fortune, I booked us into a fancy room in the most luxurious hotel in Las Vegas. The car, an old Nash Rambler with bald tires, broke down in the Black Hills in North Dakota. We had to stay three days while the car was repaired, and then the children refused to leave until they could see the end of a movie serial they had gotten caught up watching. The trip was an excellent adventure. I enjoyed myself as much as the children. Years later, Rod took his own children to visit many of the same places.

In Washington, the neighborhood was a great big playground for the children: they played soccer in the street and water polo in the pool; I was relegated to the position of goalie in water polo because the children said I did not swim fast enough. We went fishing in the Potomac River until I read in the paper about people falling in and drowning. I tried never to miss Sid Caesar and Carl Reiner in *The Show of Shows*, the best TV show and most humorous I have ever seen.

The four children emerged as distinct individuals. Rod was not quite the sweet, innocent boy he appeared to be. His shining face was belied by his involvement in regular neighborhood eruptions. And Lindsay was my own maverick. She ran away one day when she was about six. She announced her intent, and I stood on the front step and watched her struggling up the hill with her little red suitcase. It was an entrancing sight. Neither she nor I remember what dastardly act of mine had caused this defiant response from her.

We moved into a rented house in Virginia when we came to Washington, and Allan arrived home with our first TV set. He wanted to watch the World Series, a major baseball confrontation between the New York Yankees and the New York Giants. The first night, we were watching TV and unpacking the boxes when I suddenly said, "We have four children, and there are only three on the couch." Bones, then two years old, was missing. We called the police, who found him nearby, sitting on a sofa happily eating cookies, the guest of an elderly couple who lived in the neighborhood. They wanted to keep this cute little blond boy but gave him back to us.

Allan did not like being in the suburbs, so we soon moved into the Chevy Chase section of the District of Columbia and rented a house on Ingomar Street. I was astonished by and grateful to the brave woman who would rent to a family with four little children. It was an attractive family home with a wide surrounding porch and more space than we had in Rochester. The children could walk to school.

Our financial situation improved each year, allowing us to buy a house on Forty-eighth Street, where we lived for seven or eight years, and then to build a house with a pool on Forty-sixth Street. We held a membership in a golf and tennis club in northern Virginia, where Allan golfed and I belonged to the tennis team. We were able to send the children to private school, but money was always an issue. Although Allan was a gifted doctor, he was not a very good businessman, like many doctors. He invested in land in Virginia that proved to be worthless except for a farm in Loudoun County on Goose Creek, which he bought in October 1955. It seemed like a terrible waste of money that we could ill afford at the time, and I was upset about it, but it proved to be a good investment much later. My children continued to enjoy that house for years. Other investments were less profitable.

Allan did not worry about things like money. That was one of my jobs. I somehow juggled our finances to find the tuition money and keep the household running. Money had always been a means to an end for me, so I never cared much about accumulating wealth, but I have to admit, I worried endlessly about making ends meet throughout the marriage. My father's warning to me about the danger of debt always rang in my ears. Allan held the conviction that things would somehow work out, and they did.

Although my two oldest children had been born in Great Britain, all four of the children were now growing up as Americans. Allan had become a naturalized U.S. citizen, but I hesitated. My British heritage meant a great deal to me. I had served my country, and my family had worked the land in Essex County for hundreds of years. My emotional and psychic connection to Great Britain was very strong. But my children were definitely 100 percent true-blue Americans. When Rod was a youngster, he was embarrassed by my accent and used to make me stand far away at soccer matches so no one would notice when I cheered him on. To his credit, it was a passing childhood phase. He came running home from school one day and burst into the house to announce there was a new boy at school who had long hair, wore short pants, and talked just like me. My mother was very much a proper Englishwoman throughout her entire life. I wrote to her once to say I would be coming home for a visit, and she said how lovely it would be to see the children but added, "They don't chew gum, dear, do they?" My years in the United States had changed me as well. My mother once suggested I not answer the telephone at Brick House, because after living in Minnesota, I was apt to say, "Hi," and that was far too informal for her. While visiting my parents, I asked my brother Ted to accompany me to buy an antique card table, which he wanted to give me as a birthday present. When we pulled up to the shop, he instructed me to stay in the car. I was surprised. When I asked why, he said, "With that American accent of yours, they'll double the price." It had never occurred to me that living in America was diluting my English accent.

As the children grew up, they wanted me to be an American, just as they were. So I finally relented and on March 12, 1957, went downtown to be sworn in as a U.S. citizen. A friend told me it would not be too bad because the citizenship oath did not mention the queen. The oath actually required me to renounce "any foreign prince, potentate, state or sovereignty," so the friend was literally correct; there was not a single mention of the queen herself. That omission somehow made it a bit easier.

I did not tell anyone in the family that I was going to do it at the time because I had such mixed emotions. Another new citizen, a Hungarian man, standing in line with me exclaimed, "Isn't it wonderful to be an American!" At that moment, I was not sure that I could fully agree. It was a difficult decision, but I never looked back or regretted it. I have lived in the United States for 75 percent of my life and come to love and admire this country. My children, grandchildren, and great-grandchildren are blessed to be citizens of the United States. I always felt I should have been more appreciative of the opportunity to become an American citizen, given how many foreigners aspire to U.S. citizenship, but I cannot deny that I did not give up being a subject of the queen without some pain.

My father sent me a plane ticket each year so that I could return home to see my parents. There were currency restrictions, so you could not send money out of the country. My mother would say, "Do you mind eating pheasant again?" as if it were a hardship! Father died in 1958 after a brief illness. My mother stayed in Brick House for a few more years but grew isolated and lonely by herself. She stayed at Brick House one year longer than she really intended because she said she knew I needed to come home one more time before she moved. She was absolutely correct, and I always marveled at her insight and thoughtfulness in putting my needs ahead of her own. She had given up the chauffeur and car because she said it seemed senseless to drive into town for a single pork chop. When she moved into the village, she was much better off. She missed Brick House because she had lived there all her life, and it was an adjustment, but she could walk out each day for exercise and do errands and engage with the townspeople in a way that was impossible on the farm.

Allan McKelvie was a true visionary when it came to medical care. Toward the end of the 1950s, Allan helped establish the Orthopedic Letters Club Overseas Project (OLCOP). He and other doctors traveled overseas to provide treatment in desperately poor undeveloped countries at their own expense. The doctors hatched this project at the American Academy of Orthopaedic Surgeons Convention in January 1959. Allan convinced MEDICO, the charitable foundation created by the famous Dr. Tom Dooley and Dr. Peter D. Comanduras, to sponsor the project. MEDICO suggested they go to the Kingdom of Jordan, then a very poor country with extreme medical needs. We dropped the children at the Isle of Arran, the beautiful Scottish island where Allan had spent his holidays as a child, and left the youngest three in the care of Allan's wonderful stepmother.

Jill, then a high school student, and I accompanied him on his first trip to Jordan. He was the first OLCOP doctor to go there. I still have vivid memories of corridors and waiting rooms full of children crippled by polio, many carried on the backs of older siblings. The children had never walked and never gotten any medical treatment at all, and sadly they were hidden away by their families. It was somehow disgraceful to have a physically disabled child. Allan later told the story to *Look Magazine*, a very popular mass-circulation general-interest magazine. In the story, he told how the medical needs were so overwhelming that one or two doctors could barely dent the demand. He realized very quickly that he and the other doctors needed to teach orthopedic techniques and practices to Jordanian doctors. So he toured the hospitals of the country and taught the doctors. When he learned there were no crutches for the children, he found a refugee carpenter who earned a living making crucifixes out of olive wood and selling them to tourists. Allan sketched a picture of a pair of adjustable crutches and asked him whether he could make them. The carpenter did an amazing job. He was an excellent craftsman.

We stayed at the American Colony Hotel in East Jerusalem, then occupied by Jordan. The longtime proprietor, Bertha Spafford Vester, then quite old, lived there. She had a remarkable story. Her parents immigrated from Illinois to Jerusalem when the city was still part of the Ottoman Empire. She was a legendary figure in Jerusalem, well known for hospital and charity work and brimming with exotic anecdotes. Her parents lost their first four daughters at sea and moved to Jerusalem when she was three years old in 1881, so she did not remember any other place. During World War I she fed thousands of Turkish and British soldiers. She knew General Allenby and Lawrence of Arabia and met Rudolph Hess when he was a youth. She had lived the history we had only read about.

When Jill and I were not helping at the hospital in Jordan, we traveled all over the region in a rental car. We visited Bethlehem and Ramallah and rather bravely drove to Damascus in Syria.

Jordan denied it had a polio problem, but the American doctors found many, many victims, which provided overwhelming evidence of an epidemic. They estimated that more than one-third of the patients with orthopedic problems suffered from the aftereffects of polio. The doctors managed to get a personal meeting with King Hussein and explained the problem to him. Soon the polio vaccine was introduced in Jordan for the first time.

In 1963, I accompanied Allan to Algiers. It was a year after Algeria won independence from France, and we were warned not to leave the clinic where I was helping Allan to venture into town on the anniversary of the liberation day. But I ignored the advice and joined clinic staff to head into town. A frenzied, angry mob spotted me sitting in the back of a truck, thought I was French, and started to come after me. The workers with me cried out, "No, no, she's American, not French," and I'm sure they saved my life. It was a memorable experience. It taught me a lot about mob psychology and the need to appreciate the fires that burn in oppressed peoples.

During that same visit, a woman came out of a little shack near the hospital one night and invited me and a young doctor to come inside. She offered us couscous that she retrieved from a bowl kept under a bed. She only had one very dirty spoon. The doctor was about to decline, and I told him in English, which she could not understand, "You are going to eat that. We are both going to eat it." I nearly vomited but stifled the urge and accepted her gift to us.

She would have felt very sad if we had refused her hospitality. It would have suggested her offering was not good enough for us and, of course, that would never be acceptable. I am sure the young doctor does not remember me with fondness. I also went to Columbia and Tunisia, where I remember coming over a desert hill and seeing the ancient Roman ruin of the amphitheater at El Djem, which was once the center of the breadbasket of the ancient Roman Empire. It was the most extraordinary sight. I can see still it in my mind's eye. My friend Tom Soderstrom, a curator at the Smithsonian Institution, was able to cultivate some ancient seeds from there.

Once all the children were in school, I had more time for playing tennis with my female friends and volunteered at the Smithsonian. I also periodically enrolled in college classes to study geology, Greek literature, and other subjects that interested me. I went to class with a friend, Joan Shorey. We had a lot of fun. Joan was highly intelligent but could not spell, and we were asked to leave class once because I sent her a note when we were studying the Greeks to tell her the word "rape" has only one "p." Use defile, I suggested; it's much easier to spell. We made up all sorts of wonderful rhymes to remember our geology lessons. Eventually, I enrolled in the School of International Service at American University. But my husband would invite guests for dinner at the last minute to sabotage my efforts to study for exams or finish papers, so I soon had to give up on school. He never explicitly forbade me to go to school, but he made certain through his behavior that I would find it difficult to succeed. We never had a fight, so I did not have the chance to win or lose that battle. I was just frustrated.

I convinced Allan to buy a small cottage in Lewes, Delaware. I thought it would be a wonderful place to bring the children during their summer vacations. Washington gets terribly hot, and we could not really afford to send all of them off to summer camp. The city also emptied out in the summertime, when the wives and children abandoned the oppressive humidity and heat for a summer home. I wanted the children to experience something other than Washington, DC. In Lewes, they could swim and be outdoors and have fun. I wanted to buy a boat. My days navigating through the sea as a Wren had left me with a yearning to get back on the water. Allan was opposed and said we could not afford a boat, so I bought a kit in the mail and built a sunfish in the garage on Forty-eighth Street. I was so ignorant that when the instructions said you need a counter sink, I thought they meant the kitchen sink, not a special type of drill bit. Yet I thought it came out rather well. I was quite proud of it. I strapped it to the roof of the car and took it off to Delaware, where we raced across the sea. But when Allan saw the boat, he exploded with anger and exclaimed, "Nobody has a wife who builds boats!" When he said that, a penny dropped. I realized he had little interest in my wishes or happiness. It was disappointing that my own husband would not take any pride in my small accomplishment or even see the humor in my building a boat in the garage.

Lewes turned out to be a great summer holiday place; we made many friends there and started a much-repeated ritual of evening picnics on the beach with singing round the fire of "September Song" and other popular tunes. We had many happy times there, and now my son Rod has a house there and keeps the tradition alive, although we are no longer allowed to cook on the beach.

Most of the memories from those years are happy ones, but a few incidents foreshadowed the eventual end of the marriage. I once got very sick on New Year's Day, a national holiday. Complications developed from adhesions from minor surgery. I suffered exquisite pain, which literally brought me to my knees. Yet Allan refused to allow me to disturb the doctor on a holiday. When he left the house with the children to take them to dinner because I was simply too ill to do anything, I called my doctor, John W. Walsh, who immediately came over and quickly called an ambulance to take me to the hospital. I had emergency surgery and was hospitalized for weeks. Dr. Walsh said that I would have died if I had not received quick medical treatment. He was a wonderful doctor. He was First Lady Jacqueline Kennedy's obstetrician and delivered both of her children, Caroline and John Jr.

Allan was an excellent surgeon whose patients adored him. He also displayed great vision and compassion for the poor, as his international work demonstrated. But he clearly did not see me as a separate, equal human being with opinions, needs, or wishes of my own. He was a man of his times. He expected me to conform to a certain mode of behavior for a traditional helpmate wife and not deviate from it. His slights hurt me and built up over time.

Meanwhile, the children were growing up. I was proud of them. They were thoughtful, considerate, good people. No mother can ask for more. After being senior prefect at St. Georges, Rod went to Harvard. Jill studied at Connecticut College and Lindsay earned a bachelor of science degree at American University. Bones went to St. Georges in Newport for prep school and then Hobart College. Jill and Bones each spent one year at St. Andrews University in Scotland. The boys both became lawyers, and my girls earned master's degrees.

By 1967, only my youngest, Lindsay, remained at home. Lindsay absolutely hated the National Cathedral School as much as Jill had loved it. Jill had thrived at Cathedral and been head girl when she graduated. But Lindsay was in misery. She prompted me for the first and only time in my life to take on the head of a school. Lindsay won an award, and school administrators refused to give it to her because she was wearing the wrong shoes. I wrote out what I wanted to say and then pinned it to my sweater and waited for the head to call me back. Then, for the first and only time, I told her what I thought. I had great respect for authority and was definitely not one of those modern helicopter parents who whine and complain about everything involving their children. But the unfairness of that decision infuriated me.

Lindsay was so unhappy that I just had to find an alternative school for her. We finally arranged for her to attend the Purnell School, a boarding school in Pottersville, New Jersey, for her final two years of high school. This meant that when Lindsay went off to Purnell in the autumn of 1967, all of my children would be away at school. I would be alone at home with a man who simply refused to talk to me about anything that mattered and whose behavior told me he considered me unimportant and inconsequential. I was looking into an abyss.

In 1966, I had met Richard Helms, the deputy director of central intelligence, at a party hosted by the Lebanese embassy. I walked into a room and immediately noticed him standing behind a piano. He also noticed me. In fact, he winked at me, a surprising and rather flirtatious gesture. By chance, we sat next to each other at the dinner. We hit it off and had an immensely good time talking. His wife, Julia, and I were members of a group of women, called "The Minnows," who swam together. Allan and I ran into them at dinner parties. Dick and I always had a wonderful talk. He was interested in my thoughts and my activities. I never asked him about his work, which he appreciated. In Washington, dinner guests were always hounding him for a bit of inside information. Yet we never ran out of things to say to each other. These conversations had an extraordinary effect on both of us. I think he may have been as lonely in his marriage as I was. Finding someone to talk to so easily and happily was like drinking well water after wandering for years in a desert. We had the most genteel, old-fashioned courtship. We fell in love just by talking to one another.

My mother died in 1967 at the age of eighty-five. Although her death was not completely unexpected, it dealt an enormous blow. I may have been a grown woman with four children of my own, but losing my mother was very, very hard on me. I had lost an anchor. Not being able to call her or just know she was there for me was traumatic. I was not only sad but confused because I felt cross with her for leaving me. Her death closed a circle somehow. Losing my mother at the same time that my children were growing more independent made my loneliness more acute and nudged me closer to a decision to end my marriage.

For twenty-four years, I had tried to engage Allan McKelvie in a conversation about anything of consequence. I had failed. Each time I tried to talk to him, he walked out the door and went to the hospital. He refused to engage. Years afterward, I marveled that we never once had a real conversation in twenty-four years of marriage. We also never had an argument. I can remember the times he raised his voice to me. I did not believe in bickering in front of the children. With the benefit of hindsight, the absence of overt conflict in the marriage made the subsequent divorce a real shock for them.

For twenty-four years, I tried to find separate outlets for myself by enrolling in college, volunteering, or finding other activities, including building my own boat. His lack of support and occasional sabotage frustrated those efforts. Finally, I felt depleted and lacked the energy to try any longer. I no longer had the ability or desire to save my marriage. My growing friendship with Richard Helms and our engrossing conversations showed me that it was possible to engage intellectually and emotionally with another adult man. I had just turned forty-four. I had never held a full-time job outside my military service. I did not have a college degree, so my prospects for supporting myself were not great. But I still hoped that I could have a life of my own. I have always been optimistic and believed anything is possible. I was done with Allan. I could not continue to live that way any longer. I really was about to put my head in the oven. My nature is to do things, and my efforts to grow intellectually and create a satisfying life outside my role as a mother (which I always loved) had been stymied. Thanks to Allan, the children were all well educated. Despite my anguish about how divorce would cause the children pain, I saw no other way out. I realize now that Allan had boxed me into a corner, and anyone who knows me knows that I am not someone who does well in a corner. My instinct, almost an animal instinct, is to escape. All the doors I tried to open were slammed firmly shut in my face over and over again. On Labor Day 1967, I asked my husband for a divorce.

5

❦

ANNUS HORRIBILIS

Until the very end of the 1960s, divorce was an aberration. After the war, the cultural norm was to get married, produce children, and stay married. Large families with five to seven or more children were not unusual. Everyone was making up for lost time. Moreover, the legal system made divorce difficult and adversarial. The law specified that one party had to be guilty and the other innocent, except in Nevada, the home of the quickie divorce. The U.S. divorce rate fell to an all-time historic low in 1957. Not surprisingly, 1957 was also the peak year for the birth rate of the baby boomers, the huge generation of children born after the war. The year I asked my first husband for a divorce was also the year that a handful of states adopted the first no-fault divorce laws, which allowed married couples to dissolve unhappy marriages by mutual consent.

My request for a divorce both shocked and infuriated my husband. Until too late, it likely never occurred to him that I might be unhappy. He tried to convince me to change my mind. At one point in anger, Allan warned me I would never see the children again. But I had to believe that I would never lose my children, and while there might be a temporary estrangement, it would not last. Fortunately, I was right about that. Divorce is miserable, and I am sure many people say and do things they regret later after the emotions have settled down. Allan did all the things one might expect of a spouse of twenty-four years who felt blindsided by his wife's desire to end their marriage. But my mind was made up by that time. I waited until Labor Day to give the children, and myself, one last summer without anxiety and tension. I knew the divorce would be difficult for them, and it was. I will always regret the pain they experienced because it was never my intent to put them in the middle of my desire to change my life.

Allan insisted I tell the children myself on the same day I asked him for the divorce. I called them to my bedroom. It was completely dreadful. They were stunned. I had been extremely careful to avoid arguing with Allan in front of them. I felt very strongly that children should not witness bickering. So they had no inkling anything was wrong. It was not surprising. Children rarely consider the inner lives of their parents. The young take parents for granted, as they should. And young people focus on their own issues and feelings, not those of their parents, which is appropriate and normal.

That said, I do not pretend it was easy on them. Although the children were in high school and college, teenagers, particularly young teenagers, crave order and discipline. They are figuring out who they are as individuals and experiencing tremendous physical changes in their bodies and minds. While they may rebel against parental constraints, they also rely upon their parents to act as anchors in a stable, secure life. It is the security of the family that allows them to experiment, test limits, and find themselves and their place in the world. I effectively yanked up the anchors by ending my marriage and always felt, to my eternal regret, that I caused the two younger children particular anguish in those years.

Once I saw the children off to their respective schools, I left my husband and the house on Forty-sixth Street and moved into the Fairfax Hotel on Massachusetts Avenue. I had not really thought through the practical aspect of divorce, such as where I would live. Beverly Gore, the wife of Grady Gore, whose father bought the Fairfax Hotel in 1932, said she was sure Grady could find a room for me. The Fairfax, an elegant hotel near Dupont Circle, had served as a permanent residence for many prominent people, including Colonel Gore's cousin, Senator Al Gore Sr. of Tennessee, and his family, which included their son, young Al. Young Al grew up to become a senator himself and then vice president of the United States. This was long in the future, however. Grady found me a tiny room with a bed and a cupboard and a little stove that was the right price and comfortable. At the same time, it was a lonely and solitary time for me and a major departure from living in my own house, with my own garden, surrounded by the bustle of children. It often felt as though I were doing penance for my decision to divorce Allan, but I never once reconsidered.

Meanwhile, Dick Helms had moved from his home into the Chevy Chase Country Club just over the District of Columbia line. He had asked his wife, Julia, for a divorce the previous spring. Richard had married Julia B. Shields in 1939 when he was twenty-six, while he was working on the business side of the *Indianapolis Times*. He had early ambitions to become a newspaper publisher, and after working for United Press in Europe as a reporter before the war, he went to Indianapolis to learn the business aspects of newspapering. He met and married Julia, a thirty-two-year-old divorcée with two children, while he was there. They were married just over two years when he enlisted in the military in January 1942. They had one son, Dennis, who grew up to become an intellectual property lawyer. Dennis was attending law school at the University of Virginia at the time his father ended his marriage. Richard told me he decided to move into the Chevy Chase Country Club because it was a private club, and the press would not take note of his comings and goings there. He was also incredibly busy and had many issues to worry about, and the club would at least take care of his day-to-day needs, and he could get all his meals there.

I did not know it at the time, but he worried about whether his divorce would create a political problem for President Lyndon B. Johnson, who had named him director of central intelligence in June 1966. As I have noted, divorce was a bit scandalous. So he approached Johnson after one of the regular Tuesday national security lunches and told him he needed to talk to him about a personal issue. He offered to resign his position if a divorce would create a problem for the president, but Johnson dismissed the offer and told him divorce would not be an issue. It was quite a gamble for Richard. He had spent his entire career in intelligence and loved it. Later, in 1968, Dick again asked to see the president privately and told him we were going to be married. President Johnson knew me because our oldest daughters were schoolmates and close friends. I did not realize until many years later that President Johnson probably knew Dick and I would marry before I did. Dick spoke to me about marriage late that summer. He noted that the children would all be away at their various schools. He thought deeply about the decision and its impact on our families. Having his support and friendship certainly helped me screw up my courage, and falling in love with him gave me a good reason to act. That said, any number of things could have gone wrong, so I was not exactly feeling secure about my future. This had absolutely nothing to do with my feelings for Dick. But he needed to secure a divorce as well and worried that Julia might not grant him his freedom.

We were both sensitive to scandal and the appearance of two married (if separated) people being together, so we rarely saw each other. In any case, Dick was extremely busy with his work that year. The war in Vietnam was becoming more intense, and the civil rights movement was beginning to explode on the streets of urban America. President Johnson was convinced at one point that foreign interests were fanning the flames of civil discontent and responsible for the street riots taking place in the cities as well as for the intense antiwar demonstrations. He ordered Dick to uncover the foreign source of the agitation. Dick had to step very carefully. The CIA is not allowed to investigate American citizens inside the United States or concern itself with domestic security issues. He followed the president's orders and looked into it, but he found no evidence of foreign involvement. This is the operation that became known as Operation CHAOS and became the subject of congressional inquiries much later. At the time, the president's distress pained Dick, and he very much wanted to do what he could to ease Johnson's anxiety while still complying with the law. He liked and admired LBJ and always felt the president did not get the credit he deserved for his efforts to improve civil rights for all.

This was an extraordinary time in the whole country. Young people were experimenting with alternative lifestyles and drugs. Families were divided by the war. I knew of fathers who worked in government whose own children joined the antiwar marches outside government buildings. It was a time of extraordinary measures. Immediately after Martin Luther King Jr.'s death, District of Columbia mayor Walter Washington imposed an early evening curfew in an effort to get everyone off the streets.

Dick and I communicated by telephone. On rare occasions, we left the city for the suburbs for dinner in a place we hoped would be private. Dick tells of one of those dinners in his memoir written with William Hood, *A Look over My Shoulder*, published in 2003 after his death. It was August 20, 1968, the night before my forty-fifth birthday. He took me to Normandy Farms, outside the city, for dinner. I remember his beeper went off. He had a wonderful beeper. After his first beeper sounded during a congressional hearing, he asked the technicians at the agency to design a silent one so that he could be alerted without letting anyone around, including the press, know that something may have occurred. Today vibrating technical devices are common, but it was quite unusual then.

Earlier that year Alexander Dubček won election as first secretary of the Communist Party in Czechoslovakia and began introducing political liberalization. This did not sit well with the overseers in Moscow. That night Warsaw Pact forces and Soviet tanks rolled across the Czech border to stop the liberalization and set things back in order. We couldn't finish dinner. He dropped me at the Fairfax before going straight to a meeting at the White House to deal with the Soviet invasion of Czechoslovakia. I understood his need to be discreet about his work. It was simply part of what he did. I accepted that without question.

Although the twenty-four-hour gossip news cycle still remained far in the future, we were concerned about the few reporters working for the *Washington Star* and the *Washington Post* who specialized in society gossip, particularly Maxine Cheshire and Winnie McLendon, two women who had amazing sources and a nose for scandal. After Dick's divorce became official, many people put the pieces together and realized we were a couple. My friends pressed me on whether I intended to marry Richard Helms. My friend Pat Acheson, the daughter-in-law of former secretary of state Dean Acheson and wife of David Acheson, called me and exclaimed, "You can't marry him; he never says anything!" which amused me endlessly. Dick never stopped talking when he was with me, but this was not the aspect of him that most people ever saw. His public face was extremely discreet, taciturn, and understated; he was the quintessential spymaster. Margaret Jay, Baroness Jay of Paddington, once told me that she sat next to Dick at one of Kay Graham's dinner parties. Her then husband, British ambassador Peter Jay, asked her what she had learned from the former spymaster. She replied, "Nothing. We talked about tennis." For Kay and my husband, talking about tennis and bridge at these dinners was an escape from duty and work. Margaret played a footnote in American literary history. She was a thinly disguised character in Nora Ephron's best-selling novel *Heartburn.* Ephron wrote the ultimate revenge novel after she discovered her husband, Carl Bernstein, half of the famous Woodward and Bernstein investigative duo at the *Washington Post*, was having an affair with Margaret when Nora was pregnant with her second child.

I only told two close friends about our hopes and plans. Kay Graham, publisher of the *Washington Post*, who later became a good friend, tried to worm some news out of me, but I was convinced she would tell one of her reporters, so I told her nothing.

That long year I felt as though I was wandering through a deep, endless fog. Everything looked strange and unfamiliar. Any transition, even one that is desired, is difficult. There have been many studies on the physical and psychological toll of major life events, such as the death of a loved one, divorce, loss of a job, or moving away from a home. While I made a choice and felt certain about it, I still lost my home, ready access to my children, and the role that gave me status and standing in the community. With this upheaval coming less than a year after the death of my beloved mother, I felt bereft more than once, even though my warm friendship with Dick gave me hope for better times in the future.

I felt acutely my lack of preparation for the workforce. My experience as a mother and wife was not readily translatable into a real, paying job. My ability to run a household, to hold charity events efficiently, and to stretch a dollar to fit a budget and my years as carpooler extraordinaire did not warrant lines on a curriculum vitae. So I had to figure out how to support myself. There were practical reasons. Even if Dick and I eventually married, he had been a government employee most of his adult life and was not wealthy. But I also needed to get a job for my own sense of self-worth. I felt very strongly that I needed to stand on my own two feet and be independent in every way.

Friends offered me jobs, and I tried different things, including interior decorating and real estate sales. Nothing really clicked. I had long been a volunteer at the Smithsonian, and I kept up that volunteer work to keep myself busy. The volunteer work eventually turned into a real paying job. I often advise young people today to volunteer at places where they would like to work. It gives them the opportunity to meet the bosses who hire and to show what they can do.

I knew S. Dillon Ripley, the now legendary secretary of the Smithsonian, socially. He and his wife, Mary, were well-known hosts in Washington then. Ripley was a visionary, an ecologist, and a biologist with a doctorate in ornithology. Under his leadership, the Smithsonian, often called America's attic, grew into the extraordinary institution it is today. Coincidently, both Dillon and his wife worked for the Office of Strategic Services during World War II. In fact, that is how they met. It truly is a coincidence because I believe I knew Dillon before I knew Dick Helms, but it shows how small Washington society was in those days.

I spent most of my time volunteering at a new Smithsonian museum called the Anacostia Neighborhood Museum, which was set up in an old movie theater on Nichols Avenue SE, now known as Martin Luther King Jr. Boulevard, in the African American neighborhood of Anacostia. Anacostia is the section of Washington where the first freed slaves lived after the Civil War. The museum was the first federally funded neighborhood museum in the country, and twenty years after its opening in 1967, it moved into a beautiful new building on a wooded hilltop on Fort Place, where it is now called the Anacostia Community Museum. After volunteering for some time, I worked closely with the first director, John R. Kinard, a truly wonderful man who was also the assistant pastor at the John Wesley Methodist Zion Church. It was a real honor to be in on the ground floor of the establishment of a museum that celebrated and preserved the African American experience and created educational programs for the children in the area. John Kinard died tragically young in 1989 at the age of fifty-three of bone marrow disease. During our time at the museum, we became good friends. I also made friends with other members of the museum staff. Those friendships and my work at the museum opened up a whole new world for me, and I remember clearly one of the first exhibits was on the problem of rats in the neighborhood.

When an opportunity opened to volunteer at the Smithsonian's National Portrait Gallery, I jumped at it. The gallery includes the portraits of prominent, iconic Americans and opened in 1968 in one of the oldest and most beautiful federal office buildings in the city, the Patent Office Building. The portico of the building is modeled on the Parthenon in Athens. The building has a storied history. During the Civil War, it was used as a military barracks, hospital, and morgue. Abraham Lincoln's second inaugural ball was held there in 1865. The building was as extraordinary as the exhibits.

Charles Nagel, the first director, asked me to give tours until they had time to train the official docents. American history constituted about two paragraphs of my boarding school history textbooks, so I took it upon myself to study the subject quite intensely so I would be familiar with the backgrounds of all the famous faces I saw each day. It was a great learning experience and fascinating to connect the faces in those portraits with key moments in American history. In the evenings when Washington was quiet, I would often go to the Lincoln Memorial and talk to Mr. Lincoln. In those days you could drive right up and park at the foot of the steps of the memorial. Now it is impossible to get anywhere near the monument in a vehicle because of modern security. I loved that majestic seated figure surrounded by his eloquent words. I found him to be a wonderful listener.

I vowed to say nothing negative about Allan to the children. In fact, I never told them why I was seeking a divorce. It was not something they needed to know, and there was no need to adversely affect their relationship with their father. I felt strongly that the children were entitled to a good relationship with their father, and their relationship with him truly had nothing to do with their relationship with me. As Rod said to me when I visited him at Harvard, "Do anything you like, but do not criticize my father." I deeply appreciated that sentiment, and I tried to follow it. Allan would always be the father of my children, and I always believed he was an excellent doctor and a true visionary about health care. He just wasn't the right man for me. Eventually, all four children came to understand better why I did what I did. I believe they forgave me for the pain I caused them.

At the time, however, I felt somewhat ostracized. I did not know anyone else who was getting divorced. I assume there were women in unhappy marriages, but those desperate women put on a brave front and drank vodka with their breakfast orange juice to cope. There was a tremendous amount of closeted alcoholism in those years. I was mainly worried about the children and what I would do to get work. I needed a financial agreement with Allan before I could get a quickie divorce in Reno, and the lawyers were very pro-male. In fact, Allan's lawyer was so tough that I had to change lawyers to find someone more aggressive. Allan hired a neighbor, Samuel Jackson (Jack) Lanahan, who was married to Frances Scott (Scottie) Fitzgerald, the only daughter of the great writers F. Scott and Zelda Fitzgerald. Scottie, who was also a writer, divorced him in 1968. I wonder if his aggressive advocacy for Allan reflected his personal anger over his own divorce.

In the settlement, I received the little cottage in Delaware, with a considerable mortgage, and three real estate lots in Virginia, which turned out to be quite useless. They could not be built on because of a lack of potable water, so I decided to deed them to a Virginia wildlife conservatory. When the paperwork came back some time after I had remarried, the titles were all in Dick's name. In those years, an assumption was made about married women and property rights that I suspect would not be made today. That is progress.

I went to Reno, Nevada, to get the divorce in February 1968. Divorce had acted as an economic generator for Reno since the turn of the twentieth century. Many famous people had Reno divorces, including Jack Dempsey, Mary Pickford, Cornelius Vanderbilt Jr., and Eddie Fisher. In 1968, I obtained one too by living in a depressing motel for six weeks to satisfy the legal residency requirement. That residency requirement kept motels, dude ranches, and other temporary accommodations filled with men and women desperate to get out of unhappy marriages. Until the other states began to approve no-fault divorce laws, Nevada was the divorce capital of the United States. The hotels and lawyers did a tremendous business.

I could not afford a fancy dude ranch, so I arranged for much more modest accommodations. It was a lonely time, but I kept myself busy. I brought sewing and books and took a few field trips with a rental car into Indian country to scout out some Indian artifacts for my friends at the Smithsonian. I met Robert Laxalt, the younger brother of then governor and later senator Paul Laxalt, who had written a noteworthy book about their father, an immigrant Basque shepherd. The Smithsonian Folk Festival was just being introduced at that time, and one of the curators asked me to find out more about the Basque shepherds in the United States. A girlhood friend, Liz Phillips, who then lived in California, sent her husband, Emmett Caldwell, in his little airplane to pick me up and take me back to their house for dinner a few times. That was a welcome treat, but I could not stay long as I was not allowed out of the state for more than a few hours. The children wrote me letters. Dick and I spoke on the phone. I survived the six weeks. Sadly, some of the few belongings I had left at my room at the Fairfax were stolen while I was in Reno. But it was that kind of year.

I had many friends in Washington, but some of my relationships with other women largely revolved around our children. Without that connection, we really had little in common. And then, as now, married women tended to be wary of women who were divorced, as if they worried the divorcées would go after their husbands or divorce was some sort of infectious disease. I did not exactly have a big "D" on my chest like the famous "A" worn by poor Hester Prynne in Nathanial Hawthorne's classic *The Scarlet Letter*, but I did feel awkward. My instinctive reserve and sense that it was inappropriate to discuss private matters also kept me isolated. I felt the divorce was my private problem. I experienced a lot of turmoil about the children during that year too and had no one in which to confide. Dick was neutral when it came to children. They simply were not his focus of interest. He appreciated the children were important to me and respected that, but they were not a priority for him. Over time, as he came to know them, that would change, and the children became a rewarding part of his life.

Anyone who knows me knows I have a bit of a lead foot. I have always driven rather fast and had received a number of speeding tickets over the years. I didn't seem to be able to find a car that drove at twenty-five mph. In 1968, the District of Columbia ordered me to driver reeducation, and I was petrified I would lose my license to drive. I went down to the Department of Motor Vehicles to plead my case as ordered and sat very nervously in the second row awaiting my fate. Then suddenly Dick walked in. He was heading to Capitol Hill to testify before a congressional committee and knew how worried I was, so he stopped by and sat with me. It was just so thoughtful. It only took him five minutes, but he was a busy man. Who wouldn't marry a man like that?

Queen Elizabeth II called 1992 her annus horribilis because it was the year that three of her children's marriages ended and Windsor Castle caught fire. The year between Labor Day 1967 and December 1968 felt like that to me. As the very difficult year drew to a close, Dick and I decided to get married in December. There was a small window of opportunity when he could get away from his work. The children would be on school vacation, and it seemed that it was a good time. We went up to South Orange, New Jersey, where he had grown up and where Dick's mother, Marion, still lived. When we got there, we really had no idea how to arrange the ceremony, so we went to see the minister at the local church. It turned out all was arranged. He told us that Mrs. Helms, then quite advanced in years, well into her eighties, had pulled on her snow boots during a blizzard and marched over to see him to insist he marry us. After a long pause he said, "And I *am* going to marry you." Marion Helms could not be denied. We arranged a date and time. My children drove up from Washington and put on a good front. Dennis, Dick's son, who was a student at the University of Virginia School of Law, also attended. He eventually became a good friend to me and my children. The small group of family members gathered at the home of Dick's brother Gates Helms and sister-in-law Alberta for the ceremony. A very good friend of mine, Leslie Glass, and his wife, Betty, hosted a dinner for us in New York the night before our wedding. He was second in command to the British ambassador at the United Nations, Sir Alexander Cadogan, at that time.

Our marriage was duly noted in *Time* magazine the following week. I was described in the item as a "divorcée," which made me sound far more glamorous than I was in reality. But the marriage was deliberately a very low-key affair. Then we were off to Jamaica as the guests of Lord Ronald Graham, an old friend and classmate of Dick's at Le Rosey School in Switzerland. Lord Graham lent us a small cottage on the grounds of his estate high on a hill overlooking the Caribbean in Ocho Rios. We subsequently spent many Christmas holidays there with them.

In another remarkable coincidence, I learned that Ronald was born on the Isle of Arran in Brodick Castle. Allan McKelvie had spent much of his childhood on Arran, and we and the children had been there many times on holiday and loved it. Ronald was a younger son of an ancient Scottish family—his mother was the daughter of the duke of Hamilton, and she then married the duke of Montrose. Ronald's brother inherited the title and many other castles, and Lady Jean Fforde, his sister, gave Brodick Castle to the National Trust for Scotland in lieu of death duties when their mother, the dowager duchess of Montrose, died in 1958. Ronald much later retired back to Arran, where we stayed with him, and he took us to see the drainpipe down which he had climbed from his bedroom at Brodick Castle when he was younger.

When we were in Scotland with Ronald, his sister Jean telephoned and said she had Americans staying with her as paying guests. When Ronald asked their name, she said, "Oh, it is Cabot or something." Only an old British family could be so cavalier about one of the first families of the United States! Sometime later, Jean's son, Charles, visited us in Washington. Because of the distribution of their land, we had been able to get a small share in a little "croft" in Kildonan just down the coast from Brodick. Ronald's wife, Mary, was great fun and good company. She had five grown children by a previous marriage. Because he was the son of a duke, she was Lady Ronald Graham and not just Lady Graham. He made a point of insisting she be called by the correct title and name.

The day after our marriage, our flight to Jamaica from New York was delayed by a snowstorm. Dick's security platoon kept rushing around us at the airport, muttering into their radios about not being able to get the director off on his flight for fifteen hours. It was comical. The airport ran out of food. I was so utterly exhausted by the time we arrived in Jamaica at 3 a.m. that I begged to be deposited by the road so I could just sleep.

So finally, on that beautiful Caribbean island, my annus horribilis came to an end. The next phase of my life began.

6

MRS. RICHARD HELMS

After I married Richard Helms, my life changed in fundamental ways. Being married to the man who truly became my best friend in life relieved my anxiety. I now had a partner in every sense of the word. While I still worried about landing a full-time paying job, I no longer felt as though I was swinging from a high wire with no net. Being married again also removed from me the big "D" for "divorce," which had made me feel like such an outsider. It is a cliché to say Washington is a company town, but it is true. And back in the 1960s, official Washington still had a small-town, old-fashioned, somewhat formal feel to it, and many of the top government officials knew one another well and socialized together. From a strictly social perspective, it was significant that I was married to a high-ranking government official.

I also felt better about my relationship with the children. The previous summer, they had returned from their various schools and joined me at the little cottage in Lewes, Delaware. Everything was blessedly normal. They were close to their father, but they realized that I was not abandoning them and that I had not changed. I reestablished day-to-day contact with them and could be comfortable knowing they knew I loved them and was still their mother, even though I no longer lived with their father. That summer calmed me down considerably, and I felt a slow dissipation of the clammy fog that had clouded my thinking since the day I asked for a divorce more than a year earlier.

A month or so before we married, Dick suggested I find us a place to live. I still lived in my small room at the Fairfax Hotel, and he lived in his room at the Chevy Chase Country Club. I found an apartment at the Irene, an apartment building named after the developer's wife, on Willard Avenue in Chevy Chase at the Washington, DC/Maryland line. It was a comfortable two-bedroom apartment with a study. It suited our immediate needs as well as our tight budget.

I had developed an interest in geology from my exposure to collections at the Smithsonian Institution. I suspect the fascination for unusual rocks and minerals rekindled some of my earliest memories of hunting for birds' eggs with my brother Len in the fields and streams near our childhood home in Maldon. I took a few classes and went on hunts for Jurassic-era rocks and trilobites, the fossil group of extinct marine anthropoids, in Virginia with a hard hat, an archeological pick, and a good friend who shared my interest in minerals and rocks. A *Washington Post* editor had presented me with the hard hat after he mistakenly conked me on the head with a pepper mill at a dinner party. It came in handy.

In my studies, my memory for the arcane was not always as good as I would have liked, so I came up with a mnemonic technique to remember the rock eras: Paleocene, Eocene, Oligocene, Miocene, Pliocene, Pleistocene, and Recent. It was "Pour every other martini potted Paul requests." Years earlier, I had remembered the names of the wives of Henry VIII in a similar way: "divorced, beheaded, died; divorced, beheaded, survived." In an article I wrote about my interest in 1971 for the *Washington Post*, I recounted how my ability to casually toss out terms such as "orogenic landslide" and "diastrophism," a word with maximum impact when said breathlessly, so undid my youngest, Lindsay, that she studied astronomy rather than geology in college. Dick was taken aback when I showed up with a box of rocks at our new apartment. He asked, "Do we have to have those?" I mumbled a tentative, "Yes," but he became more tolerant when he discovered some prominent public officials of his acquaintance also collected minerals. I loved the mystery and history of ancient rocks and minerals. I also appreciated their beauty. I used a piece of chalcedony drusy quartz crystal as a centerpiece on my dining room table. Surrounded by votive candles that reflected the inherent glint of the crystal, it made quite a lovely display at dinner.

Neither of us brought many possessions from our first marriages. Dick actually moved in with his clothes and a cardboard box that I dusted for years without ever quite understanding its provenance. I was reluctant to pry. I respected Dick's privacy, and he was the sort of person whose sense of discretion had been honed to an art form. When we were moving to Iran, I asked him to deal with the box. I had always assumed it held old love letters or some other private matter. But alas, it held no secret. In fact, it was disappointingly boring. The box contained his white-tie formal wear. He took great pride in the fact that he'd had the striped trousers made in London in 1938 and his white-tie formal wear still fit him even in middle age. We had no furniture. So I headed to the Thieves Market, a warehouse of used-furniture shops in Alexandria, Virginia, with my friend Ruth Renwick Coster, an artist who painted a portrait of me that now hangs over my fireplace. I had met her in Algiers. Ruth had a great eye for color and design. In a matter of hours, we found enough furniture for the small apartment, loaded the furniture into the back of a rented truck, and carried them home. I still have one of the chairs more than forty years later, a real tribute to the quality and timeless style of our finds. Then Ruth and I glued tiny square mirrors in a pattern on the walls of the hallway. It gave the apartment a rather jaunty air. Unfortunately the landlord charged me a fortune to remove them when we left.

Our stay at the apartment came along with something totally unexpected. Because Dick was effectively the top spymaster in the United States, foreign governments dispatched spies to move into our building. At the time, I knew nothing of this. Years later, I found a list of the various foreign agents who moved into the Irene just after we did. This proved to be a rather peculiar side effect of being married to Dick Helms! To the best of my knowledge, the proximity of spies had absolutely no effect on our rather ordinary life. I often wonder how much time these foreign operatives wasted tracking my not-so-secret expeditions to the tennis courts or grocery store or our evenings out for dinner with friends. I am sure the agency's security officers had made certain our apartment was secure. We always had secure telephones, particularly the one with a direct line to the White House, so Dick could speak without fear of being overheard.

Dick and I had each survived a difficult year in 1968. That year was not only personally hard for Dick as he ended a twenty-nine-year marriage and obtained his own divorce but also professionally taxing. In addition to the horrific assassinations of Martin Luther King Jr. and Robert F. Kennedy, which would have been enough to mark the year in American history, the ongoing war in Vietnam drew bigger and more passionate demonstrations throughout the country. The rest of the world, which was Dick's professional focus, was hardly less tumultuous. The North Korean Communists captured the USS *Pueblo*, a naval intelligence-gathering vessel, with its eighty-three-man crew in January when the ship, though in international waters, ventured too close to the Korean coast from the North Korean perspective. The crew would not be released until three days before Christmas. The North Vietnamese launched the Tet Offensive in January, which led to the highest U.S. casualty tolls of the Vietnam War and contributed to a rise in the antiwar sentiment at home. The Czech president Antonin Novotny resigned in March, triggering the Prague Spring, which ended on my birthday in August with an invasion by the Soviet Union and two hundred thousand Warsaw Pact forces.

The political climate also changed drastically for Dick. In the spring of 1968, President Johnson announced he would not run for reelection. LBJ's vice president, Hubert H. Humphrey, became the Democratic nominee after a difficult primary fight that culminated in rioting at the Democratic National Convention in Chicago that summer. Humphrey lost the election in November to Richard Nixon. While Dick was a career intelligence officer and lifelong government employee, he had risen so high in the agency that he now served at the pleasure of the president as the director of central intelligence. This meant he could be replaced when the administration changed. He did not have a prior relationship with Richard Nixon, and Nixon was known to be suspicious of anyone with an East Coast establishment background. Nixon, a native of California, always carried a chip on his shoulder despite his considerable political success as a senator, vice president under Dwight D. Eisenhower, and then president of the United States. Richard Helms was East Coast all the way from his Pennsylvania birthplace to his Williams College degree. Nixon was almost predisposed to distrust him and harbored deep malevolence toward the agency from the 1960 campaign. He blamed Allen Dulles for feeding data to John F. Kennedy on the alleged missile gap with the Soviet Union, a major issue in that campaign that Kennedy exploited to his political advantage.

When Presidents Nixon and Johnson spoke privately during the transition, Johnson assured Nixon that he had never known Richard Helms to be a partisan. Moreover, he told the incoming president that he had always received good counsel from his intelligence chief. LBJ relayed his conversation to Dick personally, which Dick deeply appreciated. Nixon decided to keep Dick in his position. This temporarily relieved both of us. Intelligence was Dick's life. He helped make the case for an agency that engaged in intelligence gathering and espionage and for establishing the CIA. It may seem astonishing today, but the United States had no intelligence-gathering entity before World War II. Indeed, the surprise attack on Pearl Harbor by the Japanese, which drew the United States into the war, was viewed as an extraordinary failure of intelligence. While bits and pieces of information about Japanese intentions could and probably should have tipped off senior officials at the Pentagon and White House, there was no process, person, or agency in Washington to put the pieces together. The Office of Strategic Services (OSS), hurriedly put together during the war, served that function for the United States for the duration of World War II. After a great deal of hemming and hawing and a number of false starts, the CIA was eventually created during the Truman administration in the postwar period, and Dick played an integral part in it. In his 1996 book, *From the Shadows*, Robert Gates describes Dick and his peers as the stuff of legend inside the agency. Needless to say, working in intelligence and specifically in the collection of intelligence had become an intrinsic part of Dick's identity. He was fifty-five years old in 1968 and hoped to finish his career doing his true life's work.

When Dick graduated from Williams College in 1935, he wanted to become a newspaper publisher. He landed a job with United Press, then a major wire service, in Europe and learned the news business in England and Germany, where he interviewed Adolf Hitler in 1936 and got an up-front, personal look at one of the great monsters of the twentieth century. He enlisted in the navy when war broke out, and his facility with foreign languages helped him win an assignment to the OSS, where he forged early and lasting bonds with some of the other men who helped create an intelligence operation for the United States, including William Casey, Frank Wisner, and Allen Dulles. As a wire service reporter, he acquired an acute appreciation of the power and value of factual information and began to develop his amazing powers of observation, which his years working in intelligence honed to an extraordinary degree. Dick Helms believed with every fiber of his being in the importance of gathering information and always said that no satellite or technological gizmo could tell you what was inside a man's or woman's head or provide an integrated understanding of an individual's personality in the same way as a face-to-face assessment by another human being. He harbored a residual resistance to covert action because so many things could go wrong in a secret mission that often became not so secret. Moreover, covert operations unfortunately became the course of last resort for desperate presidents. When all else failed, presidents pushed for a dramatic Hail Mary pass of a secret mission. More often than not, that decision was a prescription for disaster.

During the Kennedy administration, before I knew Dick, he refused to attend a single planning meeting on the Bay of Pigs mission, which ended so disastrously. He heartily opposed it from start to finish. President Kennedy and his brother, the attorney general, were so adamant about taking down Fidel Castro and his Communist regime in Cuba that they insisted the mission go forward. I learned that Dick's colleagues had an office pool about how long he could avoid attending a Bay of Pigs meeting. Throughout his career, he held this consistent position on covert action, and more often than not his judgment proved to be sounder than that of those who pushed for such operations.

The CIA has one boss, the president of the United States. The director of central intelligence effectively has a constituency of one. Since World War II, political leaders have sometimes ignored the information they have been given, or intelligence officials have told political leaders what they wanted to hear rather than giving them the straight, unvarnished truth. Other times, presidents have ordered the agency to engage in operations that intelligence professionals felt were unwise. In his book, Bob Gates bluntly states that every time a political leader came up with a harebrained notion for a secret mission and foisted it on the CIA, it invariably proved to be a mistake. Dick reached the same conclusion, and it pained him because in every instance, from the Bay of Pigs in Cuba to the Nicaraguan Contras to the weapons of mass destruction in Iraq, the country suffered. When asked if they should do away with the CIA, one director said no, because then the political leaders would have no one to blame for mistakes.

So Dick's job seemed as secure as a political appointment can ever be. He and I could both breathe easier in 1969. We were together at last and could enjoy the pleasure and comfort of each other's presence. We began our life together.

My second marriage from the start was very different from the first. If I said I had a problem, Dick would immediately sit down and ask, "What is it?" I deeply appreciated his attentiveness and concern for me. We planned our social schedule together. Dick received many invitations, and at first we tended to accept most of them until the night when we each realized neither of us wanted to be at a particular event. After that, we decided we would never accept an invitation unless one of us really wanted or needed to attend. So we sorted through the invitations and decided together. Some decisions involved extensive negotiation, such as the time I wanted to attend a Michael Jackson concert. One day he declined out of hand an invitation to dinner with the first sea lord of Great Britain because he was not very fond of the hostess who issued the invitation. He later called me from his car and said he felt selfish making that decision and asked if I would like to go because I had been a leading Wren in the war. He was so considerate of me, my feelings, and my views. One free weekend day not long after we were married, he asked me, "What would you like to do today?" I was dumbstruck. I finally said, "I haven't been asked that in twenty-five years!" Allan had always gone golfing on his days off, and in those days women were not allowed on the golf course on weekends. I also thought golf took far too much time, and I could not leave the children for the hours and hours it took to play eighteen holes. I played tennis, so we rarely spent much recreational time together, and Allan had not sought my company. By contrast, Dick and I played tennis together twice a week at the Chevy Chase Country Club and the Arlington YMCA. We were very compatible, like two old shoes, right from the start. Neither of us had had the comfort of a confidante for a very long time, and now we just talked about everything and really shared our lives. The companionship of marriage came as just a wonderful surprise.

Since childhood, when I devoured the books at Brick House, I have always been a totally undisciplined reader with interests that ranged far and wide. In Washington, it is not at all unusual to meet individuals with deep expertise in a specific area. The town and government are loaded with experts in every conceivable area. But I had met very few people with eclectic, wide-ranging interests. One reason I warmed to Dick so quickly was that he was interested in and knowledgeable about a variety of subjects and topics. Indeed, it was his job to brief senior government officials on the state of the world, so he knew the significance of this river or the location of that desert or mountain range, as well as the histories of individuals and countries. When seated next to Dick at a dinner at the Lebanese embassy, I had found a kindred spirit. We started our friendship by talking, and during our marriage we continued to talk. That was a great contrast to when he was in public, when he spoke little. He often said that you don't learn anything when your mouth is open. He was a great listener and duly noted that listening took a lot of "ass time."

He was a sophisticated man. At Williams College, he studied art under three professors, Whit Stoddard, Lane Faison, and Bill Pearson, who trained a generation of prominent museum directors. Whit Stoddard came to stay with us often and would get me to drive him around Washington, where he had me in many a near accident while we stopped in the middle of traffic circles so he could lecture me on the local statutory. Dick enjoyed art and remembered his lessons well. He could discuss genre, color, and artistic temperament with the best. He also loved classical music. I found him a baton, and he amused me endlessly by directing the orchestra as he listened to recordings of his favorite works.

Dick was inclusive. He never disclosed anything secret to me in violation of his classified material methods and sources agreement, but he made me an integral part of his life. We talked endlessly about the news, friends, our mutual interests, and my specific interests. We would have mock arguments about who had the more interesting day. He taught me to read a newspaper in a more discerning way and to question where the stories were coming from, to consider who was leaking, and to analyze the what and why of the opinion pieces. We really enjoyed each other's company. When he came home from work, he was tired from reading lengthy documents and dispatches all day, so we would sometimes read spy stories to one another. He did not like John le Carré, the former British spy who is considered one of the great espionage writers of the day. He found le Carré too dark and cynical. But he did love P. G. Wodehouse, the prolific British humorist. His son Dennis, by then practicing law in New York, would send him hair-raising espionage novels. Dick read as much as I did. We each had three or four books going at once.

Dick was an elegant man, always perfectly turned out, though he did not really care about clothing except for his shoes. He had very small feet, a size eight, that were difficult to fit. He only had nine toes, a shortcoming the navy doctors missed when he enlisted. He had dress shoes custom made in London in 1935. He still had those bespoke shoes more than thirty years later when we married. He had them repaired repeatedly and cared for them as if they were the crown jewels. He packed the shoes in a special bag and took great care to pack his shoe bag carefully when he traveled. His security aide, Jim Cunningham, said that keeping track of the shoe bag was one of his most important jobs.

Dick loved to dance, particularly the waltz, and never stopped learning new dance steps. His nephew Gates and Gates's girlfriend at Williams College would make valiant attempts to teach him the latest dance steps on weekend visits. He loved it.

One night we went to a dance just after Dick had inadvertently angered Senator William Fulbright, the chairman of the Senate Foreign Relations Committee. Dick had signed a letter to the editor that Fulbright construed as personally critical of him, though that was not the intent. When Dick spotted the senator, he asked me to stand next to him to see if he would dance with me. Fulbright took the bait and asked me to dance.

I nearly burst out laughing as I looked over Senator Fulbright's shoulder and noticed the eyes of every CIA officer in the room following our progression across the dance floor. I'm not sure whether the dance calmed down the angry senator, but I did my bit for the agency.

Dick spoke fluent French and German, which he learned as a youth studying in Switzerland and Germany before the war. He always wore long white trousers when we played tennis. I bought him cricket trousers at Lillywhites in London. He was tall and slim and cut quite a distinctive figure on the tennis court. When he left the agency, the troops presented him with a tennis racket that had a button on the end of the handle. When pressed, it extended the range of the racket so that he could reach even more lobs.

The lacrosse team at my boarding school, Manor House, in 1938. I am the second girl from the left in the second row. I always loved sports.

My parents, Constance and Stanley Ratcliff, at the family home, Brick House, in Maldon around 1939 at the start of the war.

William Dring, a noted artist, painted this portrait of me while I was a Boat Crew Wren during World War II. Several of us were selected to represent the service. It is part of the collection of the Imperial War Museums and reproduced here with their permission. The artist wanted to redo it. He was dissatisfied with it, but there was no time. © Imperial War Museums (Art. IWM ART LD 2423).

This shows me in my uniform on the boat that carried Queen Elizabeth, the mother of the current monarch, when she and King George VI visited Plymouth during the war. This image was used to recruit women to the Wrens. I remember seeing it on the back of biscuit tins.

My brother Leonard Ratcliff in his Royal Air Force uniform during World War II. We did not know the full extent of Len's remarkable and dangerous service as a pilot and wing commander of the super-secret Squadron 161 until after the war.

I am holding my first son, Roderick (Rod), at Brick House in 1946. The hat was quite fashionable in the 1940s.

My first husband, Allan
McNeill McKelvie, in the
McNeill clan kilt. The
McNeill clan came from
the Isle of Skye.

The river behind the prefab housing where we lived in Rochester flooded when I
was at the Mayo Hospital giving birth to my youngest daughter, Lindsay, in 1951.
Our good friend Dr. Reg Bickford rescued my three older children with a boat.

One of my husband's patients invited us to the first inaugural ball of Dwight D. Eisenhower in January 1953 at the Mayflower Hotel in downtown Washington. We sat in the box next to the president. I felt quite glamorous.

Alice Roosevelt Longworth, Allan McKelvie, and myself at an Arabian horse farm in Maryland in 1960. Alice was a colorful personality who always wore a distinctive hat.

Portrait of myself, painted by Ruth Renwick Coster, a New York portrait artist whom I met in Algiers. We became great friends. Photographed by Didi Cutler.

This White House photo shows Dick dancing with me on the left; in the center is actor and dancer Fred Astaire with the glamorous *shahbanou* during a state dinner for the shah of Iran in 1974.

I am standing with Iranian women at a clinic in northern Iran. Lady Parsons, wife of the British ambassador to Iran, is with me.

I wore a *chador* in Iran (I am on the left) so that I could visit a rare and beautiful mosque.

This photo was taken at the White House tennis court during the Reagan administration. It shows Dick Helms, myself, Kay Graham, and George Schultz.

Dick Helms and Kay Graham at Kay's seventieth birthday party in 1987. Her daughter Lally is to the left. I am next to Dick on the right. Photo used with permission of Lally Graham Weymouth.

Kay Graham and Bob McNamara at Kay's beautiful oceanfront home on Martha's Vineyard. We had many good times there.

Dick and I participated in the Reagan Foundation tennis tournament in California after the president finished his terms. We saw the Williams sisters play when they were still quite young but very precocious.

My husband Dick with me in Lewes, Delaware. The little cottage in Lewes was the scene of many wonderful summer vacations for the family.

Dick and Pamela Harriman standing in front of van Gogh's famous *White Roses* painting at the U.S. embassy in Paris. Pam had a copy made when she donated the original to the National Gallery of Art in Washington, and I could never distinguish the copy from the original.

Sailing off the coast of Turkey.

Lord Ronald Graham hosted us nearly every winter at his beautiful house in Jamaica. He retired to the Isle of Arran, where he was born and where this photograph was taken.

David Packard making us pancakes one morning at his house in Big Sur, California. There is something marvelous about watching one of the wealthiest men in the country flipping his own pancakes.

A group of friends often played bridge beneath the famous paintings of naked ladies at the Alibi Club in downtown Washington. This photo shows Chief Justice William Rehnquist, Justice Sandra Day O'Connor, and retired admiral Tazewell "Taz" Shephard.

Dick Helms enjoying one of our many dinner parties at our house on Garfield Street.

This is me with my dear friend Sandra Day O'Connor.

Polly Fritchey, a marvelous and good friend, at Fishers Island, where we spent so many happy hours gathering mussels from the rocks.

I am shown here with former secretary of state Henry Kissinger at the symposium held to explore my husband's legacy in intelligence at Georgetown University.

Dick Helms with his son Dennis Helms.

This family photograph was taken at the marriage of Rory Eakin and Emily Rummo at Sundance in Utah in 2009. Rory is the son of my daughter Lindsay.

He hated excessive security because he viewed it as ostentatious and was convinced it drew more attention to the protectee. We played tennis regularly with Secretary of State George Schultz, and it always annoyed Dick that George showed up with three SUVs full of security.

Dick preferred the shadows. Once, at a big convocation of CEOs, a very elegant woman, the wife of one of the executives, became quite distressed because she could not open her locked jewelry case. I immediately volunteered Dick for the task of breaking into her jewels. He was a bit miffed with me, but I did it unthinkingly. After all, he had excellent training in the arcane specialties of spy work. He did unlock the case for her. But he did not welcome widespread knowledge of his spy skills.

For years he smoked two packs of Chesterfields a day, a bad habit that was widespread among men of his generation, particularly those who served in World War II. Tobacco was included in military rations for decades. He had long fingers, and I loved watching him smoke. Then, one day in Tehran, he stopped. He suffered from a bit of bronchitis. When I asked him about it, he said, "I stopped yesterday, and I was still alive in the morning, and I was still alive today." He never smoked another cigarette but admitted he missed smoking while drinking coffee.

To me, he was essentially conservative in taste and lifestyle, so it shocked me that so many of his colleagues viewed him as a gambler at the agency. He was a terrible card player but did try because I had been such an avid player since childhood. That is not to say he was perfect. He was utterly useless around the house. The man never emptied the dishwasher, but then few men of his generation did anything remotely related to housework. I once encouraged him to join me in the garden. He cut off every bloom, so that ended that experiment. And he was an absolutely terrible automobile driver. I suspect this is because he relied upon a government driver for so many years. He would drive right on the median strip of a roadway and insist that it was defensive and gave him the ability to go left or right at a second's notice. I always thought we'd end up in a terrible traffic accident, and my daughters simply refused to ride in any car he drove. He once came to a dead stop in the middle of a traffic circle with one of the grandchildren.

His discipline was remarkable. He was always on call, and our telephone at home rang at all hours of the night. A foreign policy crisis does not respect a nine-to-five timetable. He had a religious fealty to keeping his head clear by rarely drinking alcohol. He limited himself to a single martini on Friday night and rarely drank more than a single glass of wine. And he was conscientious about getting his sleep. Sleep was so important to him. He developed the ability to catnap. He would tell me that the president would be calling in fifteen minutes, so he intended to sleep for the next ten, and then he would do just that. I envied him for that ability to turn off his mind and rest. He taught me that one needed to put problems on a shelf at the end of the day because they would be there in the morning. Refreshed from a good night's sleep, one could tackle the problems anew. He said always to face your problems first before anything else.

He always wanted to get to bed at his regular time, so we were often the first to leave dinner parties and had to take care not to leave before the guest of honor. When we entertained, he never hesitated to hustle our guests out the door by throwing his hands in the air and pointedly asking, "Don't you have a home?" My children still break out in gales of laughter remembering this endearing quirk. More than anything, he loved to hear us laugh, and the more raucously, the better—I do not think there was much humor at the office.

Dick's anecdotes became part of the McKelvie family lore. My daughter Jill arrived at the Lewes beach house first one weekend and telephoned Dick immediately, saying, "Don't come! The plumber has made a mistake, and the toilet is in the middle of the sitting room floor." A voice replied, "Sorry about the toilet, but I am on a ranch in the middle of Montana . . . wrong number."

Another weekend, Lynda Bird Johnson, the president's daughter, was coming to stay, and Secret Service agents were all over the place. Lindsay left in high dudgeon, announcing she was not staying anywhere there were guns in the trash cans.

During my first marriage, I worried relentlessly about finances. My first husband made sufficient money to support our family, but his investments were often impulsive and not always prudent. This caused tremendous strain in the marriage. Dick was the opposite. He paid bills before they fell through the mail slot. He acutely remembered the lean years of the Great Depression and his close friends who were forced to drop out of Williams because they could no longer afford the tuition. I would joke that he still had his first nickel. He bought his socks at Brooks Brothers and when one got a hole, he would return them. This absolutely shocked me, and I was deeply chagrined when the store repeatedly exchanged the old for a new pair. He once got upset with his son Dennis because Dennis bought himself a new belt. In Dick's mind, having one perfectly serviceable belt was sufficient. When we hosted dinner parties, he thought having a single bottle of wine was quite enough for our guests. My children found this parsimony hilarious. But we were essentially compatible in our attitude toward money and debt. Neither of us put great stock in the accumulation of wealth for its own sake. We shared an interest in experience and learning. Yet we were careful about not spending more than we could afford. My father's advice to me, as I left for America, never to borrow or buy on credit still rang in my ears. It sounds incredibly boring, but this resistance to debt and innate frugality was a great comfort to me.

At the time we lived on a tight budget. A government salary only goes so far. I do not believe Dick's salary ever exceeded $65,000 a year. And I had a lot more time on my hands with my children off at school. After years of volunteer work as a den mother, event planner, chauffeur, tour guide, and keeper of the neighborhood collection of frogs (in the garage), I very much wanted to work and have a real job. I was so naïve that I did not realize being married to the head of central intelligence for the United States created some constraints on where I could work and what I could do. A friend who was an interior decorator invited me to help her, but her embassy clients were a bit taken aback by the fact that I was married to the head of central intelligence and doubtless thought I was there to plant listening devices. So that did not work out too well. I tried real estate but sold only one house.

In 1969 my friends at the Smithsonian opened a door that led to my first real, paying job since the Wrens. The Smithsonian Institution had been producing radio shows off and on since 1923. During the Great Depression, the museum worked with the Works Progress Administration (WPA) and the U.S. Office of Education to broadcast a half-hour show of stories that drew upon the eclectic riches of the Smithsonian. Smithsonian staff prepared the wide-ranging scripts, which included science, history, arts, and culture. The WPA hired out-of-work actors and musicians to perform in the broadcasts. In 1969, David Challinor, who was the assistant secretary for science and research at the Smithsonian, and William "Willy" Warner, the assistant secretary for public service, approached me and asked if I would be interested in hosting a weekly magazine-style radio show featuring the curators, guest speakers, and experts that regularly populated or visited the museum. They knew me well and deemed this position the perfect job for someone with my insatiable thirst for knowledge and interest in everything. The job drew upon my years of voracious reading, my eclectic tastes, and my innate curiosity. I was thrilled.

The Smithsonian is a bottomless treasure chest of interesting people and things. On September 7, 1969, my first show aired as host of Radio Smithsonian's new weekly interview show with Paul Johnson as the producer. I loved everything about it. The show became an amazing education for me. For one show, I interviewed a scholar who studied elephants in Ceylon. For another, I spoke to the costume curator on women's bathing costumes through the years. I did interviews on blue whales; worms; the manner in which mosquitoes communicate by stridulation from rubbing their legs together; continental drift; how smells like chocolate can add to the authenticity of an exhibit; how the Chinese kept secret the way to make porcelain for a thousand years before the Europeans discovered the technique; and about Canela Indians in central Brazil, where a son-in-law cannot remain alone in the same room with, look in the eye, or speak directly to his mother-in-law, though I never quite understood why. I interviewed British ambassador John Freeman when he presented a Hawker Hurricane to the Smithsonian. The Hawker Hurricane was a single-seat aircraft designed and built for World War II. The aircraft is credited with 60 percent of Royal Air Force air victories during the Battle of Britain. The Hawker Hurricanes were the very planes I had watched fighting in the skies over England. The interview brought full circle my own World War II experiences with my postwar life.

Dick was apprehensive on my behalf when I told him I had lined up Edward Teller, the nuclear physicist, for an interview. I told him I shared his concern and had already secured an excellent briefing from one of my friends at the agency. A few days later, Dick saw Teller at a White House meeting. When he started to speak to him about official business, Teller said, "Never mind that. How's your wife?" Dick said I must have done quite well. I interviewed Rube Goldberg just before he died at the age of eighty-seven. He was a Pulitzer Prize–winning cartoonist famous for his hilarious depictions of extraordinarily complicated inventions that performed simple tasks. He was so creative that the phrase "Rube Goldberg" entered the lexicon to refer to a complicated, unusual invention. He was still full of ideas. I remember how Jamie Wyeth, the painter, described his feelings when he painted an image of the moon after the first moon landing. I taped my old friend Dr. Reg Bickford from the Mayo Clinic talking about brain waves.

The show was broadcast on Sunday nights through public radio stations and over the Armed Forces Network, and I was continually surprised by the people who became avid fans. Cap Weinberger, who was the Federal Trade Commission chairman at the time and later became secretary of defense, always told me he loved the show. Sarah Booth Conroy interviewed me for a story for the *New York Times* that autumn. I told her I went to work at the Smithsonian because "I wasn't any good at ladies luncheons. I never could find any clean white gloves."

The Smithsonian was full of characters in those days. Congress created the Smithsonian Institution by legislation in 1846 to deal with the bequest of James Smithson, an English chemist and mineralogist, who died in 1829. He left his estate to his nephew, but his will said that if his nephew died without heirs, the estate was to go to the United States to found the Smithsonian Institution, "an establishment for the increase and diffusion of knowledge among men." The bequest of just over $500,000 grew into the nation's preeminent public museum. During Dillon Ripley's tenure, the Smithsonian underwent extraordinary expansion, with new museums, art galleries, and programs. Dillon was so charismatic, he created a lot of interest in the museum projects. But he did occasionally get in to trouble with Congress, and I was later tasked to look into some of the criticisms. When I asked the head of the zoo about some birds that had gone to Dillon's Connecticut estate, he looked at me quizzically and replied, "Well, some of them did not look quite the same when they came back as when they went up." Stewart Alsop, the newspaper columnist, used to tell the story of going to see Dillon in the hope of making some friends for the beautiful British wife he had brought over during the war. While talking to Dillon, whom he had met in the OSS during the war, he asked, "Whatever happened to that long drink of water who worked upstairs?" Dillon replied slowly, "I married her." Stewart allowed that was not the best way to make friends for his new wife.

One of the most delightful storytellers in Washington was David Challinor, the assistant secretary, a noted conservationist who held a doctorate in biology. When Congress had to be diverted from some sensitive issue, the office would send him up to testify, and he would wander off into tales of the sex life of the snake or some such arcane topic, and we knew the members of Congress would be entranced and temporarily diverted from the topic at hand.

I loved to roam through the museum corridors and watch the public reaction to the remarkable treasures. Every lunch hour I visited a different area. The Smithsonian featured an expert opinion clinic that appraised the value of family heirlooms years before the popular *Antiques Roadshow* broadcast on public television. One morning I watched a sour-looking woman shepherd her elderly father, who clutched a painting to his thin chest. She displayed no patience with her father and made us understand she was magnanimously indulging this nutty old man. The painting turned out to be authentic and priceless. With this news, she transformed into a cloying and solicitous daughter. I wanted to take the poor old man home with me.

The curator of herpetology, the study of amphibians and reptiles, installed a mini-computer to answer the questions of visitors. When someone asked, "Do snakes have souls?" he rushed from his office to find a pride of Baptist ministers waiting for his answer.

I made so many new friends in those years. My colleague Ben Ruhe became a great fan of the boomerang while traveling in Australia. He taught us to how to throw it. Ben became one of the foremost boomerang enthusiasts in the entire country. And Louis Leakey, the marvelous anthropologist and naturalist, would invite me home to talk about life and human relationships while he whipped up a soufflé. He refused to eat in restaurants after more than forty years of living in the wilds of Africa in search of signs of early primeval man. Dick and I later visited his research area in Olduvai Gorge in Africa.

I met simply extraordinary people at the Smithsonian. Some were visitors and just passing through on a lecture tour. I had my own little office tucked away in one of the warrens of the museum. One day, leaning over the balcony, I saw Charles Lindbergh, the legendary aviator, standing quietly below his plane, the *Spirit of St. Louis,* which was then being displayed in the Arts and Industries Building. Lindbergh made history when he flew the single-seat, single-engine aircraft nonstop from New York to Paris in 1927. As I looked down at him from a balcony in the Arts and Industries Building, I wondered what he was thinking. He was alone, just gazing up at his little plane. That transatlantic trip made his fame and defined his life. He died of lymphoma in Hawaii a few years later.

The Smithsonian employed or provided work space for many experts whose research was funded by grants. These experts toiled away in the back corners of the museums in virtual obscurity for decades. They were not only knowledgeable but also passionate about their areas of expertise in science or art or culture. I so enjoyed their enthusiasm and willingness to teach and explain. At lunch in the cafeteria one day, I sat next to a woman who studied the Pribilof Islands, four volcanic islands 250 miles north of the Aleutian Islands and 300 miles from the coast of Alaska. They are famous among birders for their rich bird life and fur seals. Dillon Ripley was a highly regarded ornithologist, and he came on the show to talk about birds and the ongoing research into why they fly in formation and who gets to lead. I once interviewed an expert on worms. I was so taken by his excited descriptions of these lowly creatures that I exclaimed, "You really love worms!" He agreed: he did love worms. Afterward, he asked me to take that part out of the interview before it was broadcast. I reluctantly agreed. I never could look at the humble worm in the same way after his revelatory remarks.

I spent three days a week working on Smithsonian Radio. Being able to wander through the warren of the Smithsonian museums and pluck out an interesting subject or person for an interview was a slice of heaven. The other two days I spent working on Concern, Inc., an environmental organization aimed at women that I founded with several friends in 1970. Concern grew out of a conversation I had with my longtime friend Nan Ignatius. Nan, a direct descendent of Cotton Mather, the Puritan minister, and I had a great deal in common. Her husband, Paul, served as secretary of the navy and later worked briefly as president of the Washington Post Company. Their son David, who became a friend, was just a year older than my younger daughter. David became a prominent columnist for the *Washington Post* with expertise in the Middle East and economics. Nan and I sat together on a sofa during a dinner party one night during the winter of 1969 and talked about how we were both distressed about the toxic content of everyday items used in the home by housewives. We were among many others growing increasingly concerned about the impact of pollution, sprawl, and chemical poisoning on the environment. Public awareness of the environmental price of the prosperity of the 1950s, with their rapid growth and explosion of consumer goods, grew throughout the decade of the 1960s. Rachel Carson published *The Silent Spring*, her best-selling cautionary tale about the devastating damage done by pesticides to wildlife. We realized that American housewives had great, untapped economic power and believed that many women, like ourselves, wanted to take action in some fashion. We decided we ought to try and harness the pocketbook power of the housewives who, in fact, truly made the decisions about most consumer purchases in most American families.

As mothers and housewives, we made the connection between safety and everyday use of household products instantly. The linkages were obvious to us. For example, I knew some local schools were spraying poisonous pesticides on their trees and instinctively knew there was something profoundly wrong with spraying poisons in proximity to growing children. We used products to clean our houses and laundry that contained chemicals and were having an adverse impact upon the environment. We knew children chewed on the sides of cribs as they were teething, so lead paint was an issue. We were gardeners and knew that pesticides could kill our songbirds as well as the little insects that devoured our roses.

When we started Concern, I asked Bob McNamara for his opinion. He was a big booster and told me that women in the marketplace were powerful and could be a force for real good and change. We believed this too, and I found his opinion reassuring because he understood markets far better than others. McNamara had been one of the legendary "Whiz Kids" who completely rebuilt the Ford Motor Company after World War II. He was the first non-family member to be named president of the company, just before President Kennedy named him defense secretary.

Nan and I looked around for like-minded women. We invited Aileen Train, whose husband, Russell, was then chairman of the President's Council on Environmental Quality and later became the second administrator for the Environmental Protection Agency; Joan Shorey and Peggy Mickey, whose husbands were prominent lawyers in town; and Janet Grayson, who was active in the Audubon Society with her husband, William, a Smithsonian official. Janet later married our friend Charlie Whitehouse after his first wife, Molly, followed her muse and left him. The 1960s were a decade of transformation, change, and experimentation that took many forms.

Interest in the environment was building at that time. The first Earth Day took place in April 1970, just weeks after we formally incorporated our nonprofit organization in March. That summer President Richard Nixon created the Environmental Protection Agency (EPA) through executive order.

I cannot deny that the prominence and power of our husbands opened many doors. We understood the benefit and were very deliberate in using our connections. We met with senators, congressmen, and various government officials. We did extensive research and sought out the best experts and looked for the very best data available. We were very concerned about producing the very best information from the best sources. I brought in botanists from the Smithsonian to help with gardening tips for *The Living Garden*, our environmental calendar for gardeners, which was authored by Joan Kirk with Janet Grayson as the liaison with Concern. This calendar has been copied many times since but was the first of its kind.

My husband's best friend, John W. Gardner, loaned us space at the offices of the National Urban Coalition, which he then headed. John was a remarkable man who, like Dick, worked for the OSS during World War II. In fact, they shared an office in the old temporary buildings on the Mall in Washington just after the war. He served as secretary of health, education, and welfare during the Johnson administration but resigned because of his opposition to the Vietnam War. After he left the cabinet, he established the National Urban Coalition as a kind of lobbying group before founding Common Cause in 1970. Common Cause became a public-interest powerhouse and, by the end of John's very distinguished career, was viewed as the most enduring part of his legacy.

Concern initially focused on three major issues: lead in paints, phosphates in detergents, and overpackaging. Ingesting lead can lead to debilitating developmental problems in young children, and every mother worries about a teething baby or toddler chewing on painted furniture or painted toys. Lead in household paint was not banned until 1978. After World War II, laundry detergent manufacturers created synthetic detergents. By 1959 all laundry detergents contained phosphorus, which was entering streams, lakes, rivers, and estuaries through wastewater effluent. The elevated levels of phosphorus triggered rapid growth of algae, which caused lakes and rivers to choke to death because of a lack of oxygen. For example, a *Congressional Record* entry reported Lake Erie had aged fifteen thousand years in less than fifty years, and a twenty-six-hundred-square-mile area of the freshwater lake had no oxygen within ten feet of the bottom by 1970.

The excessive packaging of grocery items was creating a massive trash problem. Data at the time shows that 46 percent of the trash in local landfills came from paper and paper products. As a native of England, I was particularly sensitive to overpackaging. The waste of materials and the extraordinary trash problems it created drove me crazy and still does. Even now I often open a package and see it is only partially filled.

Concern compiled *Eco-Tips*, a convenient, pocket-sized advice guide on how to choose store items that were sustainable and nonpolluting. We urged women to demand returnable instead of plastic bottles. This was before Oregon became the first state to adopt a beverage-container deposit law in 1972. We counseled homemakers to avoid pesticides, fertilizers, and herbicides. Our calendar provided organic gardening tips decades before organic farming became fashionable.

Concern definitely hit a chord. We were the subject of many news reports, including a splashy cover story for *Parade* magazine, the Sunday newspaper pull-out section that is the highest-circulation magazine in the United States. The cover featured a color photograph of me and my husband. The article drew ninety-two thousand letters to Concern. Lloyd Shearer, the publisher of *Parade*, called me one day and asked whether, if he mentioned our calendar again, we could fill the orders. He did, and we did. We and our volunteers worked all through Christmas to fill thousands of orders. Phil Donahue, the daytime talk show host, featured us on his television show. The *Washington Evening Star* once reported on our work on solid waste disposal in a society page gossip column and included in the item the name of a top executive from the EPA. I called him to apologize for getting his name in the gossip column. He graciously replied, "Please don't apologize. My mother just called from Florida, and she said 'you've been working in solid waste for twenty years and this is the first time it has been socially acceptable.'"

One telling detail that says a great deal about the times is that every single story about Concern published in those years identified us by our husbands' names as Mrs. Paul Ignatius, Mrs. Richard Helms, Mrs. Clyde E. Shorey,

Mrs. Paul Mickey, and Mrs. Russell Train. It was as if we did not have identities separate from our spouses. While none of us would ever be identified
as feminists from that era, we did show quite clearly the power that women
could wield in the marketplace. One day I accompanied Dick to a meeting of
the Business Roundtable at the Homestead, a resort in Hot Springs, Virginia.
The Roundtable is made up of CEOs from leading U.S. companies. We approached Bryce Harlow, the onetime Hill aide who became the face of Procter
& Gamble in Washington after he established the company's first Washington office in 1961. He also served the Nixon administration as a senior
adviser. Dick was accustomed to some deference from lobbyists, but Harlow
exclaimed, "No, no, I don't need to talk to you. I need to talk to your wife!"
I found that quite amusing. He wanted to talk to me about phosphates and
what we were proposing at Concern.

At that time, Procter & Gamble, Lever Brothers, and Colgate-Palmolive
produced about 80 percent of the total U.S. detergent market. The president
of Procter & Gamble made a public commitment to take the phosphates out
of laundry detergents in 1970, and the company literally spent millions of
dollars on research to develop effective alternates.

I suspect my interest in recycling and environmental pollution grew
somewhat organically out of my upbringing. The Foreign Service wives often remarked on how much waste they noticed when grocery shopping in
the United States after being abroad, where a loaf of bread, vegetables, and
other types of produce came without a wrapper and meat was wrapped up
in a single piece of butcher paper instead of miles of plastic wrap. European
housewives carried string bags to the grocery store to hold their purchases.
Years later, the District of Columbia passed a law requiring stores to charge
five cents for every plastic bag. Almost overnight, consumers in the city began carrying canvas bags to the grocery store, and the number of plastic bags
found in the Potomac and Anacostia rivers plummeted within months. It was
quite remarkable.

Dick took enormous delight in Concern. He began to buy his toiletries in
glass bottles that could be returned and reused. He once bought a disposable
six-pack of canned beer during a summer heat wave, but that was the excep-
tion. Of course, he was wonderfully supportive of me and my interests, but
I suspect he liked Concern because it gave him something to chat about at
social events and an excuse not to discuss his work, particularly Vietnam. In
those years of tumult, he could not venture to a dinner party without someone sidling up and trying to wheedle some tidbit of inside information from
him or voicing his or her opinion about the conduct of the war or the doings

at the White House. Dick used to describe avoiding these ambushes as "like trying to catch a fart in a mitten." As the years passed, Concern's environmental agenda became part of the mainstream, and each of us felt considerable pride and satisfaction in seeing so many others join us in taking action about waste, pollution, and chemical contamination.

When I look back on those years, I am struck by how rich they were in experiences, people, and learning. Some women at midlife, after their childbearing years are over, are at a loss, but others get a new lease on life. I happily fell into the latter category. Dick's circle of friends and acquaintances brought new people into my life.

One new friend who took it upon herself to guide me through Dick's circle was Polly Knowles Wisner Fritchey. Polly was a Georgetown hostess of some renown. She was also active in good and progressive causes. She had been married to Frank Wisner, a member of the original OSS crowd, a founder of the CIA, and Dick's boss for many years. Frank had suffered an extremely high fever during World War II, and my husband was convinced it permanently affected his mental health. Frank eventually suffered a nervous breakdown and shot himself in the bathroom at their farm in 1965. Polly came from an old Mississippi family, and she engaged in extensive fund-raising for the Kennedy Center, the Phillips Collection, and other artistic institutions. Ten years after Frank's death, Polly married Clayton Fritchey, a journalist and government official who was Adlai Stevenson's press secretary in both of his presidential campaigns in the 1950s. They stopped to visit us in Iran during their wedding trip.

When I married Dick in 1968, she hosted a dinner for us at her elegant house on P Street in Georgetown. The brick house was full of French and English antiques, and the garden was designed by Perry Wheeler, the landscape architect of choice for the private homes of Georgetown. Wheeler, a native of the state of Georgia, served in the OSS during World War II, where he did camouflage planning. But he is best known for his private garden designs in Georgetown, his collaboration with Bunny Mellon on the White House Rose Garden, and his design for the plantings around the JFK gravesite in Arlington National Cemetery. He favored English boxwood.

Polly's dinner parties were famous. She would jam four or five round tables into her dining room and invite one guest, someone well informed, like Henry Kissinger or George Kennan, to speak. One night, as the war in Vietnam continued to rage, Henry spoke after dinner about the peace he and President Nixon had negotiated in Vietnam. As we left the dining room, Dick leaned over and whispered, "Nonsense, they don't have any peace." Dick was correct.

Polly's son Frank G. Wisner became a career diplomat and served as ambassador to Zambia, Egypt, the Philippines, and India, so he and his contemporaries were always around the house and at her farm in Maryland. That sort of multigenerational socializing injected the house with great energy. Polly also had the run of a wonderful second house on the Fishers Island estate of Betsey Cushing Roosevelt Whitney, who was married to John Hay Whitney, ambassador to the Court of St. James during the Eisenhower administration. Fishers Island is located in Long Island Sound near New London, Connecticut. We spent many happy hours there collecting mussels from the rocks. Betsey was one of the famous Cushing sisters. She had previously been married to Franklin D. Roosevelt's oldest son, James.

Polly's best friend was Katharine Graham, the publisher of the *Washington Post*. I met Kay through Polly. Kay and I played tennis together every week for years. We played a foursome with Secretary of State George Schultz, sometimes at the White House tennis courts but more often at the Arlington YMCA.

Kay became close to Warren Buffett in the early 1970s, after he bought a big chunk of *Washington Post* stock. They kept company for years even though he was married to Susie. Warren and Susie had some sort of understanding. They stayed married, but she lived in San Francisco, where she had moved. He lived in Omaha, where he had a housekeeper whom Susie had arranged to take care of him in her absence. Susie occasionally came to Washington and joined Warren at Kay's dinner parties. The housekeeper eventually married Warren.

Warren loved to play bridge and urged Kay to learn. He sent Sharon Osberg, a former Women's World Bridge Champion, to Washington to teach Kay. He also arranged for Sharon to teach Bill Gates, the founder of Microsoft and one of the world's richest men. I remember poor Bill trailing around in Warren's wake at one of Kay's parties, wondering aloud why no one wanted to talk to him. Warren had that sort of effect on people.

Warren helped Kay develop the confidence she needed as a businesswoman. She often said he taught her how to read a spreadsheet, but he was much more to her than that. He guided her, boosted her spirits, and told her she was good enough. She did need that. Kay was a woman in a man's world, and her own mother had shredded whatever innate confidence she may have had at birth. Warren was fourteen years younger than she, and while their romance probably faded over time, they remained very good friends until her death.

Kay welcomed the diversions of bridge and tennis and her friendships with people who had nothing to do with the newspaper. While we played bridge, she would talk about her mother, Agnes Meyer, whose negativity and condescension left Kay, even as an adult, painfully but endearingly insecure. I remember one story she told about winning the history prize as a high school student at Madeira, the exclusive girls' school she had attended. When she rushed home to tell her mother, Agnes ignored her news and snapped, "That is a really ugly dress you are wearing." Poor Kay remembered that cutting remark decades later. Kay had psychic scars from her mother and her husband, Philip Graham. When Phil was in the throes of mental illness, his treatment of her was brutally cruel. I always found it remarkable that Kay emerged as such a good, decent woman despite that sort of treatment.

Kay's husband had committed suicide in 1963 by shooting himself in the head at their house in the country. She heard the shot and found his body. I'm not sure one ever recovers from that sort of trauma. Phil was raving mad, and the year before his suicide, he had left Kay for a young Australian journalist, Robin Webb, who was working as a stringer at *Newsweek* magazine's Paris bureau. Kay was extraordinarily kind and nonjudgmental to the young woman in her memoir, and she told me that she hoped Robin would contact her when the book was published. She very much wanted to talk to her. I believe Robin Webb returned to Australia at the encouragement of Edward Bennett Williams, who represented the *Washington Post* and Graham. But she never did contact Kay.

Kay invited us many times to visit her beautiful home overlooking the ocean on Martha's Vineyard in Massachusetts. We had wonderful, memorable times debating who should come to dinner with the Clintons during his presidency. The Vineyard is swarming with interesting people during the summer. We also shared another connection. I was very involved with the Freer Gallery of Art, the Smithsonian museum of Asian art, which also has an amazing collection of nineteenth-century American art. Her mother had been a friend of the founder, Charles L. Freer, an industrialist who became a notable art collector. The Graham family itself was not particularly interested in Asian art.

When Kay died after falling on a sidewalk during a business retreat in Sun Valley, Idaho, something in Washington died. Her house on R Street had been a gathering spot for an eclectic circle of international friends and leaders in a warm, noncontroversial setting where camaraderie prevailed. She had many friendships that sometimes surprised me. For example, her closeness to and fondness for Nancy Reagan was genuine and reciprocated.

Being married to Dick meant we also now shared friends. My friends and children enriched his life as well. I had met Alice Roosevelt Longworth before

I met Dick, but we were often invited to her grand house near the Dupont Circle neighborhood of Washington. She was born in 1884 but remained active well into her eighties. We spent election night in 1972 at a party at her house. She was eighty-eight then. She never lost her famous wit. If she liked you, she was delightful. If not, well, she could be rather acerbic. Alice lost her mother when she was two days old, and her father, the famous Rough Rider and later president Theodore Roosevelt, shuffled her off to an aunt before he remarried. She clearly missed the loving attention of her mother. She spent much of her life being outrageous, which brought her a great deal of attention. In my experience, those who lose their mothers when young, including my first husband, never seem to recover from that loss.

Dick's reputation for discretion extended to me. Supreme Court Justice Lewis Powell loved to dance, and he would regale me with stories about his days at Bletchley Park, the supersecret British code-breaking center, during World War II. In those days, the code-breaking operation, code-named "Station X" by the British, was still considered confidential. The U.S. government sent Powell, then a young military officer, to Bletchley Park for training during the war. He loved the experience and took enormous pride in his role in breaking the German and other codes. He apparently viewed me as a safe repository for his stories because I was married to the nation's most celebrated spymaster. But he was careful only to talk to me about Bletchley while we danced or sat together at dinners so no one else could overhear him. He was such a gentleman. I always kept his confidence until he himself wrote about it.

My husband knew former secretary of state Dean Acheson well. He was a delightful and interesting man who refused to take calls from "the White House" because a building could not place a telephone call. He stayed late at his office at the State Department to revise correspondence and eliminate references to the State Department's or the White House's expressing opinions or taking actions. The first time I was seated next to him at a dinner party, I was worried about how in the world I would have an intelligent conversation with this giant of foreign policy who played such a central role in the creation of the Marshall Plan, the Truman Doctrine, and the North Atlantic Treaty Organization. I had read an article in *The Atlantic* magazine about language and his fascination with it and felt I could hold my own talking about language. So I asked him about language and words. That conversation launched a rewarding friendship.

David Packard, the cofounder of Hewlett-Packard, and his wife, Lucile, became great friends when Packard served as deputy secretary of defense under Melvin Laird from 1969 to 1971. President Nixon once described

Laird as the most devious man in Washington in a conversation with Dick. I have never met anyone who disagreed with that assessment. David was quite different—an engaging, open, and wonderful man who was generous about inviting us to visit them at their homes in British Columbia and Big Sur. He admired my mineral collection. One day he took me for a ride in Big Sur, and his car broke down. He rummaged through the glove compartment until he found the owner's manual and told me that you should never buy anything if you can't understand the manual. He fixed the car, and we were on our way. One of his great interests was marine biology, and he built the aquarium in Monterey, California. When he took me to see it, I was looking forward to the exhibits. It was not to be. He took me underground and explained every pipe, joint, and fixture to me. He took enormous pride in all of it. I never did get to see the exhibits, but I am sure I could have passed a plumbing exam after his detailed explanation of the innards of the building. Dick and he enjoyed discussing the *Glomar Explorer* and the effort to raise a Soviet ballistic-missile submarine from the depths of the Pacific Ocean.

David Packard only served two years before resigning in December 1971. His resignation was unexpected, and when we asked why he was leaving, he looked a bit embarrassed and mumbled something about losing $18 million because of some trust or stock option or other. Lucile once idly told him at breakfast when we were with them that she had forgotten to tell him that she had given $1 million to the Wolf Trap Foundation for the Performing Arts, where she was on the board. We were quietly bemused that someone would "forget" a million-dollar donation, but they were very wealthy. When David died in 1996, his net worth was estimated to be $3.7 billion. He left most of his money to the charitable foundation he and Lucile had created. It was so sad to see him near the end of his life. We visited him at his house, where he still lived after his wife's death. His faithful housekeeper sent us so many dried apricots, but the flowerpots in his garden were unattended, and I longed to fill them with flowers for him.

I had always wanted to be my own person, to have my own life and make a contribution to the world. Although I viewed my experience as the mother of four wonderful children as among the most enriching and valuable of my life, this new phase that began in my mid-forties was simply wonderful. With Dick by my side, I was finally coming into my own.

7

❧❦

TWO OATHS

I n 1935 Richard Helms graduated second in his class at Williams College, and his classmates deemed him "most likely to succeed." I like to think that his classmates recognized in him the qualities that I came to admire and respect. Dick was first and foremost a great patriot. It sounds sappy, but he was. He loved his country. He was a disciplined and self-confident man who followed a clear set of principles in his life—namely, he worked for the president of the United States and believed the agency was a critical source of foreign information for the president; he took an oath to keep the secrets of the United States; he felt a deep loyalty to his colleagues in the CIA family yet recognized his obligation to keep his colleagues disciplined and accountable; and last, but certainly not least, everything he did served the best interests of the security of the United States of America. The Watergate scandal put those principles in collision and upended the old order in Washington. My husband did not know it at the time but that bungled, third-rate burglary at the Watergate office complex in the early summer of 1972 marked the beginning of the end of his career in intelligence.

By the fourth year of our marriage, I had long grown accustomed to the late night telephone calls for my husband. Notification of a crisis breaking out in some remote corner of the world or a query from the president or White House senior staff was simply part of his job. A phone call late on Saturday night, June 17, 1972, from Howard Osborn, the CIA chief of security, concerned an issue closer to home. Howard told Dick that the District of Columbia metropolitan police had arrested five men for breaking into the

Democratic National Committee office in the Watergate office building early that morning. Four were Cubans. The fifth was James McCord, a former CIA agent who had left the agency two years earlier. Osborn also told Dick that E. Howard Hunt, another retired CIA officer, was involved in some fashion. Dick knew both, particularly Hunt, and he was concerned, though more puzzled than worried. The CIA is strictly forbidden from engaging in domestic surveillance. Neither McCord nor Hunt worked for the agency any longer. Breaking into a political party office in the United States and rifling through the files fell outside the agency mandate or even its interests, so an official connection seemed unlikely—unlikely but not impossible. Things do happen. But Dick told Osborn to make certain there was no agency involvement. The CIA had ongoing relationships with Cubans in Miami because of U.S. concerns about Communist Cuba. And Hunt had obtained some surveillance-related materials from the agency in recent years as part of the work he was doing for the White House on security. Dick learned of that favor after the fact, and when Hunt's request for agency support escalated, he put a stop to it. Hunt served in the OSS during World War II and had a long career with the agency as a covert operator. The loan of materials came about in part as a kind of professional courtesy but also because John Ehrlichman, President Nixon's domestic policy adviser, instructed the CIA to help Hunt. In short, Dick had legitimate reasons for his concern. He instructed Osborn to keep him posted. Before going to bed, I noticed Dick called L. Patrick Gray, then acting director of the FBI. It was a natural gesture. The FBI had jurisdiction over any illegality involving federal matters in the United States.

J. Edgar Hoover, the much-feared director of the FBI who kept dossiers on the powerful during his long tenure in office, had died of an apparent heart attack on May 2, just six weeks earlier. President Nixon appointed Gray, then serving in a senior position at the Justice Department, to Hoover's job in an acting capacity pending Senate confirmation. Dick reached Gray through the White House switchboard. The White House switchboard and the remarkable Signal Corps had the extraordinary ability to find virtually anyone anywhere at any time. It took a few minutes because Gray was traveling in California, but Signal tracked him down to a hotel room in Los Angeles. Dick told Gray that there was no CIA involvement in the Watergate burglary but advised him to look into John Ehrlichman's relationship with McCord and Hunt. Dick already knew that Hunt and McCord had been hired by Nixon's campaign to do private security work, and he knew Ehrlichman had expressed a particular interest in Hunt's work. My husband paid close attention to anything involving current or former CIA personnel and the White House because he worked directly for the president in his capacity as director of central intelligence. Gray told my husband that he was aware of the break-in. But Dick said that Gray was nonresponsive and volunteered no information or insight of his own. This struck him as so curious that he commented on it to me. Why, he wondered, does Pat Gray seem disinterested? Pat Gray's utter lack of interest in this caper continued to puzzle Dick, and he mentioned it repeatedly. It was some time before he realized Gray had been co-opted by the Nixon White House.

To me, it is amazing that the head of the CIA and acting head of the FBI knew about the arrest less than twenty-four hours after police took into custody five men at 2:30 a.m. in what, by all appearances, was a somewhat routine burglary in a downtown office building. But, with the benefit of hindsight, it is not that surprising. That burglary was like a loose thread on a sweater. Once someone pulled at the thread, a massive conspiracy and cover-up unraveled. The Watergate scandal took down a president. Two more years passed before the true story of the Watergate burglary became widely known to the public, and it was years before all the details of White House involvement came to light. Of course, Richard Nixon was forced to resign in August 1974, as he faced almost certain impeachment. The money trail led investigators right to the Oval Office, where Nixon was issuing the orders and his two senior aides, Ehrlichman and H. R. Haldeman, his chief of staff, were carrying them out. The revelation that Nixon had actually taped conversations about the caper and cover-up provided the last bit of evidence needed to end his political career and ultimately exonerate Dick and the CIA.

By the time Nixon resigned, we were living in Iran, where Dick served as U.S. ambassador. Before Dick left intelligence and became an ambassador, I had a front-row seat to a scandal that not only destroyed a president but also changed politics and America in some fundamental ways. Watergate represented a loss of innocence for the United States. After Watergate, Americans no longer viewed their elected leaders or their president in quite the same fashion. But more important to my story, Watergate made Americans more suspicious of and skeptical toward their government. The old boys' network was utterly destroyed. The gentleman's agreement between Congress and the White House that allowed presidents to use the CIA as a personal and secret foreign policy tool effectively ended. The press became far more aggressive, powerful, and intrusive in political life after Watergate and the additional revelations about CIA covert operations. Oversight of intelligence from Congress grew substantially, which in some respects was a good thing because it curbed the more impulsive and reckless instincts of presidents.

But there was a downside. Watergate unleashed forces that deeply hurt my husband and his reputation and damaged the U.S. intelligence-gathering operation. There is no need for me to defend Richard Helms, but I would be remiss if I did not say I firmly believe that any objective reading of the record will show that he behaved honorably and stuck to his principles throughout the entire mess.

In oral histories recorded by agency historians that were declassified in 2008, Dick described his view of the role of DCI as "the principal intelligence officer for the president." He explained that he did not take a position on policy or engage in partisan activities because he viewed his role as "keeping the game honest" by supplying hard factual and accurate data on world conditions and history. Dick often said he had one boss: the president of the United States. Regardless of political party or persuasion, he served the president and felt it was his obligation to do whatever the president asked. Of course, he would not break the law or take actions that would hurt the CIA or the intelligence community, and there were times when he veered awfully close to the line to accommodate a presidential demand. Many times he complained that the lashes on his back due to Attorney General Robert F. Kennedy's relentless obsession with Fidel Castro were still visible years after the Kennedy administration. Dick made little secret of his view that the Bay of Pigs invasion of Cuba was a mistake. Indeed, his refusal to attend a single planning meeting on that debacle quite clearly reflected his opinion. It is worth noting that every single operation undertaken by the CIA was done with the approval of the president of the United States. Dick always told me that key members of Congress had been briefed on every secret mission. This was not "a rogue agency," even though individual agents might need to be reined in from time to time.

There is great debate about the role of a secret intelligence operation in an open society like the United States. There are those who question its value. My husband viewed those people as impossibly naïve. I agree. As someone who grew up in Great Britain, I also sometimes can recognize the impulse in Americans to believe that this country is different and better than others and never would, as a matter of policy, engage in matters like a military coup or political overthrow of an unpleasant foreign leader or the assassination of a dictator. In his book on my husband, *The Man Who Kept the Secrets*, Thomas Powers refers several times to the "child's view of history," the innocent belief in the essential superiority and goodness of the United States. But the world contains many threats and dangers for those who embrace freedom. Dick Helms understood this, believed this, and acted accordingly. In my view, this pragmatic realism is the mark of a true patriot.

While only Congress has the constitutional right to declare war, presidents, in the conduct of foreign policy, often need to take action far short of sending in the marines. The conventions of diplomacy can only go so far. Intelligence, both the gathering of data and covert operations, is frequently used by presidents, including our current president, Barack Obama, as a way to achieve foreign policy aims without taking direct military action. This is not necessarily a bad or unwise thing. Dick viewed the CIA as the equivalent of a finely honed tool for presidents and did what he could to help presidents further their foreign policy aims, even if he sometimes privately questioned their judgment or policies.

There is a story that reveals this impulse. During the Johnson administration, Dick wanted to do something to relieve the anguish of President Johnson over the war in Vietnam. Johnson had named Dick deputy director and then director of central intelligence, so my husband felt a particular obligation to LBJ, but he also liked Johnson and viewed him as an effective, thoughtful, and well-intended leader who made conditions better for the poor and minorities in the United States, although at times his methods were close to bullying. But to help Johnson, Dick asked one of the top analysts at the agency to prepare a secret memo in 1967 analyzing the price to the United States of a loss in Vietnam.

Lyndon Johnson hosted a regular Tuesday luncheon at the White House with his most trusted and closest advisers. He knew they could be trusted not to leak. Unlike the more inclusive cabinet meetings, he handpicked the people to attend these luncheons. This select group included Dick. Johnson was an astute observer of human nature and a deft politician. He knew that most of his aides and advisers would tell him what he wanted, as opposed to what he needed, to hear. He wanted Dick and others in the group to give him their best, unvarnished advice. While precious few survive for long in Washington without a substantial amount of self-editing, this group of individuals had the president's ear and the liberty to offer him their honest views. The Tuesday group included Secretary of State Dean Rusk; Secretary of Defense Bob McNamara; General Earle "Bus" Wheeler, chairman of the Joint Chiefs of Staff; Walt Rostow, the national security adviser; and George Christian, the White House press secretary. Tom Johnson, a deputy press secretary, also attended as note taker. In his own memoir, Dick said he was unaware of a single leak from those lunches, a tribute to the president's judgment and the discretion of the participants.

After one meeting, Dick handed the president a sealed envelope containing a thirty-three-page paper with a brief cover memo from him. The paper was declassified in 1993, and Dick's cover memo was declassified in 1999. The paper, titled "Implications of an Unfavorable Outcome in Vietnam," concluded that the United States could "lose" the conflict in Vietnam without sustaining any fatal blow to its prestige or power. In the final point to Johnson in his cover memo, Dick revealed a great deal about how he viewed his job: "I would emphasize that the paper was not intended as an argument for ending or for not ending the war now. We are not defeatist out here. It deals narrowly with the hypothetical question which the author put to himself, i.e., what would be the consequences of an unfavorable outcome for American policy and American interests as a whole. It has no bearing on whether the present political-military outlook within Vietnam makes acceptance of such an outcome advisable or inadvisable." In other words, Dick was not taking a policy position. He just wanted to ease President Johnson's mind and make it easier for him to make decisions about the war. Johnson was loath to be the first American president to "lose" a war. He was also aware that the war pulled resources from his war against poverty at home and undermined his domestic agenda in general. The war was tearing apart Johnson's administration, destroying his popularity with the public, and eroding his political standing. Indeed, just six months later, on March 31, 1968, Johnson announced he would not seek reelection.

The paper has certain shortcomings given that it was submitted to Dick on September 11, 1967. It reflects the times and its biases, assumptions, and mis-assumptions. But it was also prescient. One concluding paragraph suggested the long-term damage to the United States would be in its ability to fight the next war. It said, "The worst potential damage would be of the self-inflicted kind: internal dissension which would limit our future ability to use our power and resources wisely and to full effect, and lead to a loss of confidence by others in the American capacity for leadership." This proved to be true.

This Vietnam effect did constrain American military action for decades until the Gulf wars of the 1990s. Years later, after the top-secret memo was opened in the files of the LBJ Presidential Library, our telephone at home rang. It was Bob McNamara calling from Texas, where he was researching his own book on Vietnam at the LBJ library. McNamara may have been in charge of the military as secretary of defense, but he came to recognize the folly of the war and struggled mightily to find a way out. McNamara's son actively protested the war that his own father supervised. McNamara never knew about the memo that Dick had marked for the president's eyes only because Walt Rostow, the national security adviser and a hawk on the war, had deep-sixed it. The president had clearly read the document. He left his initials on it. Bob was so upset; I could hear his shouts from across the room. "Why didn't

I know about this? This would have helped me! I should have known!" Dick did not view it as appropriate for him to get involved in the administration's policy battles, but I felt great sympathy for Bob.

The war proved to be so unpopular that Johnson's men engaged in a certain amount of revisionism after the fact. Clark Clifford, one of the so-called wise men of Washington, replaced Bob McNamara as secretary of defense and as a participant in the weekly Tuesday lunches. In his memoir, Clifford claimed he spoke up and advocated for U.S. withdrawal from Vietnam during those lunches. This apparently was not true because I witnessed an interesting exchange between LBJ and my husband just a few years later.

While en route to a vacation in Mexico before we moved to Iran, Dick and I visited President Johnson and Lady Bird at their ranch in Texas. Johnson had left office and would die of heart disease about a month later. I watched as President Johnson brought up a question he had asked Dick privately on an earlier visit. He asked Dick if he recalled Clifford arguing for withdrawal from Vietnam or anything remotely like that at the Tuesday lunches. Dick rarely forgot a thing. He said he had no memory of it. Johnson had earlier asked if he could check his notes, and Dick told him that he had taken no notes because the president had asked him not to do so, but he would have remembered Clifford making that kind of assertion. I asked Tom Johnson, the deputy White House press secretary who later ran CNN, if his notes showed Clifford ever making such a bold declaration. He said they did not.

Clifford embellished, as do so many. Clark Clifford had one of those storied Washington careers that biographers favor. He enjoyed a reputation as a canny political operator. He worked as a key strategist for Harry Truman in his successful and unexpected upset election over Thomas Dewey in 1948. He served Presidents Truman, Kennedy, Johnson, and Carter and became one of Washington's most prominent superlawyers, who typically practice very little law but wield enormous influence because of vast connections and political skill. In his later years, Clifford tried to recruit Dick to the board of the Bank of Credit and Commerce International (BCCI). I flatly opposed it because Dick knew nothing about banking, and fortunately my husband agreed with me and declined the offer despite Clark's repeated requests. The BCCI scandal destroyed Clark. The bank turned out to be controlled by foreign investors and deeply involved in money laundering, bribery, arms trafficking, and many other illegal activities. Clark said he had been deceived, but he was indicted anyway. The indictments were eventually laid aside because of his ill health. He died in 1998 at the age of ninety-one, a significantly diminished and lonely man, no longer the superlawyer.

Although Dick felt an obligation to carry out the president's wishes, he also understood presidents are not always right. And he felt an obligation to protect the CIA and its agents. He eventually decided to resign as director of central intelligence because Nixon and his men made demands that he simply could not accept. This is now a matter of public record, but Nixon, through his aides, demanded that Dick come up with the money, presumably from unvouchered funds, to pay for the legal defense of the burglary team. Dick flatly refused to do this. The agency always had access to a lot of cash, but these accounts were approved by the congressional appropriations committees, and he could not conceive of using the money for unauthorized purposes, particularly something so far afield from the agency's responsibilities. I remember him on the phone with Haldeman with his voice slightly raised, which was a shout for him because he never shouted, saying, "The president needs to tell me that directly." That never happened. Nixon was clever enough to have his aides make those requests. The president also tried to blame the CIA for the burglary, co-opted the FBI acting director, tried to get the CIA to slow down the FBI investigation, and engaged in many other illegal acts as part of the cover-up. I remember so clearly Dick fretting about Pat Gray. He could not understand why Gray was so reluctant to do his job on Watergate. It became clear much later that Gray, a former career military man, had unfortunately saluted when White House officials asked him to cover for them. For example, he burned the contents of the safe of E. Howard Hunt in his fireplace in Connecticut at the behest of John Dean, the White House counsel, and Ehrlichman. Gray had a remarkable life story. He was a self-made man who rose to the highest levels of government, but Watergate nearly destroyed him. There were times when Dick had an almost impossible task to serve the president but avoid hurting his agency or doing anything illegal. He stepped very carefully.

Dick felt his days were likely numbered with Nixon after his refusal to comply with the Watergate demands and other orders that he found distasteful, and we had many long discussions about the future. Dick had absolutely no idea of what he might do for work if he left the government, and he felt ethically bound to not put out any feelers for private-sector jobs so long as he held his position. We decided he would retire from his job sometime after the November election in 1972. Dick was fifty-nine years old that year. He had a number of reasons for deciding to retire from intelligence. He was uncomfortable with the instructions he was getting from Nixon and the president's men. He did not relish the idea of what Nixon might demand of him in a second term, when Nixon would be even more emboldened and freed from the constraints of a reelection campaign. Dick also had a practical reason. We were still living in a rental apartment. He wanted to earn some money while he was still able in order to provide for a more secure retirement for both of us. Moreover, the CIA had a mandatory retirement age of sixty, and he would reach that milestone at the end of March 1973. In October 1972, he told me to find a small house for us anywhere but Georgetown and buy it. We kept our decision quiet and told no one of our retirement plans. There are few things worse in Washington than being perceived as a lame duck, and Dick's decision to retire from government could be interpreted as a reflection of Nixon during a reelection campaign.

Our real estate agent lived across the street from the house we bought on Garfield Street, just off Foxhall Road in northwest Washington. An elderly couple lived there and wanted to sell quietly, and our agent persuaded them to allow me to take a quick look at the house. I put on my running shoes and literally galloped through the house. It was small, the least expensive house I could find, and crowded with large pieces of old furniture. Getting that oversized furniture out made it seem positively roomy. We later enlarged it with a wonderful bright and airy two-story sunroom to replace two useless screened porches. The owners did not want to settle until January 1973, which suited us. Ultimately, our move into that wonderful house was delayed by four years. When we moved to Tehran, we rented it.

Dick thought it unseemly to resign during an election season. This reflected his belief that he ought not to engage in policy or political fights. He decided to wait until after the election, which is a natural time for turnover between presidential terms. Nixon, however, had his own ideas and timetable. He demanded the resignations of his cabinet and senior staff immediately after the election. It was the practice of administrations to keep on the FBI and CIA directors, however, as a matter of continuity and an implicit acknowledgment that appointment to those positions ought not to be viewed in the same way as a political favor to a supporter, so Dick did not submit his resignation at that time. Just weeks later, however, Dick was called to Camp David to meet with the president, ostensibly about the agency budget.

He later described to me and in his own memoir the rather odd scene of a stiff president who never did become comfortable with small talk or interacting with people. Nixon was a very awkward, socially inept man. In all the times I spoke to him, he always struggled to find something to say. Nixon told him he wanted "new blood" at the CIA and asked him what he thought of bringing in a new DCI. Dick was a little surprised but did not let on that he had already decided to leave the agency. He only said he would be reaching the mandatory retirement age of sixty the following March, and if he could serve until his birthday, it would keep the position out of the other more political appointments and be best for him after his long service in government. Nixon, with Haldeman by his side, agreed to let him serve until his birthday in March 1973. Dick said that Nixon seemed completely unaware of either Dick's age, which he would have thought was quite obvious, and of the fact he had served in intelligence for almost thirty years dating back to his war years in OSS. Almost impulsively, Nixon, also a veteran of World War II, asked him if he would like to be an ambassador. This had never occurred to my husband. In general there are two types of ambassadors: political appointees, who are frequently wealthy supporters of the president who can afford to pay out of pocket for the cost of entertainment overseas, and career Foreign Service officers. Nixon suggested Dick might go to Moscow. This struck Dick as peculiar and totally inappropriate, and he immediately advised Nixon that the appointment of a career spy would likely not be welcomed by the Soviets. Dick countered with Tehran. He later said it was a somewhat unusual choice on his part, though he had many reasons for requesting this assignment. Iran holds special geopolitical significance because of its history and physical location. Its borders touch Russia and what were then several Soviet satellite nations, as well as Afghanistan, Pakistan, Iraq, and Turkey. A tiny bit of water, the Persian Gulf, separates Iran from Saudi Arabia. It also holds enormous reserves of natural gas and petroleum. It has been an important Muslim nation since the Muslim conquest in AD 651, and even then Dick recognized the significance of the world's growing population of Muslims. He asked Nixon for time to speak with me and consider the offer.

The notion of moving to Tehran initially upset me. The first four years of my marriage to Dick had been among the most personally rewarding and enriching of my life because of the radio job at the Smithsonian and volunteer work with Concern. I was disheartened at the idea of leaving either. And although my two older children and my stepson were married, my two younger children were still not settled. Bones was still trying to figure out what he would do with his life, and Lindsay was still in college. I could not imagine voluntarily being thousands of miles away from them. And Iran seemed so far away and so alien. I wondered aloud why he hadn't picked a nice country in western Europe that would have fitted more easily within the comfort zone of a native of England.

I have initially resisted every major physical move in my life, which I view as a character flaw. Excessive caution is so inhibiting. I think I was afraid that I would not succeed in a new place. I always had a panicked feeling of loneliness at the notion of moving. It took me awhile to warm up to the idea of leaving England as a young wife and mother, but once I settled into life in Rochester, Minnesota, I thrived. Each time, my instincts shouted no, but I eventually came around, and every move became an opportunity to learn and grow. I suppose I have something of the spirit of an adventurer, albeit a very cautious one. While I have not always been game for the idea of trying something new, Dick and I had already shared some wonderful overseas adventures in our marriage. We agreed he should accept the offer. He did. The State Department cabled the shah of Iran, whom Dick had known for some time; the shah commended the choice, and within a matter of days, the deal was done.

Of course, it was not completely done. Although the appointment was the president's decision, the U.S. Senate had the constitutional responsibility to review the appointment under its advise-and-consent authority. Dick was a well-known commodity on Capitol Hill. He had briefed senators and House members with oversight of the CIA for years. But his testimony before the Senate Foreign Relations Committee would prove to be anything but routine.

Dick often told me that Nixon constantly disparaged the executive branch of government in front of other people, complaining and criticizing this agency or that official. He knew that he regularly trashed the CIA. To replace Dick, Nixon appointed James R. Schlesinger, a Harvard-educated economist with limited experience in intelligence, to be director of central intelligence and ordered him to "shake things up." With virtually no notice to Dick, Schlesinger was sworn in as DCI on February 2, 1973. Dick learned of the appointment from the WTOP morning radio news. No one from the White House extended the courtesy of a phone call. He barely had time to pack up his office and say good-bye to his colleagues. The commitment to let him serve until his March 30 birthday had been broken, probably deliberately. Dick moved into a temporary office at the State Department, pending his approval by the Senate and our move overseas.

Schlesinger held the position for only a few months but did an astonishing amount of damage to the agency in following Nixon's instructions. Schlesinger was not a very congenial man. In fact, he was rude, abrasive, insensitive, and cruel. He never displayed a trace of good manners or acknowledged the service of fine men and women who had put their lives on the line for their country. Schlesinger's initiative led to a major reduction in force at the agency and the loss of many gifted experienced agents, which, from the perspective of long-time employees, effectively dismantled the counterintelligence operation. He also ordered compilation of a list of every historic action taken by the agency or its personnel that might be perceived as illegal or flirted with the fine line of legality. Known as "the family jewels," this list included twenty-five years of operations under five presidents, both Democrats and Republicans, from Truman to Nixon. Every single act had been ordered or approved by a president of the United States. Members of Congress had been briefed on each and approved the funding of every operation. Not that anyone could tell that from the leaks to members of the news media and sensational headlines that cast the CIA as a rogue agency engaged in systematic illegal acts without the knowledge of the American people or its representatives. It is true that the public and rank-and-file members of Congress had no knowledge and likely little suspicion of the agency's covert operations, but that was precisely the point. They were secret. But the secrets were known by every president and by some appropriate members of Congress.

In the climate of the times, journalists and politicians made and burnished their reputations by trashing the CIA and, many times, distorting and exaggerating agency behavior while totally ignoring the fact that presidents ordered these missions and that duly elected members of Congress had signed off on each and every one. Perspective and balance were notably lacking. One incident I learned about concerned the unfortunately titled Operation CHAOS, where Johnson had the agency look into student demonstrations. Dick knew this operation would be controversial, so he deliberately kept it under his personal direction to maintain control and make certain the buck stopped with him. However, others persisted in believing that James Jesus Angleton was responsible.

Schlesinger was named secretary of defense in the spring of 1973 and left the agency within months. Bill Colby, the new director, went even further in disclosing classified information. Colby dumped an astonishing amount of classified data on the congressional committees and Justice Department. This data included Dick's testimony before the Senate Foreign Relations Committee, in which the Justice Department took a particular interest.

Senators can question nominees on virtually anything, and at this hearing, the questions dealt with agency operations in Chile, which were still top secret. The question came during an executive session of the committee from Senator Stuart Symington, a Democrat from Missouri. Senator Symington asked, "Did you try in the Central Intelligence Agency to overthrow the government of Chile?"

Dick replied, "No, sir."

He then asked, "Did you have money passed to the opponents of Allende?"

Dick again replied, "No, sir."

Then Symington asked, "So the stories you were involved in that war are wrong?"

Dick replied, "Yes, sir."

Dick tried to thread a needle by responding to the questions in the narrowest way possible because the Senate Foreign Relations Committee was not the forum for disclosing classified information; nor was it cleared to hear classified information. Moreover, Symington already knew the answers because Helms had briefed him in his capacity as a member of a Senate subcommittee, which was authorized to learn classified information.

My husband believed in keeping members of the House and Senate fully informed about agency operations. But there was a system in place, and he followed the established practice of divulging secret matters only to a select handful of senators and House members. For many years, including during his tenure as director, Dick's principal Hill contact was Senator Richard Russell, the powerful conservative Democrat from Georgia. Russell was one of the last of the great, powerful congressional barons, many of them southerners. He chaired the Senate Armed Services Committee and later the Appropriations Committee and, from all accounts, wielded a tremendous amount of power. He assembled a carefully handpicked group of senators for briefings by the agency. They never leaked, so Dick trusted them. Every dollar spent by the agency was overseen by these lawmakers. In other words, they signed off on everything. There was never a "secret war" against Laos, for example, because senators, including Stuart Symington, who would later wail about this "secret war," had been thoroughly briefed about agency operations in Laos. This is a bit of a diversion, but Symington actually visited Laos, was given a guided tour of the Laos operations by agency officials, and personally commended Dick for the Laos activities before he expressed his outrage over the "secret war." There are honorable men in Washington, but there is little honor in this type of behavior by politicians more concerned with currying public favor who sway like fragile flowers in the winds of public opinion.

This subcommittee knew all about Chile. And there was a great deal to know.

Salvador Allende Gossens was a Chilean physician, a lifelong politician, and a Marxist who favored nationalization of major industries and collectivization of land in Chile. This did not sit well with certain U.S. business interests. Notably, Donald M. Kendall, the CEO of PepsiCo and a prominent member of the U.S. sugar lobby, passionately opposed Allende's election because it would affect the price and availability of sugar for his most lucrative product, Pepsi-Cola. Kendall had given Richard Nixon his first big corporate account when Nixon practiced law in New York City.

Nixon later publicly denied he was acting at Kendall's behest, but the facts suggest otherwise, and my husband believed Nixon acted because his old patron was concerned. Calvin Coolidge once famously said that the business of America is business, and there have been many times in the history of the United States, as well as Britain, when economic interests have driven foreign policy decisions. In my own lifetime, military intervention has been undertaken more than once to guarantee access to shipping lanes and control the price of critical raw materials, such as oil. Dick had met with Kendall at the request of senior White House officials. And President Nixon called Dick to the White House and ordered him to do whatever possible to prevent Allende's victory in a three-way election in 1970. The CIA was already engaged in activities in Chile because of U.S. concerns over the spread of communism in the Americas. The extra, secret effort specifically ordered by Nixon was called Track II to differentiate it from Track I, the ongoing activities. Despite extensive efforts to disrupt the economy and support for his opponents, it was too little, too late, and Allende narrowly won his race. The United States spent $11 million all told, but its efforts were not in vain. The Chilean military eventually did mount a coup, which succeeded on September 11, 1973. Allende committed suicide on the same day. A dictator, General Augusto Pinochet, came to power and ruled for seventeen years in a regime characterized by unprecedented suppression of human rights. It is not for me to say that policymakers need to worry about unintended consequences, but the facts do speak for themselves.

The Senate Foreign Relations Committee was not authorized for briefing on agency secrets, and the questions on Chile came as a surprise, so Dick had a split second to consider his response. He was accustomed to wending his way carefully between classified and unclassified information after spending thirty years in intelligence work. It was second nature for him to deflect questions, avoid sensitive areas, and say just enough to stay firmly on the side of disclosing nonsecret data. He had a reputation in Washington for being unusually quiet. Even in talking to me, his confidante, he never disclosed classified information.

Dick knew that refusal to answer Symington's questions would amount to a tacit confirmation. He did not want to mislead the committee, but he could not disclose secrets. His sensitivity to protecting covert operations was particularly high at this time because the agency was being decimated by Schlesinger, Allende was still in power, and agency operations were still taking place in Chile.

Dick swore to tell the truth to the Senate Foreign Relations Committee, but he had also taken an oath when he joined the intelligence agency back in 1947 to "forever keep secret any information" obtained in the course of his service. The secrecy oath was made even stronger when he became director. He also signed a secrecy termination agreement when he resigned, which said, "I will never divulge, publish or reveal by writing, word, conduct, or otherwise any classified information or any information, concerning intelligence of CIA that has not been made public by CIA, to any unauthorized person including but not limited to any future governmental or private employer or official without the express written consent of the Director of the Central Intelligence Agency or his representative."

Dick never harbored a bit of confusion about his obligation or duty. He did not hesitate to tell Senator Symington and later Senator Frank Church that the CIA did not attempt to influence the vote in Chile because he felt a higher obligation to the oath he swore to protect the nation's secrets. It is important to add at this point that it was not Richard Helms's secret operation in Chile: it was an operation taken at the specific direction of Richard Nixon, a duly elected president of the United States.

Sisella Bok, the brilliant philosopher and ethicist who wrote *Lying: Moral Choices in Private and Public Life*, a book on the ethics of deception, viewed my husband's case as a classic moral dilemma faced by a public official. In fact, a case study was developed at Harvard University called "The Two Oaths of Richard Helms," and public policy students study it to understand how difficult it can be to balance conflicting obligations.

At the time, I did not give his testimony a second thought. But Dick did. He always asked the agency general counsel to review his Hill testimony, and Lawrence Houston advised him that the Chile answers might be a problem, but Dick let his remarks stand. Many years later, in 1983, after President Ronald Reagan had awarded Dick the National Security Medal, he received a letter from President Nixon saying, "You suffered a great injustice simply because you were carrying out the assignment which I felt was vitally important to the nation's security. The attempt to castrate the CIA in the mid-seventies was a national tragedy."

This window of time before we left for Iran was an extremely busy one for me. I had to deal with the logistics of a move. We would not be able to move into our new house, so it needed to be rented; personal items and furniture not going to Iran needed to be put into storage. We arranged for my children to visit us in Iran. I sought out the curator of the Smithsonian's Freer Gallery for tutelage on the art of Iran. Dr. Esin Atil, the very bright and attractive young curator of the Persian collection, gave me a wonderful grounding in the art and culture of Iran.

In the middle of all this, my doctor ordered me to undergo a hysterectomy to rectify physical problems from earlier ailments, so I had major surgery. This left me feeling weak and unwell, though I really did not have time to be sick. The prospect of running an embassy and the entertaining it entailed was enough to keep me up at night. I needed clothes of all sorts for traveling in the mountains and desert and for formal evenings, as well as hats to take tea with the empress. Bill Blass, the clothing designer, invited me to New York to pick out whatever I would need from his collection. He designed modern, wearable American sportswear and dresses with excellent, classic lines. His designs suited me, and I wore those outfits for years. Dick actually came with me to New York, and he was suitably attentive until the beautiful Faye Dunaway, then a thirty-two-year-old actress moving into the prime of her fame, appeared on the other side of the clothes rack and left him utterly distracted.

The logistics of running an embassy were daunting, and I received a great deal of advice from friends and colleagues about how to avoid personal bankruptcy during Dick's tenure in Tehran. It is a little-known fact that the State Department budget for embassies is very tight and covers the bare minimum for entertainment, an important part of any ambassador's job. The best advice came from David K. E. Bruce, a seasoned diplomat who had served in London in the OSS during the war. He is the only American to have served as ambassador to Great Britain, France, and Germany, and he also was the U.S. envoy to the People's Republic of China in 1973 and 1974. He was a truly experienced man. He told me two things: First, keep the guest list for the traditional July 4 Independence Day celebration to the bare minimum, because that one event can bust the entertainment budget for the entire year if the guest list gets out of hand. Second, only invite your dearest friends to stay with you. The cost of feeding an endless stream of houseguests can break the bank.

Dick was sworn in for his new position in the beautiful Diplomatic Reception Rooms on the eighth floor of the State Department by Secretary of State William Rogers. Just before leaving the house, a State Department official called to ask if I knew I needed to provide all the salt and pepper for the embassy. I raced out to buy thirty-six salt and pepper shakers, a set for each person at a huge formal dinner table that seated thirty-six. My son Bones offered to drive me down to the State Department for the ceremony. I accepted his offer with gratitude, forgetting momentarily that he was driving a jeep at that time. Having just undergone surgery, that bouncy ride downtown in a vehicle that appeared to have no suspension system whatsoever was memorable. Bones had graduated from college, but he was still hazy about his future. I did not want to lecture him, but I did remind him that my portrait was hanging at the beach house, and I was keeping an eye on his activities. Bones later told me that he looked up at my image more than once, and it effectively dampened his more adventurous instincts. On that day Bones dropped me by the State Department entrance. I dodged a few black limousines while carrying the thirty-six sets of salt and pepper shakers that I hoped I could stick into a diplomat pouch heading toward Tehran.

Just before our departure, the director general of the Foreign Service phoned Dick with the latest news. President Nixon had decided that the American government would not ransom any diplomatic appointees who happened to be kidnapped during their service. This did not seem to upset Dick, though it caused me a bit of concern. We broke up our long flight to Tehran by spending a day with Dick's brother Pearsall and his wife, Marianne, in Geneva. Pearsall woke us up at 3 a.m. so Dick could take a call from the U.S. embassy in Bern. The caller told my husband that he had been targeted by Black September, the Palestinian terrorist group. Black September was making headlines in those years. The organization took credit for killing eleven Israeli athletes at the 1972 Summer Olympics in Munich, as well as for any number of murders, shootings, acts of sabotage, and letter bombs that often targeted envoys. As usual, Dick was unperturbed. He went right back to sleep. I stayed up all night wondering just what lay in store for us in our next adventure.

8

EXPLORING THE WORLD

As a child, I traveled the world vicariously through books. Sparked by words on a page, my imagination carried me to exotic and exciting places. As an adult, I actually experienced more of the world by traveling with Dick. Accompanying the head of central intelligence for the United States is a great way to travel. It offered an intimate look at international leaders, opened opportunities to see some of the wonders of the world with sophisticated and knowledgeable guides, and often took me to rare spots inaccessible to the average tourist. The experiences enriched me, and the memories from those trips have remained with me for the rest of my life. My husband often said it was impossible to understand, never mind anticipate, the actions of a foreign leader without first understanding the history and culture of his land. I heartily agreed with his view, and the more I traveled, the more I appreciated Dick's acute insight into the importance and value of having deep knowledge of the complete environment of one's enemies and allies.

My first overseas trip with Dick took place in June 1969, just six months after our marriage. In the telling, it sounds like a Marx Brothers movie. We went to Mexico. I was a bit nervous and unsure of what to expect or exactly how the wife of the DCI was supposed to behave on an official trip. Security seemed absurdly high, but the Mexican government, a conservative authoritarian regime, labored under considerable internal pressure at that time because of its oppressive security practices. The previous year, Mexico had hosted the Summer Olympics in Mexico City. A determination to keep order at all costs during the games had led to heavy-handed tactics to quell street protests. This crackdown culminated in a virtual massacre of hundreds of unarmed students by Mexican soldiers, who fired into the crowds of protesters on October 2, 1968. Needless to say, Mexico still felt tense when we arrived, and our hosts were determined that nothing should go wrong for my husband's visit.

We flew into Mexico City, weary from almost a full day of traveling with virtually nothing to eat. After a convoluted, high-speed ride from the airport that taught me a quick lesson in evasive driving tactics, we entered a hotel room crowded with local officials. Our hosts offered Dick a sandwich and tray full of goodies. They offered me nothing, and I morosely wondered if the still emerging Mexican culture viewed women as so insignificant that they did not warrant feeding. Of course, unwilling to risk a diplomatic faux pas or to offend local sensibilities, I said nothing. I was just famished.

While the men stayed at the hotel to discuss serious issues, I was taken on a sightseeing tour by the wives of the officials and an enormous team of security guards. One conscientious male guard accompanied me right into the ladies' room. At one point I dodged behind a potted plant at a museum to hastily swallow every airsickness pill scrounged from the bottom of my handbag as a food substitute and to quell the waves of nausea rising from too much travel and not enough food.

Back at the hotel, Dick had left me a note on the bed pillow with a postscript noting he had left me half his sandwich, just in case. I tore apart the room in a fruitless search, but someone, probably a diligent security aide, had apparently swept it up. I considered calling room service, but I did not even know my room number. I opened the door to look for it, and two men, my guards evidently, nearly fell into the room. They spoke no English. I spoke no Spanish. I was at an impasse. I slammed the door shut and took a cold bath.

When Dick returned and asked how I was, I reported that I was "fair" and had taken two cold baths in his absence. He knew what that meant. Since my boarding school days, a cold bath was my way of coping with over-the-top stress. He expressed sympathy. We dressed for dinner. I was weak with hunger but hung in there. The Mexicans drove Dick to the nearby residence for dinner, but I walked with others and made a mental note to pack color-coordinated walking shoes with my evening clothes on future trips. They drove Dick for security reasons, reluctant to let the United States' spymaster risk any exposure on the short walk. The spymaster's wife evidently raised no similar concerns. Security was omnipresent. I spotted a large number of young men with earpieces and only much later realized they were U.S. Secret Service agents. Our government had some concern for Dick's safety as well.

Dick got very sick that night, an often inevitable side effect of traveling in foreign countries where water, sanitation, time changes, and local cuisine can wreak havoc on the hardiest intestinal systems. I considered calling for medical help, but it seemed much too complicated. Dick was valiant and rode out the illness. The next morning as we left, we passed an ambulance that had been parked next to our hotel all night in the event of an emergency. I wondered aloud about the security precautions, given that there were large name tags on our luggage. It would have been so easy to identify one of our bags and wire it with an explosive device. Dick shushed me. "They are enjoying this," he drily intoned.

With each trip, I relaxed more and discovered ways to maximize my travel experiences. Of course, I could never resist poking a bit of fun at the ever-so-serious government handlers. Just before our next trip overseas to an Islamic country, I was instructed to pack a long skirt and boots. I facetiously asked, "Do they need to match?" The very somber response was, "Mrs Helms, I will call you back."

It was not unusual for me to be the only woman on many of those trips. In the 1960s, men still dominated the professions. I would love to say that my husband ushered in a new era for women at the CIA, but that was not the case. He and the other men of his generation frequently did not realize how painfully difficult and inequitable the workplace was for professional women. As time passed, I gradually learned more about the plight of women at the agency. The CIA was not unique. Men had dominated the high-paying jobs in law, medicine, law enforcement, and the military for eons. The agency grew out of an arm of the military during World War II, so the culture remained resolutely male, even though women played critical roles, then as now, in analysis and intelligence-gathering operations. My brother flew many courageous women into occupied Europe during the war on his secret missions. The bravery and patriotism of women had never been in doubt. To his credit, Dick did make certain that the families of agents who lived overseas had appropriate housing and the very best available health care. He recognized that no woman would be comfortable living abroad with her children without some guarantee of those basic services. The agency was slow to adjust to the changing roles of professional women, but eventually it did. I recently learned that the agency now routinely briefs the spouses of agents, both male and female. This may seem like a small thing, but it was long overdue and an acknowledgment that even spies need a family life. There has been an enormous generational change in the workforce of the agency. A majority of the analysts at the CIA are now women, and women make up half the workforce, filling a growing percentage of the operational slots and a significant number of supervisory positions. In fact, it was a female analyst from the CIA who accompanied the Navy Seals on the Osama bin Laden mission in Pakistan. It is a radically different workforce. The old boys' network is long gone.

We typically traveled on a small air force jet, the usual mode of transportation for U.S. officials, including members of Congress, on official overseas trips. On one trip, the crew fixed up a small area with a curtain and a mirror so I could change clothes before touchdown. It was a lovely and sensitive gesture by the male crew. As the trip progressed, camel saddles and other purchases took over my ad hoc dressing room and squeezed me out, so I no longer changed on the plane.

I eagerly anticipated a trip to Israel because I had read so much about it and had visited Jordan with my first husband years earlier. The Israelis included me in all the activities, and we flew all over the small country in a large army helicopter. By now I had conquered airsickness, so it was the poor helicopter attendant who was overwhelmed by airsickness rather than me. We visited Moshe Dayan, the brilliant, charismatic former defense and foreign minister, at his home. Dayan was just as compelling as his reputation. With the signature black patch covering the eye he lost fighting the Vichy French in 1941, he still cut a dashing figure in his fifties. He had a reputation as a bit of a ladies' man, so I should have expected he would lavish his attention on me at our first meeting.

He virtually ignored Dick and greeted me, saying, "Oh, I hear you are interested in archeology. Do come out to the back of the house with me, and I will show you some of my collection." This was not a come-on line. Dayan escorted us to a garden filled with the most stunning collection of artifacts, including Roman columns, pottery, a sarcophagus, and many bronzes. After he died in 1981, his family sold the collection to the state. He was an avid but amateur archeologist and sometimes added items to his personal collection with the help of Israeli soldiers. While I commend his work in saving these treasures, I do have to note the manner in which he assembled these remarkable ancient pieces was quite naughty. He did not exactly follow the law, and it would have been far more appropriate to donate the collection to the state at no cost, which I believe had been part of the understanding at the time he scooped up these treasures.

He spent two hours chatting about archeology and explaining the provenance of this piece or that before he and Dick got down to discussing security issues.

His daughter Yael Dayan, a novelist, later visited me at the Smithsonian and wrote me a charming note afterward thanking me for introducing her by her own name and not as the daughter of Moshe Dayan. She became a political leader in Israel as well and wrote a book called *My Father, His Daughter*. I thought she handled herself well. She was far from the first child of a famous parent I met in my life. I often felt a pang of compassion for such children. They were privileged in many respects and usually afforded the best of schools and a comfortable upbringing, but sometimes they were neglected emotionally and took a back seat to their parents' careers. From those to whom much is given, much is expected, and some of the children were crushed beneath the burden of excessively high expectations. Yael was not one of them. She enjoyed significant success.

I met Prime Minister Golda Meir on that same trip. It was sobering to meet a living legend. She was then in her seventies. She had been born in Kiev, raised and educated in public schools in Milwaukee, Wisconsin, where she worked as a school teacher, and then moved to a kibbutz in Palestine with her husband in 1921. She was one of the founders of the modern state of Israel and highly respected for her toughness and intellect. I sat at the back of the small living room to listen and watch quietly. I learned this technique from Dick. Dick often said that you did not learn anything when your mouth was open. I smiled to myself as the high-ranking Israeli officials who accompanied us, who had previously been so articulate and opinionated, sat in dead silence in her presence, perched on the edges of their seats like little school boys, hanging on her every word. Of course, I did the same.

She smoked the same old-fashioned, nonfiltered Chesterfield cigarettes as Dick did and made note of that coincidence right away. They smoked companionably together as the aides sat around on chairs like so many courtiers and she held forth. She wore no makeup, and her hair was pulled straight back in a severe, no-nonsense style. She had a ramrod straight back. There was nothing fluffy about this formidable woman. She talked about world affairs with tremendous ease, displaying an extraordinary grasp and understanding of history and current events with personal observations about her experiences and views. I wish I could hear her views today on illegal building in the occupied territories. She was amazing, almost like a dowager queen mother, stately, dignified, and commanding. I don't believe there was a single woman in the United States who held comparable status at that point, though it was satisfying for me, some years later, to see women like Justice Sandra Day O'Connor and Hillary Rodham Clinton eventually rise to the level warranted by innate talent, intellect, and ambition.

One of the most memorable parts of that visit was a trip to St. Catherine's Monastery on the Sinai Peninsula. The original chapel was built by the emperor Justinian in the sixth century on the site reputed to be the spot where Moses saw the burning bush. The monastery is located in a remote, rugged section of the desert. As visitors come in by air, the monastery's bulk and high, impassible walls loom in the distance next to Mt. Sinai and Mt. Horeb. It's an extraordinary sight. The monastery is an untouched example of early Greek and Roman architecture and design, and it remains flawless after seventeen centuries, thanks to the dry, desert environment and remote location.

The monastery is named for an early Christian martyr, St. Catherine, who was sentenced to die on the wheel; when that did not work, she was beheaded. The myth holds that angels carried her remains to this location. The monastery has an exquisite collection of ancient manuscripts, some of the earliest records of Christianity still in existence, and magnificent icons dating back to the Crusades. The books are perfectly preserved because of the arid climate. When we visited, the hand-painted chapel ceiling had just been cleaned by a Princeton University restoration team. It was breathtaking.

Until the twentieth century, the monks kept the gates of the monastery blocked and lowered a basket by hand from the top of the wall for visitors or provisions. The monks have always lived in peace with the Bedouin tribes that live in the desert. We were astonished when the monks lowered their basket full of freshly baked bread, and previously unseen Bedouin tribespeople appeared, almost magically, to retrieve it.

We were fortunate to have memorable trips to that part of the world, including to Petra, the religious capital of the Nabataea's ancient civilization of wealthy spice traders that once, around the sixth century BC, ruled much of Jordan. I got to know King Hussein of Jordan better than I knew most leaders because he often came to Iran during our four years living in that country. He was an attractive, trim man with an athletic grace, lovely manners, and an ease with Western ways, doubtless picked up during his years as a student in England. He impressed me with his personal bravery. King Hussein was a direct descendent of the Prophet Mohammed. His great-great-grandfather was guardian of the Holy Places as ruler of Mecca before World War I. When Hussein was only fifteen years old, he narrowly escaped an assassin's bullet, which killed his grandfather, during a visit to Jerusalem.

On our first visit to Jordan, the king offered to take us to see Mount Nebo, the spot where Moses was given a glimpse of the Promised Land, which he was never to enter. We expected an entourage with multiple cars, guards, and drivers. But the king picked us up by himself, driving his own car. The king kept a Sten gun, a deadly, British-made submachine gun, on the floor next to him. He often drove around without guards or security agents. I still find that remarkable. We had lunch that day with Wasfi Al-Tal, the Jordanian prime minister, who was murdered not long afterward on November 28, 1971, outside a Cairo hotel by Black September, the PLO terrorist group. So the dangers and risks were real. I wonder if Hussein's early brush with violent death as a teenager inured him to the security risks. He himself once told me that he believed his position as a descendent of the Prophet protected him from danger.

The next day the king invited us to stay with him at his summer place on the Gulf of Aqaba, a spectacular but low-key resort located on the northern tip of the Red Sea. We brought our suitcase to the helicopter, and King Hussein himself grabbed and stowed it. This left us utterly befuddled and tongue-tied. It seemed so inappropriate for a king to be carrying our bag, but he dealt with it too quickly for us to do anything but sputter our meek protests. The king piloted the chopper himself. We flew south to the Gulf of Aqaba to his waterfront beach house, which looks out at Eilat, the Israeli port. To the west sprawls a vast and endless Saudi Arabian desert. From the air, one appreciates the remarkable proximity of national borders in the Middle East and how that closeness complicates international relations.

The king invited me to go waterskiing with him one day. Dick rather stuff-ily advised me not to fall. His tone of voice made it sound as though the honor of the United States rested upon my ability to stay upright. Fortunately, I did. The king drove the boat, and I had a really wonderful time skiing behind him. I was rather proud of myself, and it gave me bragging rights with the children, who found the image of their middle-aged mother waterskiing behind a king rather funny. The boat he piloted that day earned a footnote in history. The CIA had arranged for Jordan to acquire that boat so that the king and Golda Meir could meet on it. Given the geopolitical realities of the time, they could only meet on neutral territory, which the open water of the gulf between their two countries constituted. Prime Minister Meir later complained that the boat was much too small, and she got wet during those secret meetings.

The king was still a young man when I first met him. He was only in his thirties. He followed an informal, relaxed lifestyle at his summer place. Every member of each traveling party ate together at a long table. After a long day and delicious dinner, Dick and I went for a walk on the beach thinking it would be courteous to give the king some private time. We later learned that after we left, he took our two guards into his ham radio studio. They stayed with him until 3 a.m. working his radio and marveled all the way home about the remarkable experience of hanging out with a real king. At that time he was married to a British native, Antoinette Avril Gardiner, who was known as Her

Royal Highness Princess Muna al-Hussein. They divorced in 1971. She is the mother of King Abdullah II.

I was traveling as something of a consort to Dick, one step behind him, like Prince Phillip trailing around after Queen Elizabeth II. But I found I had my own unique role to play in international affairs. We stopped in Fiji on our way to New Zealand in the summer of 1972, a long trip that took Dick away from Washington just after the Watergate burglary. Before leaving town, I listened as he lectured his deputy, the charming and multilingual Vernon A. Walters, that he absolutely could not, under any circumstances, agree to anything even close to illegal demanded by the president's aides in his absence. Vernon was an army general who spoke six languages fluently and became close to Richard Nixon when he interpreted for him on a key trip to Latin America during Nixon's time as Eisenhower's vice president. Dick always told me that Vernon was put at the agency to "keep an eye" on Dick and be the president's man in the CIA. Vernon, however, to his everlasting credit, followed instructions and did not buckle to White House pressure.

In Fiji, I met Prime Minister Ratu Sir Kamisese Mara, the man considered the George Washington of Fiji. The prime minister loomed over everyone. He stood well over six feet tall. This handsome and commanding man with deep roots in the tribal culture of the islands had been educated in New Zealand and England. He pulled me aside to ask if I would do him a personal favor. I readily agreed. He complained that the wife of the U.S. ambassador to Fiji wore sheer blouses, and the sight of her undergarments and skin beneath the flimsy fabric deeply offended local sensibilities. Her husband was a wealthy Texas oilman and philanthropist who had been named ambassador by President Nixon. The prime minister asked if I would deliver this delicate message to the secretary of state. Upon my return to Washington, I told Secretary of State William Rogers of the prime minister's concern. I never did hear what happened.

Dick was an excellent traveling companion. His knowledge of the world was deep and extensive. He had a firm belief that everyone needed to study geography, and during his high-level briefings he was always dismayed by senators and members of Congress who hadn't a clue about the places he spoke of, particularly the rivers that play such a crucial role in commerce and history. We often saw this lack of knowledge when lawmakers stopped in Tehran. We had an ongoing bet as to how long it would be before the visiting senator or representative referred to the Iranians as "Arabs." It is a common error, but the Persians are most definitely not Arabs. They trace their heritage back to the ancient Iranian peoples who lived in Iran thousands of years before the time of Christ. Such distinctions were enormously important in the geopolitical stew of the Middle East. Fortunately the public now knows more about the countries of the Middle East. It is one good outcome of the terrible years of turmoil in the region.

The agency had some history in Iran. In 1953, the governments of Winston Churchill in the United Kingdom and Dwight D. Eisenhower in the United States cooperated in orchestrating a military coup against the democratically elected government of Prime Minister Mohammad Mosaddegh after he nationalized the oil industry. Iran's oil was then controlled by the British-owned Anglo-Iranian Oil Company (AIOC). Iran only received a small percentage of the AIOC's profits from its oil. The disparity between the value of this national treasure and the benefit to Iranians drove the call for nationalization in Iran, and the government responded to it. Kermit Roosevelt Jr., an agency intelligence officer and grandson of President Theodore Roosevelt, was the key U.S. agent on what was originally a UK operation but became a U.S. operation. This was far from the first time that Western governments perceived a threat because Western profits happened to be at stake. And it was far from the first time much a mission triggered unintended consequences, namely, the furtherance of autocratic government and deep anti-Western sentiment among the local peoples.

Mosaddegh held office for just over two years. He was subsequently convicted of treason, held in solitary confinement for three years, and then placed under house arrest until his death at the age of eighty-four in 1967. History will judge whether that was appropriate. The shah gradually became more and more authoritarian, with an intelligence service that tracked down dissidents and a system that prohibited more than one political party. With the benefit of hindsight, I believe his repressive style led directly to his overthrow in 1979, just two years after we left.

Dick and the shah had attended the same prep school in Switzerland, Le Rosey, but, contrary to many reports, not at the same time. The shah was a contemporary of Dick's younger brother, Pearsall, but Dick and the shah had a long relationship. They first met in the 1950s. Dick briefed the shah on many occasions. During Dick's tenure as ambassador, he often met with the shah. They always spoke alone without any aides. My husband spoke candidly to the shah, as he had spoken to presidents of the United States. He never thought it made any sense to shade the truth in speaking to those with true power. He warned the shah about the insidious cancer of corruption in Iran and advised him to loosen his autocratic style and allow more than one political party.

The shah was a reticent, almost shy man. He was not a strong leader and came to power by accident of birth. I sat next to him at many social events, and he was always charming. He told me that he firmly believed that he would be a success and enjoy the support of his people if he expanded education, health care, and economic opportunity. He made great progress toward his three goals, but it was not enough.

The money generated from the sale of oil accelerated the shah's ability to modernize his country and simultaneously created a larger and more educated middle class with greater expectations. The land-reform initiatives he had launched back in the 1960s had also increased the number of landowners. But these new landowners never received the modern agricultural and technological support they needed to make the most from their land. As a result, many rural people, particularly the young, migrated into the cities in search of better opportunities. Tehran became a center for these disaffected people. They found common purpose with the shah's opponents. I saw some of these young people at Tehran University. They were my classmates, and they became part of the opposition to the shah. His policies denied them a role in political life, so when he needed them, he found no support among their ranks. Because there was no mainstream outlet in the form of an alternate political party for expressing views, concerns, and desires, all of the diverse opponents of the shah, regardless of motive, ended up consolidating in a massive move to oust him.

The shah mistakenly thought the moderate Shi'ite clergy would be his ally, particularly against radical Marxism and communism. The Soviet Union bumped up against Iran's borders, so the threat of communism was more immediate and real in Iran at that time.

Ayatollah Ruhollah Khomeini became the vessel that held all the varied opponents to the shah. Khomeini was shrewd. He stopped mentioning his most controversial views, such as his opposition to land reform and voting rights for women and his fundamental belief in *velayat-e-faqih*, which holds that an Islamic country should be governed under the principles of the sharia and the guardianship of Islamic jurists, who are heirs to the mantle of the Prophet. He elaborated on this theory in a series of lectures and in a 1970 book, *Islamic Government: Velayat-e-Faqih*. This theory was incorporated into the Iranian constitution adopted after the Islamic Revolution in 1979, and Khomeini became the first "guardian" of Iran.

The United States was little help to the shah because U.S. policy shifted so often. John Kennedy had encouraged movement to a constitutional monarchy, but Richard Nixon stopped the push toward democracy, and Jimmy Carter was so focused on human rights that his administration's policy left the shah confused about U.S. motives. Then the shah got sick, and his illness compounded his inherent weaknesses as a leader.

We could see the signs of trouble when we lived there. The shah did many good things in his country, and he was understandably proud of the universities and medical clinics he founded and improvements in the country's infrastructure. But history shows that people cannot be denied basic human freedoms—not in the United States and not in Iran either. The shah believed that modernization could only take place if he had absolute authority. He was not the least bit subtle about it. To his credit, he was loath in the end to use the military against his own people. But that concession made little difference to the many, many discontented and unhappy Iranians. The opposition came to be personified by the Grand Ayatollah Ruhollah Khomeini.

Khomeini believed firmly in an Islamic theocracy. His strong resistance to the shah's "White Revolution" of 1963, which included land reform, enfranchisement of women, and profit sharing for industrial workers, resulted in his exile by the shah. For most of his nearly fifteen-year exile, Khomeini lived in Najaf, Iraq. He communicated with the Iranian people through taped sermons that were smuggled into Iran and played at all the mosques during Friday services. The alienation so many felt, including the opposition of many educated women, empowered him. Saddam Hussein in Iraq wanted to get rid of Khomeini, who was stirring up Iraqi Shia. At first, Khomeini was to move to Kuwait, but the Kuwaitis would have no part of him. The shah would not have him back in Iran, so he ended up in Paris when the French agreed to accept him. This was a big mistake for the shah. Khomeini moved to a suburb of Paris in 1978, and that is where the Western media discovered him and enhanced his standing internationally. The shah left Iran in 1979, ostensibly on vacation but never to return, and Khomeini returned to consolidate his power after the Iranian Islamic Revolution.

Dick and I made a very quiet visit to New York to see the shah in his hospital room toward the end of 1979. He was being treated for a terminal form of cancer and would die in Egypt in July 1980. He was bitter and felt abandoned by the United States. One characteristic I noticed about Iranians that could be seen in virtually every one, from the humblest to the highest, was an innate sense of conspiracy, almost a paranoia, that ominous outside powers were controlling the country's destiny. If anything went wrong, it was the fault of the Russians, the English, the United States—anyone except themselves. The shah was dying and desperate to understand what had gone wrong. He did not think the United States and its confused policy and lack of advice had been helpful in the end. He seemed to have no appreciation that he had made some fundamental errors in quashing any political opposition, ignoring the fundamental role of culture and religion in his own country, and allowing the

gap between the haves and have-nots to widen. Without the development of
a political system to handle the modernization, and without a way to bring
some level of opportunity to the masses of desperately poor rural Iranians,
he did not stand a chance. His departure from Iran left behind a massive political vacuum, which the ayatollah and mullahs effectively filled. I leave it to
policymakers to debate whether it is prudent for the United States to support
autocratic regimes. I know that historically the United States has gotten into
bed with distasteful allies in order to gain strategic advantage over an enemy
considered more dangerous. But history has shown this strategy has backfired
as often as it has served its purpose.

What remains part of me decades after moving from Tehran is a deep appreciation for the richness and antiquity of the Persian culture, the vital and
central role of religion in the lives of Iranians, both rich and poor, and the
tunnel vision of the shah, who was so fixated on modernizing his country that
he never realized the discomfort it caused among the people and the deep
hostility it engendered among the powerful mullahs.

The distance the shah had traveled from his own people was demonstrated
by the extraordinary party he threw some years before we arrived, between
October 12 and 16, 1971, to mark the twenty-five-hundred-year anniversary
of the Persian Empire founded by Cyrus the Great. Ten years in the planning,
the event set a new world standard for opulence. The shah erected a tent city
in Persepolis decorated by a French interior designer with materials flown
in from Paris. This is the equivalent of a U.S. president holding a Fourth of
July party with materials purchased in China. The guests were a who's who
of kings, queens, princesses, and heads of state. A fleet of 250 bright-red
Mercedes-Benz limousines fetched guests from the newly renovated airport
and sped them down a brand-new highway. The dinnerware was designed
by Limoges, the linens by Porhault, the staff uniforms by Lanvin. This richness was lavished on foreign guests at a time when the rural people barely
eked out a living, without clean water or sufficient food. No wonder the
Ayatollah Khomeini called it the "devil's festival." The tent city remained
in place after the party, and I visited it during our time in Iran. Years later,
it was still amazing.

While we lived in Iran, the empress, or *shahbanou*, was patron to the Shi-
raz Arts Festival. The festival was ambitious and well intended and featured
Iranian and Western music, dance, and theater. She deserved credit for
highlighting native arts and crafts. But even I was taken aback by some of
the avant-garde material featured at the festival, and I talked to Dick about
it. I know it deeply offended the culturally conservative sensibilities of many

in the Islamic country. Such insensitivity to culture seriously damaged the shah's standing with his people. I always thought his wife should have known better. Her father was an army colonel, so she came from modest middle-class roots. But she got swept up in the glamor and, as they say, believed her own press clippings.

I immersed myself in Persian culture. Although I was not allowed even to walk down the street without a guard, I managed to see and experience a great deal and met a cross-section of Iranians. I first ventured out to the bazaar, the eclectic and colorful shopping district, after a search of the embassy revealed no suitable table linens. The bazaar has a worldwide reputation, and for good reason. It is six miles of covered streets and alleys bustling with vibrant humanity. It smells of spices, animals, sweat, and people. I am convinced there is nothing that cannot be found there: gold, copper, and other metal goods; rare books and coins; gorgeous rugs; crafts; clothing; every imaginable type of household items tools and decorative arts; and the most delicious food in the world.

On my first visit, I found hand-blocked material called *qalamkar*. It could be turned into beautiful tablecloths and placemats that reflected Iranian craftsmanship, color, and materials. Because the U.S. government did not provide many basic items needed to run an embassy and entertain large numbers of guests, I had to be creative in repurposing existing items or finding local and inexpensive ways to meet the needs of the embassy. The bazaar became my go-to place and favorite way to give visitors a look into the Persian psyche.

The *bazaaris*, the merchants who operated and worked in the bazaars, played a key role in the Iranian Revolution in 1979. They were traditionalists and quietly supported anti-shah forces when the shah ignored their concerns about religion and introduced new big-money players into the markets.

Before leaving Washington, I borrowed modern American paintings and prints from the private collection of Stanley Woodward, a Foreign Service officer who served as ambassador to Canada during the Truman administration. Ambassador Woodward was a charter member of the State Department's Fine Arts Committee, which brought contemporary American art to embassies around the world. We were far from the only ambassadorial couple without the personal fortune to decorate the embassy public rooms from personal collections, so we deeply appreciated his efforts.

I prevailed upon my friends at the Smithsonian to loan me some wonderful George Catlin paintings of Indians and the American West. The curators were loath to let the pieces go because other ambassadors had not treated borrowed artwork with the care it deserved in the past. But I promised to protect the art with my life, and they agreed. I thought Iranians would find the images of Native American Indians and cowboys as fascinating as I did. In fact, those paintings were great favorites of our Iranian guests. We often invited Iranian artists into the embassy to see the paintings. Most of them had never seen original American artwork.

We also hosted movie screenings. The residence in Tehran had unused space in the basement that we turned into a small movie theater to show American films, one of the most popular U.S. exports. We started happily with American films, but I quickly realized that most violated Islamic values with scenes of sex, nudity, or excessive drinking of alcohol. I was really embarrassed, so I then found a few films from museums. In my search for appropriate movies, I discovered Iranian films. Initially, they were on subjects we wished to learn more about and included such titles as *Cyrus the Great*, the first Iranian film to be shown at the Cannes festival, and *The Hajj*, a documentary on the pilgrimage to Mecca that all Muslims aspire to make at least once in their lifetime. When I showed that movie, Shoja ad-Din Sheik-holeslamzadeh, a medical doctor who served as the health minister, said, "Cynthia, thank you for showing that film. We have forgotten about those people." The health minister and I became great friends because he said I was the only Westerner who could pronounce his name correctly or, indeed, even remember it.

I then discovered modern Iranian films. I showed the acclaimed short film *The House Is Black*, which is about a leper colony and directed by the poet Forough Farrokhzad, who died tragically in a car accident at the age of thirty-two in 1967, and Amir Naderi's *Harmonica*. Regardless of the subject, Iranian filmmakers retain an ingrained sense of their culture and literature; it is in their DNA. It was a natural progression for them to move from classical subjects to the interpretation of modern poetry and literature. Hamid Dabashi of Columbia University once said that Iranian filmmakers tell the story of modern Iran through their films. "We are in fact currently in contemporary film washing our dirty laundry right in front of the whole world," he said.

They continue to do so to this day. Iranian filmmakers, both inside Iran and in exile, use their talent to bring real Iranian concerns to public attention at film festivals throughout the world. It did not surprise me when an Iranian drama, *Separation*, written and directed by Asghar Farhadi, won the eighty-fourth Academy Award for Best Foreign Language film. This remarkable movie was made by Iranians inside Iran. Another filmmaker, Abbas Kiarostami, has made dozens of movies inside Iran that have attracted international acclaim. It is difficult for these filmmakers. They need to follow strict rules and subject their films to certain editors and avoid anything derogatory about the government. The penalty for violating Islamic sensibilities is heavy. A well-known Iranian actress, Golshifteh Farahani, who was the first Iranian actress to appear in a major Hollywood movie as Leonardo DiCaprio's love interest in *Body of Lies*, was banned from Iran after she appeared partially nude in a French art film and magazine. Iranian filmmakers in exile and in Iran have really put Iran on the international cultural map. This is probably more appreciated abroad than at home.

I wanted to take full advantage of this extraordinary opportunity to live in such an ancient land, so I took Iranian language lessons each week and sponsored a poetry club to read and interpret the remarkable Persian poetry that every Persian, regardless of gender, social station, or income, seemed able to recite from memory at the drop of a hat. Professor Jerome Clinton acted as our poetry guide. We read the poets Hafiz, Saadi, and Rumi. My embassy colleague Marian Wrachi remembers that Professor Clinton translated and transliterated the prose so that we could see the verse structure. Poetry allows one to peek into the Persian soul. I still remember the lyricism of Rumi, who wrote of his relationship with God, and how his words still resonate in the twenty-first century.

> There is a way between voice and presence
> Where information flows
> In disciplined silence it opens
> With wandering talk it closes.

I had read Omar Khayyam (1048–1131) in my youth. He was a philosopher, poet, mathematician, astronomer, and scientist who challenged the hypocrisy of the clergy and religious doctrine, a brave thing to do in those days. He wrote some of the most important treatises in algebra. He developed a solar calendar that experts say is even more accurate than the Gregorian calendar, with only a one-day error in five thousand years. An English writer and poet, Edward FitzGerald, translated Khayyam's works in the nineteenth century, introducing this remarkable body of work to the West in *The Rubaiyat of Omar Khayyam*. That book was in our family library at Maldon. His lyrics had fired my imagination as a girl.

> The sphere upon which mortals come and go
> Has no end or beginning that we know
> And none there is to tell us in plain truth
> Whence do we come and whither do we go!

His questioning and searching nature has not been in fashion in Iran, and I was disappointed to discover that Iranians actually prefer other poets to him. It did not diminish my deep appreciation of his work. Visiting Khayyam's tomb in his mausoleum in Niphapur made a lifelong dream come true for me.

I adored the Persian bread. Lunch was the main meal of the day, and hot, fresh bread from a local bakery was often an intrinsic element. I learned the differences between the various types of unleavened flat bread; leavened *barbari*, named after the Berbers who settled in Iran; and *sangak*, which is cooked by stretching the flat dough on stones called *sang*. All were delicious. Unleavened bread was quite exotic to Western tastes then but has become far more commonplace as the smaller world has brought greater interaction between great cuisines.

The cuisine reflected the culture and the geography. Despite the vast area of desert, the soil is generally quite good, and the Iranians became practiced at drying vegetables, herbs, and fruit, so those crucial ingredients were always in ample supply. The countryside is not suitable for raising cattle, so the Iranians cook mostly lamb and chicken and an astonishing array of vegetable soups and stews and rice dishes. Many recipes, including *chelo kebab*, pounded lamb served with white rice, have been handed down through the ages from the days when the Silk Route went through Iran and Saudi Arabia to China and India. I approached every buffet, the traditional way to serve dinner, with anticipation because I loved the different rice dishes spiced with saffron, coriander, dill, chives, and parsley. The lima beans and rice dishes sometimes were served with a wafer-like crust called *tahdig*. I still serve Persian food in Washington to my friends and to the family at Christmas.

The one popular drink I did not like was a yogurt drink called *doogh*. The yogurt was too salty and sour for my taste, even with its characteristic tiny sprig of fresh mint. I stuck with the little glasses of tea, though I did find the local custom of sipping it through a cube of sugar held in your teeth made it much too sweet. It always disappointed me when nervous American visitors would order a bacon, lettuce, and tomato sandwich or another sorry facsimile of a familiar American dish rather than partake of the local fare. Trust me, a hamburger in Tehran is neither the same nor as good as one in New York.

I had always admired Persian carpets but was a bit embarrassed as I realized how little I actually knew about them. I learned that each carpet tells the story of its origins. The merchants offered tea in glasses known as *estekaan* and kindly taught me how to examine, feel, and understand a carpet. When buying a Persian carpet, one is not just engaging in a commercial enterprise; the buyer enters into a tender, loving relationship that is spoiled if lust is heavy and knowledge light. The designs revealed geography. The floral designs of Tabriz and Sanardaj are different from those of Mashhad. Each tribe produces a different geometric pattern. There is a significant difference between classical carpets and tribal pieces. The wool comes from fat-tailed sheep, and the thousands of knots are tied with lightning dexterity and speed, sometimes by small children. As I learned more, I earned the respect of the merchants, who began to treat me as a friend rather than a tourist. I brought home as many carpets as I could. They reflect a marvelous culture and history and provide endless enjoyment.

My love of the food and carpets came together in the picnics Iranians held in gardens and parks, in the countryside near the *qanats*, the underground aqueducts that carry fresh water from the mountain streams, in use since Roman times, and sometimes by the side of a road. A Persian picnic is an event that begins with a live chicken, always includes flat bread, and ends with lush grapes, melons, and dates. The most delicious grapes I ever ate in my life were served at a picnic near the home of Court Minister Alam, the shah's top aide, in Birjand, an eastern province near the Afghanistan border. Dancers from Afghanistan entertained us, and when I asked if it was difficult to cross the border, the minister laughed, pointed to a bush, and said, "That is the border." In 1975 the distinctions between national boundaries were not always precise.

When the Iranian bridge team won the world championship the first year we lived in Iran, I invited them to the embassy to teach the ambassador how to play bridge. Dick was never a great card player, but he enjoyed the lessons. The bridge team members had never been inside the U.S. embassy and seemed delighted by the invitation. I played cards once a week with a group of Iranian women who were fierce card players. Card games were great entertainment for people of different languages because the cards speak an international language known to all.

Since the Iranian Revolution and the 9/11 attacks on the United States, Americans have learned a lot more about Islam, the world's second-largest religion, with more than 1.5 billion adherents. The view of Islam, however, has often been distorted by the most extreme elements, such as the Taliban in Afghanistan and al-Qaeda, the organization headed by Osama bin Laden, the mastermind of 9/11. Most Americans reflexively view the *hijab*, the head scarf worn by many Muslim women; the *chador*, the full-length cloak Iranian women pull over their clothing; and the *burqa*, the head-to-toe covering that obscures everything but an Afghani woman's eyes, as symbols of oppression. I learned it is not that simple.

To distinguish the role of religion in the oppression of women from the power politics of traditional patriarchal societies is difficult because, throughout history, men have used Islam as a cudgel to deny women basic human rights and to keep them under control. The most extreme Islamic sects still oppress women and girls by denying them education and treating them worse than chattels. Like many Americans, including current American leaders, I worry about the fate of women in Afghanistan if the Taliban regains its old influence. The oppression of women was historically true in Iran as well. The Qur'an itself does not condone mistreatment of women, but interpretation of the sacred word has been disputed for centuries and remains a heated topic of disagreement among Muslims. It is clear that the men who would oppress women interpret the Qur'an to serve their own purposes.

The more exposure I had to the Iranian culture, the more I realized how important culture and tradition were to the people. For many young women of college age whom I met when I took classes at the local university, the head scarf was a sign of modesty and respect for their heritage. My language teacher told me that her mother suffered terribly when Reza Shah, the shah's father, abolished the veil. My teacher and her siblings got their mother dressed in Western clothes, but she literally could not pass the door frame to leave the house. She felt undressed and ashamed without her traditional covering. I felt such sympathy for her.

Women in Iran did acquire some rights slowly over time. Women gained access to education around the time of the Constitutional Revolution of 1905 to 1911. The shah's father, who was forced to abdicate by the Allied powers in 1941, banned the veil in 1936 as a way to draw more women into the workforce. The Allies smeared him as a Nazi collaborator, and this charge has been discredited. But his insistence upon neutrality and the large German presence in his country did not square with the Allies' wartime need for an overland route to Russia to supply the Soviet Union, then a partner with the United States and Britain.

Other rights for women did not come until the 1960s, when Reza Shah's son, the shah, granted women the right to vote and the right to be elected to Parliament. The Family Protection Law passed in 1967 raised the marriage age from thirteen to fifteen for girls, abolished the practice of awarding child custody only to the fathers, gave women the right to sue for divorce, and limited polygamy by requiring the permission of a first wife for a husband to take a second spouse. This law was suspended after the revolution in 1979, and the Ayatollah Khomeini attempted to roll back the clock for women in Iran.

While the most extreme and conservative form of Islam denies women education, the right to vote, the right to inherit a fair share of property, and the right to make fundamental decisions about their lives, the rank-and-file Islamic view of women is far more respectful and far more complicated. I discovered that many women liked wearing a *chador* because it gave them a protective cover out of doors, keeping them from prying eyes and allowing them freedom of movement that might otherwise have been difficult. Many Muslim women told me they wore the *hijab* because it was culturally comfortable, like blue jeans for Americans, who wear them from infancy to old age.

As a woman, I was particularly sensitive to the status of women in Iran. The longer I lived there, the more aware I became of how much more complicated gender politics is in an Islamic nation. Dick and I viewed the Islamic culture and religion as seamless. This is difficult to appreciate in a secular society, where religion is separated into a different sphere from government and the rest of society. In a diverse culture like the United States, a true melting pot of many cultures, religions, ethnicities, and races, a separation between religion and government is not only prudent but also necessary to public order. It would probably be impossible to respect the diversity of beliefs and backgrounds in the United States without the brilliant Bill of Rights authored by the Founding Fathers, which has made diversity and tolerance so crucial to the American way. But Iran is a far older country with traditions, beliefs, and cultural touchstones dating back thousands of years. This leads to a way of life that may seem oppressive to outsiders but makes perfect sense to the natives.

My friend Haleh Esfandiari, an Iranian academic and scholar who left Iran on the eve of the Islamic Revolution in 1979 and now directs the Middle East Program at the Woodrow Wilson International Center for Scholars, has written eloquently of women's rights in Iran. She returned to Tehran to visit her elderly, ailing mother in 2007 and was arrested and held in solitary confinement in prison for 110 days. It took international pressure to secure her release. She says that women were an intrinsic part of the Islamic Revolution, caught up like many hoping for better times, but they assumed, mistakenly, that the revolution would lead to more rights for women and equality for all citizens. This sadly proved to be a wrong assumption. When the ayatollah began to pull back the few rights women enjoyed under the shah, women resisted, and slowly but surely over the course of some years, the government has had to back off. The economy needed the participation of its educated women, and the march of history proved stronger than the conservative theocratic interpretation of the Qur'an. It makes me hopeful that the women of Iran will eventually enjoy the full rights they deserve.

I had a singular experience when I visited Mashhad, one of the holiest cities for Shia Muslims and the resting place of the martyred Ali al-Reza, the Eighth Iman. Western and non-Muslim visitors very rarely had the opportunity to visit the shrine, so Dick accepted the invitation of the governor of the province of Khorasan. Each mosque is strictly divided by gender, so I could only go with the wife of the governor into the female section. Our visit was scheduled for early afternoon, when the mosque would be least crowded. I wrapped a *chador* over my long-sleeved Western clothes. I never did acquire the skill of the Iranian women, who twisted the fabric so deftly they were able to keep their hair completely covered by holding the *chador* closed in their teeth. I was nervous because I had heard stories of religious fanatics attacking those who were not dressed conservatively enough. The shrine was packed with pilgrims, and all, rich and poor alike, wailed, prostrated themselves, and prayed in waves of emotional religious fervor. I almost envied them for their passionate belief. The crowd swept me along with a group receiving glowing candles. I put out my hand like the others, not knowing what else to do, but the donor looked up, noticed my green eyes, and passed me over. A green-eyed redhead was clearly not Persian. I walked by Dick three times, and he did not recognize me in my *chador*.

The Ayatollah Khomeini feared the effect on Islamic values of a creeping Western influence and the onslaught of the crudest elements of Western culture. The relative openness of surrounding Arab countries to the West has been viewed with contempt by the Islamic revolutionaries in Iran. I consider myself unusually broad-minded but do sometimes find myself in sympathy when I see the degradation and incivility that so often passes for "freedom" in Western culture in our times.

It is clear to me that Iran still wants respect, a place at the table, and recognition from the outside world. The long history of manipulation and intervention by foreigners, including the Russians, Turks, British, and Americans, has made them understandably suspicious of outsiders. I do not view this as unwarranted paranoia. I have been told that the Iranian fixation on developing nuclear capability probably has much more to do with national pride than obliterating the Jewish state. Many disagree with that, but it is clear Iran wants to be a regional leader and to keep up with its neighbors. Mahmoud Ahmadinejad, the current president, has been misquoted on his view of Israel. He said he believed Israel would disappear as a failed enterprise. This is quite different from vowing to wipe Israel off the face of the earth. But those with different agendas interpret his words to serve their own purposes.

In the spring of 1976, Dick and I decided it was time to wind down our diplomatic service and think about going home. It was an election year in the United States, and we appreciated that President Gerald Ford, the accidental president who came into office after Nixon's resignation, would likely lose the election in November. He did. Jimmy Carter, then an almost obscure one-term Georgia governor, won. He was the quintessential Washington outsider who became popular precisely because he had nothing to do with Watergate or Washington. We were also tired of the diplomatic life, and I was eager to get back to Washington, where my children were beginning to produce the next generation of our family.

After we moved to Tehran in 1973, Dick had been required to travel back to Washington dozens of times to testify before various committees on Capitol Hill investigating various aspects of intelligence "revelations." His testimony on Chile before the Senate Foreign Relations Committee had proved to be more problematic than he initially realized. The Justice Department was seriously considering criminal charges that would threaten his pension, his reputation, and his freedom. It was time to go home.

9

THE LEGAL CASE

I was certainly aware that Congress and the press subjected the agency to far more intense scrutiny while we lived in Iran. But until I returned, I did not fully appreciate how much the political climate had changed in Washington. Of course, the outward signs remained the same. Many of our friends still held positions of power and responsibility. Washington looked the same, as beautiful as ever. But something fundamental had shifted in the political atmosphere during our absence. The old rules that had governed relations between the Central Intelligence Agency and Congress had gone out the window. The old champions of the agency on Capitol Hill had literally died or been cowed into silence by the lust for exposés. The old, implicit respect for an experienced Washington insider, the gentleman's agreement that one could take the word of a man of integrity, had utterly disappeared.

While we were away, President Richard Nixon resigned from office in disgrace in August 1974; the 1974 off-year congressional election in November brought the largest class of freshman Democrats to Washington since World War II; and Gerald R. Ford, the accidental president, lost the 1976 election to Jimmy Carter, a somewhat obscure one-term governor from Georgia. But there was something different about this traditional shift of power and administrations. The suspicion and skepticism triggered by the Watergate affair spread like a virulent infection, poisoning the once cordial relations between the administration and the Hill. This was reflected and exaggerated in Congress, then as now a raw nerve ending seeking to appeal to and appease the masses through whatever means. I do not dispute that the era certainly called for more transparency and more oversight of intelligence from Congress. Indeed, not one of the intelligence community's most controversial actions would have taken place had a president of the United States not issued a direct order. This includes the order to kill Patrice Lumumba in the Congo during the Eisenhower administration, the plot to kill Castro during the Kennedy administration, the investigation of foreign involvement in the antiwar and student movements during the Johnson and Nixon administrations, and the effort to oust Salvador Allende in Chile during the Nixon administration. It is entirely possible that no president would have ordered the intelligence community to do those things had he known the action would be second-guessed or scrutinized by Congress. The Founding Fathers of the United States were absolute geniuses in constructing a system of checks and balances for the new government. For the first twenty-five years of the CIA's existence, presidents had precious few checks on them. And while I appreciate as much as anyone the importance of excellent intelligence to the conduct of foreign policy and national security, I also recognize that presidents are human beings who make mistakes.

Individual members of Congress are also very human and sometimes deeply flawed. I learned that many are often driven by more than a love of country and desire to shape public policy. Indeed, in those grim days it often seemed as though personal political agendas took priority over the nation's well-being. For example, Senator Frank Church, a Democrat from Idaho who became such a thorn in the side of the intelligence community, planned to run for president in 1976 and used his special committee as a platform to craft a national public image and reputation. Church's campaign never really got off the ground, and there was a certain karmic justice in that failure.

His committee, however, was prolific. The Church Committee published fourteen reports, scoring sensational headlines, on the history of the out-of-control "rogue elephant," as he described the CIA. As usual, the facts rarely caught up with the allegations. In one of the more egregious incidents, Senator Stuart Symington, the Democrat from Missouri, aggressively criticized the "secret war in Laos," even though he had repeatedly been fully briefed on CIA activities in that country and actually received a rare, in-depth, personal guided tour of the operation in Laos by the CIA. Secret? Not quite. There was a suggestion later that Symington, then seventy-five, had simply forgotten what he knew. He did not seek reelection in 1976, and he offered Dick's legal counsel his help in persuading the government to not pursue charges against my husband.

As a leader in the agency since the beginning, Dick became the target of much of the congressional grandstanding and theatrics. A declassified internal CIA history of Dick's tenure at the agency concluded, "Helms was a man of the system who took charge of CIA just as the old rules governing CIA's relations with Congress were collapsing. His were the years of the gathering storm, and he left just before the deluge."

In 1975 and 1976, Dick traveled from Tehran to Washington sixteen times to testify before investigative committees on thirty different occasions for more than one hundred hours. A single trip was grueling. It took as many as eighteen hours, with a brief stop to switch planes in London. Dick usually traveled nonstop, went to bed soon after he arrived, and then testified before one of the committees the following day for hours on end. There was an 8.5-hour time difference. He sometimes completed the 12,680-mile round trip in four days. It took a terrific toll on him both physically and mentally and was difficult for me to watch.

We were both somewhat relieved by Nixon's resignation, though it was odd to experience it from the cocoon of the ambassador's residence in Tehran on August 8, 1974. We had spoken by phone to a friend in Washington that day, longtime *Time* magazine correspondent Hugh Sidey, who alerted us to Nixon's intent to address the nation on television that night. Hugh had very kindly called constantly to keep us updated on political news in Washington. There was considerable speculation as to what Nixon might say. Dick, as usual, was unperturbed and went to bed at his normal time. I arranged for the young marine who stood guard throughout the night to wake me at 4:15 a.m. The president was scheduled to speak at 9 p.m. in Washington, which would be 4:30 a.m. our time. Wearing my dressing gown, I grabbed a large short-wave radio, took it into the garden to find a spot where the radio reception was best, and found a station in Sweden that was carrying the broadcast live. Sitting in that fragrant garden beneath a starry sky more than six thousand miles from Washington, I listened to Nixon announce his resignation. The suspense finally got to Dick, who threw open the upstairs bedroom window with a clatter during the speech to lean out and ask me what had happened. Nixon had no love for my husband, so we were glad he was gone, but we did hope that Gerald Ford, the former House Republican minority leader and then vice president who became president upon Nixon's resignation, would keep Henry Kissinger on as secretary of state. We felt Kissinger provided continuity in foreign policy, and we respected his intellect and sophistication.

With the benefit of hindsight, it is now clearer that Watergate and its aftermath contributed heavily to the relentless attack on Dick and the intelligence community. The Watergate burglary proved just one element in a White House effort to crush Richard Nixon's political opponents by illegal means. For a time, there was deep suspicion that the CIA had somehow been behind the Watergate burglary. Eventually all of the investigations concluded that the CIA had nothing to do with either the break-in or the cover-up.

But the investigative fever was indiscriminate, and it spread to the CIA itself and twenty-five years' worth of secret intelligence. Dick was repeatedly called on to explain decisions made years earlier in a very different Cold War era, when the Communist threat was seen as real and imminent. While the Soviet Union had not yet crumbled beneath the weight of its own oppression, the inexorable march of time had shifted the perception of the old enemy, and the Cold War era was passing. The widespread suspicion of "the establishment" also cast the worst possible light on the past. Sadly, there was a striking lack of perspective and history in these investigations, and the young congressional staffers, particularly those working for the Pike Committee, were almost comical in their lack of knowledge and understanding. For example, the committee staff interpreted the phrase "people were detailed" as "people were tailed." None of the young staffers had served in the military, so they misunderstood the meaning of the verb "to detail," which is when one is temporarily assigned to a specific task, usually outside of customary duties. The selective leaks to the media, the headline hunting, the rivalry between the House and Senate to score points with the public, and the incompetence of the reviewers damaged the agency as well as Dick's hard-earned reputation.

Needless to say, the headlines were merciless, and every past action and decision came across as malevolent if not blatantly illegal. The press onslaught began with a *New York Times* article by Seymour Hersh, published on December 20, 1974, about what was known as Operation CHAOS. The operation was ordered initially by President Lyndon Johnson and continued by President Richard Nixon. Both men were convinced that foreign interests, probably Communists, were inciting young Americans to oppose the war and demonstrate against the government. Dick was caught between a direct presidential order to investigate this alleged infiltration and his mandate to comply with the law forbidding the agency from spying on Americans at home. The *New York Times* article was followed by a Daniel Schorr story on CBS on February 28, 1975, charging that the CIA had been responsible for assassinations overseas. This proved to be wrong. The CIA had contributed to coups and assassination plots, but the agency never killed a foreign leader. The allegations were really never effectively disproved for most members of the public.

Dick could not abide Daniel Schorr. Years later, he got a little bit of satisfaction when CBS subpoenaed him as part of its defense against a libel lawsuit brought by General William C. Westmoreland. Dick agreed to be questioned but flatly refused to allow his testimony to be videotaped for fear it would be used in a fragmentary, distorted way. After prolonged legal wrangling, CBS was ordered to reimburse Dick for legal fees.

Politicians love to be seen as righting wrongs and fighting for the public. Needless to say, members of Congress mostly fanned the flames. The feeding frenzy of investigations included probes by the House Armed Services Committee's Special Subcommittee on Intelligence, known as the Nedzi Committee; the Senate Select Committee to Study Government Operations with Respect to Intelligence Activities, or the Church Committee; and the House Select Committee on Intelligence, or the Pike Committee. In an effort to get on the right side of public opinion, President Ford created the Rockefeller Commission headed by Vice President Nelson Rockefeller. Of course, the whole Watergate mess warranted its own investigation: the Senate Select Committee on Presidential Campaign Activities, or the Ervin or Watergate Committee.

Meanwhile, another issue festered like a low-grade fever: Dick's testimony before the Senate Foreign Relations Committee, during his confirmation hearing, about agency activity in Chile. During his brief, destructive tenure as DCI, James Schlesinger had demanded a report on every single agency act that might be perceived as illegal or exceeding its charter. The document, which came to be known as "the family jewels," was a litany of covert operations and included information that revealed a contradiction between the agency's actual involvement in Chilean politics and Dick's parsed testimony to the Senate Foreign Relations Committee.

In 1974, William Colby, the career intelligence officer who replaced Schlesinger, forwarded the report on Dick's testimony to the Justice Department. The agency's legal counsel and others suggested he put the documents in a safe and forget about them, but he decided to share them with the new congressional oversight committees that proliferated like summer weeds after Watergate. At the time, my husband and many of his colleagues were horrified by Bill Colby's decision to include him among the "family jewels" cases. They viewed it as a personal betrayal. I'm quite certain Dick never forgave Bill, whom he had mentored. They never spoke again. I understand why he felt deeply wounded by a decision that set in motion a career- and reputation-crushing criminal investigation.

But time brings insight and perspective. Bill Colby died after an apparent boating accident in April 1996 near his home on the eastern shore of

Maryland. I have never questioned Colby's integrity. He and my husband represented two sides of a fierce debate within the agency. I suspect Bill Colby also had the best of motives. He wanted to do whatever he could to protect the agency so it could thrive and be productive in the future. Disclosing all the secrets to members of Congress, who promptly leaked them, may not have been the most prudent course, but it is important to remember that Bill spent most of his intelligence career overseas. Unlike my husband, who was steeped in the political ways of Washington, Bill was not a Washington insider in the same way. I often wonder if he even realized how damaging and damning the disclosures would be for the agency, its reputation, and its ability to function in the future. Bill Colby was something of a Boy Scout who believed that the truth and a righteous cause would prevail. In Washington, this view was simply naïve.

The Helms case festered at the Justice Department for two years. All changed in March 1976, when the former ambassador to Chile, career diplomat Edward M. Korry, concerned that the full extent of U.S. involvement in the plot against Allende would never be exposed, sent a detailed letter to Gerald Ford's attorney general, Edward H. Levi. Korry had been kept in the dark about the full extent of the Track II operation, the one that involved active CIA engagement in a military coup ordered by Richard Nixon. Nixon himself had insisted Korry not be informed. The letter piqued interest, and the government began to present testimony to a grand jury in the summer of 1976. None of this was known publicly. We were ready to go home, so Dick submitted his resignation to President Ford in October, and on Election Day the president announced Dick would leave Iran at the end of the year.

We left Iran just before Christmas of 1976 and stopped on the way for a vacation in Morocco in northern Africa. Our house on Garfield Street, which we bought just before leaving four years earlier, had been rented while we were away, and it needed a lot of maintenance work before we could move in. So we stayed with my daughter Lindsay and her family, who lived just blocks away, for a few months. The day our possessions arrived from Iran coincided with a rare and huge snowstorm in Washington, DC, and our crates were dumped in the snow in the front yard. It was quite a mess, and I spent most of 1977 organizing the logistics of our house and life and renewing our garden.

After our return to Washington, Dick's legal jeopardy became clearer to me. The Justice Department formally notified him during the first week in January that he was a target of an investigation. It was some welcome home. As a result, we were in a holding pattern for most of 1977. President Jimmy Carter took office in January and inherited the case. His Justice Department tried to figure out what to do with the allegations against Dick. It was not an easy call. Going forward with the case threatened to expose national security secrets, and Dick's "guilt" was by no means certain or clear. He had taken an oath to keep the secrets. Prosecuting a government official for doing his job set a dangerous precedent that would affect future presidents and their ability to work with the agency, as well as adversely affect our allies' willingness to share secrets with us. Attorney General Griffin Bell later told Dick that he was anguished by the case, and it was one of the toughest issues he inherited from the previous administration.

Gerald Ford was an accidental president and proved to be a weak one. He did nothing to protect my husband or the secrets of the country. Dick was convinced that disclosure of these secrets would put at considerable risk not only CIA agents in the field but also their sources in foreign lands. This proved to be sadly true. Richard Welch, the station chief in Greece, a brilliant, Harvard educated classicist, was murdered in Athens by a Greek terrorist organization on December 23, 1975, as he returned home from a party. His identity had been revealed in a magazine. Seven years later, Congress passed the Intelligence Identities Protection Act of 1982, making it illegal to expose a covert agent. It was too late for Mr. Welch.

During Dick's tenure, the CIA was the only Western intelligence organization that had not been penetrated by foreign spies, or at least it wasn't known to have been penetrated. Dick attributed this long streak of success to James Jesus Angleton, the longtime chief of counterintelligence. I met Jim after he was pushed out of the agency by Colby. He taught me to cast for fly fishing in the Potomac River. Jim's precision, exactitude, and perfectionism were readily apparent that day. He made me cast over and over and over again until I hit the exact right spot, a particular daffodil. He brought that same concentration and focus to his work. Jim was brilliant but also eccentric. His eccentricities and middle name proved to be irresistible to reporters with a preconception about spies and the agency. He never used his middle name, a reflection of his mother's Mexican heritage, but it was always used in news accounts. Indeed, I know that the agency told Seymour Hersh that Dick Helms, not Jim Angleton, was in charge of Operation CHAOS, but Hersh chose to ignore that fact because it did not fit with his view that Angleton was a rogue spy.

Angleton was considered a bit paranoid, and I really cannot disagree with that view. Dick was aware of the critics' views, and he did modify Angleton's responsibilities and keep him close in order to monitor his work, but he often told me that he was confident he would never have a mole so long as Jim Angleton was on the job, and he would take any heat necessary to keep him on the payroll. This proved to be true. I am certain Jim would have spotted double agent Aldrich Ames's Jaguar automobile and lavish lifestyle and figured out he was a Soviet spy long before his perfidy was finally uncovered. Ames was exposed in 1994 after compromising more CIA assets than anyone in history, until Robert Hanssen, the FBI agent who spied for the Soviets for twenty years, was caught seven years later.

It was a stressful time for us. Dick established a consulting practice to advise corporations on international affairs, and we set him up in an office downtown with an able assistant. Dick spent a lot of time talking to lawyers. He was represented by the best. Dick had gone to Clark Clifford early on, seeking his counsel; Clifford told him he needed to hire the best lawyer in town and recommended Edward Bennett Williams, the founding partner of Williams & Connolly, and one of the top defense lawyers in Washington. Ed was a true superlawyer before there was such a term. He was a remarkably skillful trial lawyer who understood politics and power as well as the law. He represented a number of high-profile clients, including the *Washington Post*; teamster boss Jimmy Hoffa; Senator Joseph McCarthy; the Reverend Sun Myung Moon, head of the Unification Church; and Adam Clayton Powell Jr., the scandal-plagued congressman from Harlem. He owned the Baltimore Orioles baseball team and was part owner of the Washington Redskins football team. Ed was an engaging and delightful raconteur, as well as a shrewd lawyer, and would prove to be a truly great friend.

My husband worked closely with Ed's gifted associate, Greg Craig, then a thirty-two-year-old lawyer just five years out of Yale Law School, where his classmates included Bill Clinton and Hillary Rodham. Much later Greg became legal counsel to President Barack Obama and represented as many famous people as his old boss and mentor with the same flair and excellence. Because Ed Williams had many cases, it fell to Greg to do the background work on the Helms case. Greg compiled the data, conducted the interviews, and took Dick's calls when he remembered a fact or incident that he felt was essential to the case. Greg remembers that my husband was simply incredulous that this was happening and was most concerned that his lawyers have all the facts so they would understand what had really happened and why. Dick could trust Ed and Greg to keep his confidences because of the attorney-client privilege.

We worried about money because Ed Williams was not only one of the best lawyers in Washington but also one of the most expensive. I remember 1977 as the year we ate a lot of hot dogs and cut back on our personal expenses to save as much money as possible to pay what we were certain would be an enormous legal bill.

I remember little else from that dreadful year. Much like 1968, 1977 was for us a year of major transition in which our fate was being determined by forces beyond our control. The experience gave me an acute appreciation for and understanding of those who get caught up in the criminal justice system. The legal system is an inexorable force that cannot be stopped or changed in any fundamental way once a case has been launched. I did a lot of gardening that year. Digging in dirt, growing plants and flowers, and redesigning the landscape around our small home were things I could control. Dick and I certainly talked about the case, but it did neither of us any good to obsess about the details, so the case hung over us like a bad weather system that just refuses to go out to sea.

Our family and many friends sustained us during that difficult year. There is a transient quality to much of official Washington. People come and go, ebbing and flowing like the tides with the change in parties and administrations. But there is also a permanent Washington of career government employees, lawyers and lobbyists, reporters and columnists, and the sort of "normal" people who make up any community. That was the world in which we lived. Others have referred to us and many of our friends as belonging to the "Georgetown set," which annoys me to this day. We never lived in Georgetown, and only a few of our friends lived in Georgetown, the village-like, pricey neighborhood that became famous during the Kennedy years. The term is not only sloppy shorthand but also implies an extreme degree of wealth, exclusivity, and elitism. We did have some wealthy friends. Some of them were powerful and influential. But they were also real people, not caricatures, and their loyalty and friendship meant a great deal at a stressful time.

Once when we were back in town briefly for a visit during Dick's time as ambassador to Iran, I ran into Joan Braden, who was hosting a dinner party and invited us to attend. Joan and Tom Braden were longtime friends. Tom had served in the OSS during the war and worked for the agency in the early 1950s. They were very close to the Kennedy family, particularly Robert F. Kennedy. Tom Braden later became a well-known newspaper columnist and television commentator. He wrote the best-selling book *Eight Is Enough* about the adventures of a family with eight children, which later became the basis for a popular television series. Joan was a bone-thin whirling dervish of energy. She and Tom had some sort of understanding that she could see other men. She had well-known dalliances with Nelson Rockefeller and Bob McNamara and traveled extensively with Bob after Bob's wife died. I never quite understood how she pulled it off.

It was later mistakenly reported that the Bradens arranged the dinner party as a way to show support for Dick. In fact, our invitation came almost by accident. But the dinner proved to be a wonderful and memorable evening as Henry Kissinger, Bob McNamara, and Averell Harriman each got up and toasted Dick. William Safire, the *New York Times* columnist, described it in print as "a moving and courageous display of support for one of those embattled members" of the Cold War–era foreign policy establishment.

By the summer, Dick's case had begun to move forward. We later learned that it had been debated at the very highest levels of the government. Discussions included President Jimmy Carter and Vice President Walter Mondale. When elected public officials are involved, all sorts of different agendas come into play. President Carter had campaigned as a Washington outsider who would bring more transparency and honesty to government. In his famous words, he wanted to provide "a government as good as its people." I never really understood what that meant. The new administration did not want to promote the notion of two types of justice: one for the insiders, another for everyone else. Greg Craig believes that National Security Adviser Zbigniew Brzezinski played a pivotal role in convincing the president to resolve the issue in a quiet, humane way with as little damage to the government and Dick as possible.

In September, Ed Williams and Greg Craig went to the Justice Department for a meeting with Benjamin Civiletti, then the deputy attorney general in charge of the Criminal Division. Civiletti eventually served as attorney general and, after his government service, earned some notoriety as the first lawyer in Washington to charge $1,000 an hour. Williams and Craig wanted the case dismissed, but a dismissal would have been politically difficult for the Carter administration. At that meeting, Civiletti laid out the government's case in great detail for three hours. The evidence included all sorts of intelligence data, such as secret cables concerning CIA activities in Chile as well as Dick's testimony before the Senate Foreign Relations Committee. Greg remembers taking frantic, detailed notes while Williams listened intently.

At the end of the presentation, Civiletti abruptly said, "The attorney general, Griffin Bell, wants to see you." So the four of them went upstairs to meet with him. Bell told them the government wanted to resolve the case in a way that met the requirements of the law but did not punish a patriotic man who had served his country. The government proposed that Dick plead guilty to the charges of not testifying "fully" to Congress, a misdemeanor. But Williams and Craig argued successfully that Dick would plead nolo contendere to two misdemeanor charges; in return he would get neither jail time nor a fine.

By pleading no contest, Dick would not admit guilt, but the plea would clear the way for a resolution of this long legal nightmare. It was as good a resolution as we could expect. Greg says it was obvious to them at the time that this had all been carefully choreographed in advance by the Justice Department and the White House.

Dick and I discussed this case at length, and we wanted him to be vindicated, so we wanted the case to go to trial to prove Dick was an honorable man with the purest of motives and noblest of intentions. Clark Clifford and Ed Williams dissuaded us, however. They argued persuasively that no District of Columbia jury could possibly appreciate the nuanced position Dick took in balancing his two oaths to testify fully to Congress and to protect the nation's secrets. Dick could never be judged by a jury of his peers. Few people in the world shared his perspective. Precious few career spies are called to jury service. We had to agree. We also wanted this case to go away. It was so exhausting. I could see the strain on Dick, who was never a robust man. A trial would be costly and prolong the agony for another eighteen months to two years. And neither of us cared to wake up in the morning again to a pack of television crews and reporters on our front door step. The first time the media stakeout came to Garfield Street coincided with trash day in the District of Columbia. I stopped Dick before he could perform his routine chore of wheeling a big plastic trash bin to the curb. All I could imagine was a front-page photo of Dick in his suit and tie with our household trash.

Dick was worried about the effect of a plea on his government pension. He had worked in government for most of his adult life, and he was counting on his pension to support us for years to come. The government agreed and obtained a legal opinion saying the plea would not affect his pension, and the deal was struck at the end of October 1977.

All that was left was an appearance before a federal judge to seal the deal. The first appearance was scheduled for Monday, October 31, 1977, at 9:30 a.m. before Judge Barrington D. Parker Sr., an African American jurist known for his fearlessness. Judge Parker had lost a leg two years earlier when struck by a car while crossing a downtown street. I had gone back to work at the Smithsonian and went to my office. I was jumping out of my skin all day with anxiety. Dick called me every half hour or so from a pay phone to give me an update. This was long before the ubiquity of cell phones and texting. They finally went before the judge at 2:30 p.m., but Judge Parker was having none of this quiet, low-key plea. The courtroom was virtually empty. He ordered them to return on November 4. Needless to say, on that day the courtroom was packed with press. In fact, the press showed up at our doorstep to catch the defendant leaving for the courthouse. The stakeout trapped us in the house. The son of a neighbor brought us our newspaper. He changed his clothes in order to look good in front of all the TV cameras.

This time I was present in the courtroom. I knew it would be dreadful, and the idea of not being there for my husband was more than I could bear. Judge Parker had his audience and tongue-lashed Dick for ten minutes, describing this man who had served his country unstintingly for thirty-five years as being "in disgrace and shame." He ignored any extenuating circumstances and lectured Dick about the responsibility of all public officials to honor the laws of the land. He also ignored the sentencing recommendation and added a $2,000 fine and a two-year prison term, which he promptly suspended. Dick was stunned. When he came over to me in the front row of the courtroom, he was literally shaking. It was a devastating experience for him. When they left the courtroom, Ed Williams told the press that Dick would wear the conviction "like a badge of honor." I'm not sure Dick viewed it as such. Yet, for all the personal distress caused by the case, Dick never wavered. He always said the risk of leaks was too great to have testified in any other way.

While the legal case damaged Dick, it did not destroy him. His own sense of integrity and duty sustained him, as did an extraordinary support system of friends and colleagues. After leaving the courthouse, Dick had a long-standing commitment to attend the regular luncheon of the Central Intelligence Retiree Association at the Kenwood Golf and Country Club in nearby Bethesda, Maryland. The last thing he wanted to do was talk about the case or even see anyone, but he was a man of routine and duty, so he went. When he walked in the door, nearly four hundred of his former colleagues jumped up and greeted him with a thunderous standing ovation. The association members passed around two large wicker baskets and gathered up donations in cash and checks to pay his legal fine. Dick rarely displayed any emotion in public, but the ovation moved him almost to tears. The opinion of his associates from the agency probably mattered more than any other. I was so happy for him and grateful to his friends and colleagues for supporting him.

There was one last task. A few days after the court appearance, Dick got dressed to go downtown and told me he was going to see Ed Williams to find out how much he owed him. We had been steeling ourselves for this moment for a year. Afterward Dick told me that when he asked what he owed him, Ed looked puzzled. "You don't owe me anything, Dick," he said. "And I really mean it." We were overwhelmed by his kindness and generosity. I hosted a dinner party for him later as a way to offer some thanks for his incredible services. He regaled the gathering with hilarious stories from his legal career, including one memorable tale of an organized crime figure who bribed a judge. I made the mistake of setting up tables in two rooms. I only regret all our guests did not hear about his many legal adventures.

The resolution of the case allowed the sunlight back in our lives. We were able to move on, adjust to life out of government, and enjoy a new phase of our marriage and lives. Six years later, President Ronald Reagan presented Dick with the National Security Medal, the highest award in the intelligence community for "exceptional meritorious service." With that gesture, the entire affair came full circle. Finally, the man who kept the secrets had won official vindication from the country he so loved.

10

⁂

LIFE GOES ON

W e felt liberated by the resolution of the legal case. We could finally move ahead with our lives. Dick built a consulting practice and provided counsel to corporations doing business overseas. At the time, many Americans still had little knowledge or understanding of Islam and the histories and rivalries of the Middle East and other hot spots around the world. His transition to private life after a long career in government went well. The four years spent as ambassador to Iran helped to wean him away from the intelligence world. And the government often called upon him to serve on various boards and commissions.

I felt enormous relief and looked forward to picking up the pieces of my own life. I had returned to the Smithsonian to work part time in the communications office. I wanted to write a book about my experiences as the ambassador's wife in Iran but initially could not get a publisher interested. Just when our life seemed to be settling down, I experienced an unexpected reminder of my own mortality. In 1978, my husband noticed a mole on my left leg was bleeding and suggested a doctor check it out. I had stage-four melanoma, a potentially deadly form of skin cancer. The doctor recommended immediate surgery to remove it. We had previously scheduled a dinner for Supreme Court Justice Lewis Powell, so Dick hosted the dinner himself. I set the table, put the name cards in place, and checked myself into Georgetown University Hospital. I still remember someone spilled red wine on my best tablecloth, leaving the most awful stain. It is odd how one remembers the silliest, most mundane things at such times. The surgeons had to dig deep to remove every bit of cancer from my leg and then graft skin to cover the open wound. That surgery forced me to wear pantsuits before they became ubiquitous. At the time, I felt badly that the scar would not allow me to wear a skirt any longer. This says something about my state of mind. I hardly thought I might die.

I woke from the surgery to find Vernon Walters, the former army general and Dick's former deputy at the agency, perched at the end of my bed with an enormous bouquet of flowers. At that moment I honestly thought I had died. It was such an utterly strange sight. Vernon was a garrulous fellow and an extremely large man with great hanging jowls. The bed sagged beneath his weight. I thought, I must be dead. But my mind could not come up with any other explanation for the incongruous sight of Vernon waiting at the foot of my bed.

The first doctor told me that my condition was probably not survivable. Obviously, advanced melanoma can be fatal, but I was incredulous that this mere mole on my leg might kill me. I was still physically active and otherwise healthy and, from my perspective, not the least bit old in my mid-fifties. I spent hours on the telephone researching various treatment options. This was long before a Google search would provide that sort of information with the click of a mouse. A close friend recommended I go to Duke University, where they were experimenting with a vaccine. I flew down to Duke twice a month for the injections. They worked. The Duke University Melanoma Clinic developed adjuvant therapy to treat cutaneous melanoma. After more than twenty-five years, the treatment had a 19 percent survival rate. I was among the fortunate survivors. I receive periodic letters from Duke asking if I am still alive. It feels very good to be able to respond in the affirmative.

It was a disquieting episode. At one point, I called Dick at his downtown office and asked him to please come home immediately. For once in my life, I felt overwhelmed and a bit desperate, which was so not like me. Dick came at once, and his presence reassured me. I wonder if the stress of 1977 and the court case had some correlation with the cancer. Allan McKelvie sent me a thoughtful letter urging me to get a second medical opinion. In 1971, Allan had married Helen Niblack, an art collector and avid horsewoman, so we had both moved on from the difficult time of our divorce. I very much appreciated his kind letter.

My illness brought challenges but proved to be just a bump in the road. We were getting older, but we had great energy and a zest for life. With my children now settling into careers and busy raising their own families, and with Dick free of middle-of-the-night emergency calls from the agency and White House and his old responsibilities, we experienced a different type of freedom to enjoy our travels and our friends. We also watched remarkable change taking place both at home and abroad. The Cold War ended as the Soviet Union crumbled, ending an enmity that had dominated Dick's adult life and upending a lot of old assumptions. Women and minority group members continued to make extraordinary strides toward full equality. However, it was not all positive. There is crudeness to the culture that accompanied greater openness and a loss of civility that is painfully obvious in the political sphere but also permeates so much of everyday life. The lack of manners and the respect and dignity that they convey to each individual is sad and a true loss.

Those years were busy and happy ones. We traveled back to Iran three times in 1978. We dined with our old friends among the ruling elite and in the world of journalism in Tehran, and it eventually became clear to me that they still had no idea of what was happening in their own country. This surprised me because the rhetoric at the mosques provided a compelling early-warning system of trouble.

After the shah went into exile in January 1979 (he piloted the plane himself, and there was no food as the caterers had refused to deliver it) and the Islamic Revolution took place, a publisher expressed an interest in my book proposal. There was growing interest in Iran after Iranian students took fifty-two Americans hostage at the U.S. embassy in Tehran in 1979. So I took a year to write *An Ambassador's Wife in Iran*, which was published by Dodd, Mead and Company in 1981. I was eager to share my experiences and help Americans understand the ancient Persian culture and people. I sent the chapter on Islam to three different professors to read, and each one came back with very different views. This impressed us again with how even scholars could not agree on a single interpretation of Islam.

The prominent banker David Rockefeller was among those lobbying the Carter administration to grant the shah permission to enter the United States for military treatment. After we returned from Iran, David hosted a dinner for us at his elegant apartment in Manhattan. I was seated between David and his brother Laurance. A few days earlier, a human rights organization had approached Laurance to support an effort to stop female genital mutilation (or female circumcision), which was then attracting the attention of the international community. Laurance asked me if I was familiar with the issue. I was. He wanted to know what exactly the process entailed and I explained that it involved cutting the clitoris and other female organs. At that time Laurance was approaching seventy and deaf as a post. In a booming voice in the middle of this genteel dinner party, he asked, "What is a clitoris?" Dick's head reared up in surprise across the table. I had to raise my voice so Laurance could hear but was reluctant to attract attention from the other guests. My halting explanation of female sex organs must have been satisfactory because I later learned he gave the group $50,000 for their work. But I could only imagine what my mother would have thought of this dinner conversation.

Our friends still enjoyed hosting dinner parties, and my own circle still loved bridge and tennis. We were all involved in many civic affairs and often pulled one another into specific causes. For example, my friend B. A. Bentsen brought me into one of her favorite causes, the U.S. Botanic Garden. I played tennis for twenty-four years with B. A. She was a former fashion model, a tall, strikingly beautiful woman who was married to Lloyd Bentsen, the longtime Texas senator and Treasury secretary. B. A. had grown up in an orphanage and overcame a tremendously difficult childhood. She was known for her devotion to her husband. They were an unusually close couple. She traveled with him when he was selected to be the vice presidential candidate by Democratic nominee Michael S. Dukakis in 1988, and I'm told the press corps adored her. B. A. worked with Mary Johnston, the wife of Louisiana senator Bennett Johnston, to raise money for the beautiful garden that is part of the U.S. Botanic Garden at the foot of Capitol Hill. The Botanical Garden was first proposed by George Washington in 1796 and became a reality in 1820. B. A. and Mary worked with the American Rose Society to designate the rose as America's national flower. The garden offered a three-acre tract on the south side of the Mall to create a National Garden, which opened in the fall of 2006. B. A. invited me to help, and I served for more than ten years as a board member of the National Fund for the U.S. Botanic Garden, which raised $11.5 million in private-sector funds to create the National Garden. I was privileged to donate the trees, and I love to watch them grow and enhance the beauty of the Washington Mall.

The end of the Cold War turned the world upside down for old spymasters like Dick. Former enemies were now allies. Secret files were opened both here and abroad. It was a chance for Dick, who had lived long enough to see this turnabout, to tie up some loose ends, answer long-unanswered questions, and solve a few mysteries. We hosted several fascinating dinners with former KGB officers at our home. It was surreal to listen to these former spies, both American and Soviet, compare notes and talk candidly about what was really going on when they were such fierce adversaries. I planned those dinners carefully so the food and wine flowed smoothly and freely and our guests could speak in comfort and candor about the past. I always kept the guest list small to keep the dinners intimate so that everyone at the table could engage in the conversation. Needless to say, I hung on every word.

We hosted the last KGB chief for dinner one night in 1995. Mikhail Gorbachev had selected Vadim Bakatin, then a thirty-four-year-old Communist

Party official, to be chairman of the KGB in 1991 with the specific job of shutting down the once-feared secret police organization. He held the job for about seven months before his position was eliminated by the Yeltsin administration. The old KGB forces proved too entrenched to eradicate completely. Indeed, a former KGB officer, Vladimir Putin, has held an iron grip on Russia since 2000, a real testimony to the insidious influence of the intelligence agency in that country.

Bakatin was a tall, handsome, sandy-haired man with a charming and appealingly open personality. We were intrigued as he told his personal story and answered Dick's careful, probing questions. Bakatin said that on his first day on the job as chairman of the KGB, he called for the file on his grandfather, a provincial school teacher who had been tried and executed during the Stalin purges of the 1930s, ostensibly for being a foreign spy, a ludicrous charge. He told us that the file included his grandfather's "confession," signed with a shaky hand that he recognized from his own signature he had made in family documents, including a family Bible.

Bakatin turned a page for the KGB when he took the extraordinary step of showing U.S. Ambassador Robert Strauss the diagrams of the U.S. embassy with all the covert listening devices planted by the KGB. This was wildly controversial in Russia at the time. Some old spies likened it to treason. He viewed it as a goodwill gesture toward a former enemy who was now a friend.

As Bakatin left the house after a revealing evening, he paused at our doorway to thank me personally. "Thank you, Mrs. Helms," he said. "I cannot tell you how much this evening has meant to me." He told me that he had memorized every bit of my decor, the location of every candle and the placement of every piece of pottery, and looked forward to describing it in detail to his wife. He explained that their lives had been harsh during the difficult years of Soviet rule, and his wife longed for attractive surroundings and would vicariously take pleasure in the description of our home. It was a reminder of my good fortune. My heart went out to Mrs. Bakatin.

Another Russian guest one lunchtime was the Soviet general Vadim Kirpichenko, who told us he had led the Soviet army into Afghanistan in 1979. The U.S. war in Afghanistan could not have been imagined at that point. We, after all, had armed the side battling the Soviets in one of the many proxy skirmishes and wars that took place in that era. But I later remembered his observations about the challenges of Afghanistan when the United States had spent more than ten years mired in its own difficult war there.

On another occasion, we hosted a KGB defector for dinner. These dinners were always sanctioned by the CIA, and our guests always included a watchful

State Department or agency official. Dick was eager to learn what had happened to a Russian defector named Nikolai Artamonov. He had defected
to the United States in 1959 and gone to work for the Defense Intelligence
Agency, an arm of the U.S. intelligence community, where he was known
as Nicholas Shadrin. The KGB approached him in 1966 to spy for them as
well, and the FBI decided to turn him into a double agent. He disappeared
in Europe in December 1975. Subsequently, there had been charges and
countercharges about whom he really worked for. That evening, Dick found
out. He learned the KGB had kidnapped Artamonov/Shadrin in Vienna and
tossed him into the trunk of a car, intending to take him back into the Soviet
Union. But he died. They were not sure whether the cause was car exhaust or
an overdose of the drugs used to pacify him. That he died by accident solved
a twenty-year mystery.

At that same dinner, Dick asked about Lee Harvey Oswald, the man who
assassinated John F. Kennedy in Dallas in 1963, and his involvement with the
KGB. Oswald had moved to the Soviet Union, where he married a Russian
woman, but soon tired of the harsh life and moved back to the United States.
He was an avowed Marxist and had attempted to offer his services to the Russians and the Cubans. The KGB defector confirmed that the KGB had indeed
talked to Oswald, a former marine, and considered using him as an agent, but
they concluded that he was too mentally unstable to be of use to them.

Dick was now on a roll, his curiosity increasingly sated with each course
of the dinner. So he asked about Alger Hiss, the U.S. government official ac-
cused of being a Communist spy in one of the most highly publicized cases
of the Cold War era. Oh, yes, said the KGB agent, Hiss had worked for them.
Hiss maintained his innocence until his death in 1996. Some of Dick's dear
friends, particularly Dean Acheson, defended him to the end. We had no
reason to doubt the veracity of the former spy enjoying our hospitality on
Garfield Street so long after the fact.

We met President and Nancy Reagan socially at a dinner hosted by George
Will, the syndicated columnist. We ended up becoming good friends. One
time we invited Rex Harrison, the British actor whom we had met in Iran,
over for dinner while he was in town appearing in a play. We wanted to
invite other people who might be interesting to him. Ronald and Nancy
Reagan were the only former actors we knew. Dick decided he had been in
Washington long enough to invite the president to dinner. Moreover, Mike
Deaver, the president's deputy chief of staff, had been encouraging me to invite the Reagans to dinner for some time because he said they felt isolated in
the White House and were eager to socialize. I did get a sense from Nancy of

how they suffered from cabin fever at 1600 Pennsylvania Avenue. I once casually said, "You should come to dinner sometime." Nancy shot back, "When?" leaving no doubt about her eagerness to get out of the house. Nancy was very fond of Dick because he helped her straighten out an administrative problem with her "Just Say No" antidrug campaign.

For that first dinner for Rex Harrison, Mercia Harrison, the wife of the actor, said we were not to tell Rex that the president was coming because if he knew, he would give his costar, Claudette Colbert, a miserable time all week with his one-upmanship. Each time the Reagans came to our house, the Secret Service and metropolitan police took over our street like an invading force. It was an utterly exhausting exercise. There must have been sixty-three support and security people crowding into our garage and little house. We warned the neighbors in advance, and they were good sports about the bustle and inconvenience, although our next-door neighbor did stop by to affirm that he was not a Republican. Everything was carefully scripted, even the chair where the president would sit. The Secret Service wanted to make certain he was not seated near a window. Of course, the president ignored that carefully designated chair and sat in another. I was bug-eyed when the president took a very large helping of dessert. When he noticed my reaction, he said, "I have to do that because Nancy won't let me have seconds." I was worried there wouldn't be enough.

For one of the Reagan dinners, I invited Larry McMurtry, the novelist whose fiction is often set in the Wild West, because I thought President Reagan might enjoy talking to him about cowboys and such things. It was a disaster. McMurtry never opened his mouth. Sandra Day O'Connor later told me McMurtry knew nothing about cowboys. It was all an image. Sandra knew what she was talking about. She grew up on a real cattle ranch in Arizona.

We were frequent guests at the White House in those years. We played in the White House tennis tournaments and enjoyed many casual family dinners and movie nights. It is well known that the Reagans loved movies. The ritual was always the same. The president sat rapt with his bowl of jelly beans, and afterward everyone discussed the film. I sat next to him during the screening of an early Rambo movie, sharing his jelly beans. I hated that movie and could not wait for it to end. The president adored every second of the action movie. He paid such close attention he could repeat entire chunks of dialogue afterward.

The Reagans graciously included us in a state dinner for the last Soviet leader, Mikhail Gorbachev, in December 1987. It was a coveted invitation at the time. Nancy told us of the infighting involved in getting an invitation to that dinner. I was seated at a table with Gorbachev and Nancy Reagan when

Gorbachev began to describe to Nancy in some detail the operation of the politburo through his translator. I sat on the other side of him. I knew that the CIA had spent endless hours trying to figure out the internal politics of the Soviet Union and immediately got up to find an American who spoke Russian to listen to his explanation. I appreciated after all those years with Dick how valuable this information about the inner political workings of the USSR would be to agency analysts even then. I don't think Nancy realized the significance of Gorbachev's confidences that night.

The Reagans included us in a small dinner party on election night in 1988 when Vice President George H. W. Bush beat Massachusetts governor Michael S. Dukakis in his bid for the presidency. The president, aware his days in the White House were now numbered, spoke charmingly about "the people's house" and welcomed George and Barbara Bush in absentia. When the Reagans returned to California, they invited us to visit. We played tennis in tournaments organized by Merv Griffin, the singer and talk show host and close Reagan friend. One time the Williams sisters, who were quite young and precocious then, participated. They later became world champions.

We had some wonderful times with the Reagans at their favorite table at Chasens, a celebrity hangout in West Hollywood. Ronald Reagan proposed to Nancy Davis at Chasens, and the "Reagan booth" where he proposed is now on display at his presidential library. The Reagans completed each other as a couple. They really needed no one else, and there was little room for others. They were devoted to one another, and Nancy was extremely protective of him. You could stay on her good side so long as you did nothing to hurt her Ronnie. Those who fell out of favor were cut off immediately, without another good word. I admired her loyalty but questioned her unblinking judgments at times when she dismissed individuals who had served her and her husband for years because of an unfortunate personal problem.

Reagan was more intelligent than many people believed. He knew exactly what he was doing, though some people thought he was oblivious or unthinking. At the first Reagan dinner at our home, Reagan talked incessantly to me about Gorbachev and how he was completely convinced he could do business with him. Of course, Secretary of State George Schultz made it clear that he was terrified Reagan would give away the store when the time came to negotiate new treaties and agreements with Russia. George's fears proved to be unwarranted.

I am among those who question Reagan's explanation that he did not know what Bill Casey was doing during the Iran-Contra affair. Skeptics insisted the president had to know that arms were being sold for money for the Nicaraguan Contras. But Reagan told me that he had not understood Casey when he explained the operation to him. I would like to believe him because no one could understand a word Casey said; he mumbled.

We still got an occasional White House invitation after Reagan left office. When Sandra Day O'Connor resigned from the Court, President George W. Bush hosted a farewell dinner for her at the White House. I took my son Rod to make certain I did not get arrested for saying something rude to Vice President Dick Cheney, whom I could never abide. Rod was seated next to Marilyn Quayle, the wife of former vice president Dan Quayle. Mrs. Quayle pointedly told Rod that he could take his place card home but needed to leave the metal holder in place. Rod is a quiet man, but these instructions left him speechless. She acted as though he was a country bumpkin who had ventured into the big city on holiday. Rod is a prominent intellectual property lawyer, and he had recently resigned after ten years as a federal district court judge. To this day I have no idea whom she thought she was talking to.

Those dinner invitations often showed a private side of public people. I was a guest at a small dinner hosted by Porter Goss, who became head of the agency during the George W. Bush administration. The former president and father of George W. Bush, George H. W. Bush, a lovely man who had served as head of central intelligence himself, was among the guests. He rose to speak about the war in Iraq, which even then, around 2005, was being viewed as an enormous mistake, but he was overwhelmed with emotion. Tears streamed down his face. He did not, or perhaps could not, explain why this subject so distressed him, but we all felt his pain. He gave up trying to talk and sat down.

The world was changing in those years, but we often heard an echo from the past. When Dick was director of central intelligence, I accompanied him on a trip to Vietnam and Laos and, at one event, sat next to a large man who was an official with the agency. He said he did not know what to discuss with the director's wife. So I said, "I will keep talking until you think of something." I invited him to come see us in Washington some day. Years after Dick had retired from the agency, that operative showed up on our doorstep on Garfield Street just dying to talk to Dick. They had a wonderful chat.

While my husband was no longer on a government payroll, he remained engaged with the government as a member of many boards and commissions. He traveled with a delegation to Moscow to assess the security of the U.S. embassy there. They had electronic equipment to show the presence of bugs. He said the entire board lit up like a Christmas tree because the building was so loaded with electronic listening devices. It was hardly unexpected because the KGB chairman had told them the place was bugged, but Dick said they all burst out laughing at the sheer excess of the KGB diligence.

He was at the White House attending one of those commission meetings on the day in 1983 when a suicide bomber drove a truck loaded with more than two thousand pounds of explosives into the U.S. embassy in Beirut. The blast killed sixty-three people, including seventeen Americans. One of the dead was Robert C. Ames, the head of the agency's Office of Near East and South Asia Analysis and a longtime friend of Dick's. Bob Ames was brilliant, and Dick always said he was the best Middle East analyst in the agency. He had hoped Bob would be assigned to a post in the region when we went to Iran, but the White House insisted he stay in Washington. Bob was attending a meeting at the embassy when he died at the age of forty-nine, leaving six children. Four years later, Dick went to a testimonial dinner in Bob's memory at La Salle University in Philadelphia. He spoke about a paper that Bob had written on the understanding of Arab culture. William Casey, then director of central intelligence and a friend of Dick's since OSS days, when they shared an apartment in London, called and offered him a ride in the agency airplane. Casey was then seventy-three years old and under considerable pressure from grueling hearings on the Iran-Contra scandal, in which senior Reagan administration officials had facilitated the sale of arms to Iran in defiance of the arms embargo and used the money to fund the Nicaraguan Contras despite the legal ban on U.S. funding.

Dick raced up the stairs to our bedroom when he got home. I had rarely seen him so agitated. He said, "Something is wrong with Casey!" He said Casey could not hold his martini glass upright on the plane. Casey loved his martinis. I agreed it sounded as though something was physically wrong and suggested it was some sort of motor problem. The following day, Dick called Robert Gates, then number two at the agency, and told him not to let Casey talk to anyone but to get him out of the office. Casey never saw a doctor. He inexplicably went to his weekend home with his wife. When he returned to the office on Monday, he collapsed and was carried out of the agency on a stretcher. Doctors diagnosed a brain tumor and did surgery that week. He never recovered and died the following May. To me, that anecdote says a great deal about Dick's powers of observation. No one knew Casey had a brain tumor at that time, but Dick could see and sense something was profoundly wrong with his old friend.

One day, as a member of the board of the Freer Gallery of Art, I was invited with two or three others to meet the Dalai Lama, the Tibetan religious leader, who was visiting the United States. I took my granddaughter Cynthia, or "C2," as I call her, who is now a doctor. What a great privilege. The Dalai Lama, whom many believe to be the living reincarnation of Buddha, was joyful and smiling and spoke movingly in a both intellectual and analytical way. When we were introduced, he recognized my name. Dick had helped to bring him out of Lhasa and get him across the dangerous mountain passes into India in 1959, when he was a young monk. As we took our leave, he shook my hand and, smiling that extraordinary, beatific smile, said, "Thank you." My granddaughter and I went out onto the Washington Mall, spread our blankets, and with thousands of others listened to his message.

Public officials in Washington have always harbored secret lives. Openness and transparency are now taken for granted, as many reveal virtually everything there is to know in public. Then, however, many private people had personal secrets. Looking back, I am bemused by how much people knew but did not discuss. Joseph Alsop, for example, one of the most celebrated journalists of his era, a highly influential syndicated columnist for forty years, was gay at a time when no one publicly acknowledged homosexuality. Of course, there were many gay people, but it was rarely acknowledged. Gay people were firmly "in the closet," as they say. In his book, Dick described Joe as "a scrupulously closeted homosexual." Joe married Susan Mary Patten, the widow of his college classmate, Bill Patten, when he was fifty-one. They were married for twelve years before divorcing. Joe was related to the Oyster Bay branch of the Roosevelt family, and Alice Roosevelt Longworth was his first cousin. Susan Mary was a descendent of John Jay, the first chief justice of the United States.

In 1957, during a trip to Moscow and during Joe's heyday as an influential columnist, the KGB set up a tryst between Joe and a gay man and took photographs. They attempted to blackmail him into becoming a spy for them. Joe was having none of that and went straight to the embassy to inform them. He also told Frank Wisner, then head of the Directorate of Plans at the agency, where Dick was his deputy. Wisner advised him to let the FBI know. Unfortunately, J. Edgar Hoover thrived on that sort of private information. Some years later, the KGB tried to blackmail him again with the photographs. Joe considered going public with his sexuality, but Dick advised him to keep it private to spare his family the public embarrassment. Dick did inform President Johnson. The American Psychiatric Association did not declassify homosexuality as a mental disorder until 1973. The World Health Organization did not do so until 1990. But decent people do not discriminate against anyone based upon sexual orientation. Dick went to New York City himself to personally tell the KGB that they were to cease and desist unless they wanted the CIA to pull the same stunt on several of their own KGB officers. They backed off.

Joe was obsessed with the war in Vietnam. He was a strong hawk and always pressing his views on Dick. Dick told me one day he'd discovered that if he sat and listened and said absolutely nothing while Joe held forth on his views of the conduct of the war over lunch, it was far less tiresome than trying to argue with him. Joe was something of a mixed blessing in our lives. He was very conservative and very vocal in his views, which were strongly held. But he could also be charming. The extraordinary dinner parties at his house in Georgetown were truly memorable and, as a high official once said to me, "better than any college course." Susan Mary was a legendary hostess as well. He lined the brown felt walls of his dining room with portraits of people he called his "instant" ancestors. Some were real ancestors, but many were strangers. He said that their faces were so ugly, he had to use them as wallpaper. He always served dinner on white china and used tablecloths with a paisley print. One friend compared them to cowboy bandanas, but they were far nicer than that. His table seated twelve, and the dozen guests included senators from both political parties, State Department officials, cabinet secretaries from different administrations, an occasional army general like William Westmoreland, and prominent thinkers and scholars like Sir Isaiah Berlin, one of the most brilliant social and political theorists of the time. The conversations grew heated, and guests often came close to blows. Soon after we were married, we attended one of Joe's dinners, and I got up and went to Dick and told him we needed to leave. He remonstrated with me because he was enjoying himself, but I was acutely uncomfortable and told him, "Bob McNamara is about to hit someone!"

Joe stayed at our house a few times and never failed to tell me the house was far too small, but he envied the maidenhair fern in my garden, which he had been unable to nurture successfully in his own. He so despised azaleas, except white ones, which are ubiquitous in Washington in the springtime, that he would stay indoors when they bloomed. He died of lung cancer in August 1989, and during his final months, Polly Fritchey and I would go sit with him. He lost all interest in politics but held forth until the end on art and archeology. He was a man of eclectic taste and talents and truly one of a kind. Washington lost a memorable character when he died.

Dick had known W. Averell Harriman, the former governor of New York, presidential candidate, and diplomat, for some time. Harriman, the son of a railroad baron, served as secretary of commerce under Harry Truman but is best known for his role in key diplomatic moments during World War II and the Cold War. He served as ambassador to the Soviet Union and Great Britain and took on special diplomatic missions during the Kennedy and Johnson administrations. Averell's second wife, Marie Norton Whitney, died unexpectedly of a heart attack at the age of sixty-seven on September 26, 1970.

Many years earlier, during World War II, Averell had an affair with Pamela Digby Churchill, the young wife of Randolph, who was the son of Winston Churchill. After that marriage ended, Pamela was involved with many prominent and powerful men, including legendary CBS journalist Edward R. Murrow, John Hay "Jock" Whitney, Prince Aly Khan, Alfonso de Portago, Gianni Agnelli, and Baron Elie de Rothschild. She is now viewed as one of the greatest courtesans of her time. I often watched in utter amazement as enormously powerful men of all ages simply melted in her presence into pools of helpless goo. Pamela was a good-looking woman but not movie-star beautiful. But she made the most of her looks. She had one of the best facelifts I have ever seen. She was bone thin. A story about her once described her as a bit chubby, and she was so stung that she just stopped eating. She served delicious food at her dinner parties but only sipped on a cup of bouillon herself. I once asked Dick why she had such power over men. He believed it was her ability to focus intensely and exclusively on the person to whom she was speaking so that he believed no one else in the world existed at that moment.

Pamela became a good friend. We were close in age and both English, and with some reservations, I have never been one to judge another. Pamela's many romances were simply part of who she was. She enticed Leland Hayward, the Broadway producer, away from his wife, Nancy "Slim" Hawks, and remained married to him until his death on March 18, 1971. After Leland's death, some say literally the day after, though that must be exaggerated, she arranged to run into Averell Harriman at a dinner party at Kay Graham's house. They immediately picked up where they had left off and married on September 27, 1971.

Marie Harriman had purchased an extraordinary Vincent van Gogh painting titled *White Roses* in 1930, and it hung for years in their Georgetown house. It is an oil painting with masses of white roses against a green background. Van Gogh painted it during his final weeks at the asylum in Saint-Rémy in 1890. It is fair to say that it is priceless.

The painting apparently was always intended for the National Gallery of Art, but Pamela was reluctant to let it go too soon. J. Carter Brown convinced Pamela to donate it to the National Gallery in memory of Averell. The gift was announced in 1989, but the painting continued to appear periodically at her house. Carter arranged for a flawless copy to be painted. He negotiated a deal that allowed Pamela to take back the original from time to time. When the original was hanging in the National Gallery or on tour, she used the copy. I gave up trying to tell the difference, though she and Carter insisted they could. My untutored eye never could see a single distinguishing characteristic between the copy and the original.

Pamela and Carter spent a great deal of time together after Averell's death. It was a relationship of convenience. She gave him entrée to the great houses of Britain, and he guided her in the art world. They were tremendously good fun as traveling companions. She had houses in Barbados, New York, and Idaho, and we were frequent guests. We once accompanied them on a cruise. Pamela chartered a yacht, and we sailed from Istanbul to Rhodes. She arranged for a Mercedes sedan to follow us down the coast so we could sightsee in comfort. It was beyond luxurious.

Pamela had her flaws. She was very short and abrupt with her household staff and with Averell's daughters. I found that unnecessary and probably counterproductive. But she was a very generous friend to me. One day we were visiting in Barbados, and Claudette Colbert, the actress, invited us to lunch. One of her houseguests was Slim Hawks Hayward, who by then had remarried and was known as Lady Keith. To this day I have no idea if Claudette knew or remembered that Pamela had stolen away Slim's husband. I can report they both behaved impeccably and never let on they had shared a spouse.

Pamela became a U.S. citizen the year she married Averell, and she later became a major fund-raiser in Democratic Party politics. She introduced a rather obscure young governor from Arkansas to the Washington elites. When Bill Clinton became president in 1993, he named her ambassador to France. Pam served with great distinction until her death from a cerebral hemorrhage while swimming in the pool at the Ritz in Paris. She had great personal discipline and swam virtually every day.

My dear friend Dorcas Hardin, who operated a high-end boutique in Georgetown for years, had a lengthy love affair with Paul Mellon, one of the wealthiest men in the country. It was an open secret. He had a direct phone line installed in her living room. When it rang, everyone fell silent because we knew it was Paul calling. I was told by a lawyer who had some insight into Mellon's affairs that he could never get a divorce because his estate was so complicated. His second wife, Bunny, got caught up in John Edwards's campaign-expense scandal when his aides used her money to hide Edwards's pregnant mistress during the 2008 presidential campaign. Dick and I played Scrabble with Dorcas and Paul at the home he kept in Washington to house part of his private art collection.

Dorcas had impeccable taste and always dressed beautifully. One day she tried to give me a brand-new coat. Paul did not like it, so she would never wear it again. She had a lovely disposition and was so charming. Her house was delightfully attractive, and I don't believe she had any interest in politics at all. One of her frequent guests and my friend was Harry Covington, a partner in the law firm Covington & Burling. He regaled me with tales of the escapades of New York and Washington socialites who used to cavort together in a most outrageous manner in Philadelphia hotels. These hilarious tales gave me a whole new perspective on some of the pillars of society.

Dorcas was very discreet about her relationship with Paul until much later in life. One day while eating lunch with me at Listrani's, an Italian family-style restaurant in the Palisades section of Washington, she talked loudly about the relationship while everyone in the restaurant listened. She had become quite deaf. It seemed impossibly rude to hush her, and by then no one cared.

My friendship with Sandra Day O'Connor, which continues to this day, allowed me a look into the very private lives of Supreme Court justices. Of all the public figures in Washington, perhaps none are more discreet than the justices. Sandra had been friends with Chief Justice William Rehnquist since their days at Stanford Law School. The chief talked a lot about his happy days at her family ranch and how like her mother she was.

Her husband was another Stanford Law School student, John J. O'Connor III. John was a wonderful raconteur and storyteller who gave up a thriving law practice in Arizona to move to Washington when Sandra became the first female member of the Supreme Court. I believe it always bothered her that her husband made such an enormous professional sacrifice for her. He later developed Alzheimer's disease. We knew something was wrong when John could no longer remember the punch lines of his marvelous jokes. As his disease became worse, she wanted to leave the Court to care for him, but resigning from the Supreme Court is a highly political and delicate matter that is not done lightly.

The chief justice was diagnosed with thyroid cancer in 2004, but he was determined to fight it and stay on the Court. Sandra felt she could not resign if Rehnquist was going to leave. So her decision was very much up in the air. One morning in 2005, after the Court had recessed for the term, she called me and instructed me to find a fourth for bridge and meet her at the Court in an hour so we could play with Bill Rehnquist, who had returned to work but was still quite sick. Sandra called me three or four times during that period to play bridge at the Court with the chief. It was always last minute and always to distract the chief for an hour or so. It was a challenge to find a fourth on such short notice. I could not call a lawyer or anyone who might have any conflict with the Court. On this day, I wracked my brain and came up with retired admiral Taz Shephard. Tazewell T. Shephard Jr., a career naval officer who was decorated for bravery during World War II, had served as a naval aide to JFK in the White House. I had to find someone appropriate on short notice and knew Taz would be discreet. His wife never forgave me for inviting him and not her. While we played cards, the chief suddenly announced that he had decided to stay on the Court for another session. His wife, Nan, had died in 1991 of ovarian cancer, and I suspect his work was even more important to him than ever because it gave him a reason to get up in the morning.

As we left his chambers and walked down the corridor to her chambers, Sandra turned to me and said, "Well, if he is going to stay, I can resign." She announced her intent to resign on July 1, 2005. Bill Rehnquist lost his battle with cancer on September 3, 2005, so President George W. Bush had to make two appointments to the Supreme Court. That was never the intent, but fate made it so.

Sandra Day O'Connor was acutely aware of her role in Bush's election in 2000 and, I believe, always felt conflicted about it. The outcome of the presidential election of 2000 was so close that it hinged on the results from Florida. The Republican-appointed majority on the Court stopped any attempt to recount the votes in the state of Florida and declared the Republican candidate, George W. Bush, the victor over Democratic candidate Vice President Albert Gore in December 2000. Sandra went along with the Republican majority, but I believe it bothered her greatly. Dick and I had been part of a small group that brought potluck supper and played bridge on Friday nights at the Alibi Club with the chief, Sandra, Justices Stephen Breyer and Anthony Kennedy, and a few other friends. Sandra has been a wonderful, loyal friend for thirty-one years. She remained active after leaving the Court. Her husband died in 2009. That same year she founded iCivics, a website with educational video games and other interactive materials aiming to teach young Americans how government works and how the individual can be part of it. It is fun, productive, and free to use. Sandra was an elected public official before becoming a judge and has a former politician's acute awareness of the importance of a participatory democracy. She tells me the educational program is the most important thing she has ever done.

My husband kept one more secret in the last years of his life. In 1993, we learned he had multiple myeloma, a cancer of the plasma cells, the white blood cells responsible for producing antibodies. Dick did not want anyone to know. He would not even tell his own son. He swore me to secrecy. He just did not want people constantly asking him about his health. Fortunately the disease and its treatment did not interfere with his living a full life until the final year before his death in October 2002 at the age of eighty-nine. We traveled a lot in those last years, both with and without the family. I even got him to the Arctic Circle and eastern Russia, although he preferred a warm climate.

He had always vowed never to write a book. He took his pledge to keep the nation's secrets seriously and suffered greatly for his commitment. But he changed his mind after the end of the Cold War. There had been a great deal of misreporting and misinterpretation of events. He very much wanted to make certain that the history of the science and technology evolution at the agency was told properly and to do his bit to set the record straight. He recruited William Hood, a former OSS and CIA officer who became a novelist after retiring from the agency, to help him. With his customary focus, he worked on the book every day. At first, he dictated to me, and I faxed the pages to Bill. Then he wrote his own material out longhand, and I faxed the pages to Bill. Dick, like many men of his generation, never got the hang of technology for his own personal use. The book, *A Look over My Shoulder: A Life in the Central Intelligence Agency*, was published in 2003 after his death. I asked Henry Kissinger to write the foreword, and he delivered a gracious and excellent manuscript within twenty-four hours. Henry has been unfailingly supportive and helpful through the years, and I am most grateful to him. I am very glad Dick wrote the book. It was honest and enlightening to anyone who wanted to understand the motives of and pressures on the Cold Warriors. In a small way, it offsets the distorted view of the "rogue elephant" portrayed by congressional investigative committees in the 1970s.

The lead up to the U.S. invasion of Iraq throughout 2002 attracted a great deal of comment in the press, and our phone rang constantly with journalists, particularly reporters from the British Broadcasting Corporation (BBC), eager to talk to Dick about the unfolding events and the presence of weapons of mass destruction in Iraq. I thought talking about the region to reporters might distract him from his illness, but he refused all the calls. I finally asked him why, and he said, "Because I can no longer remember what is classified." He feared he might make a mistake and disclose too much. His memory may have gotten shaky, but his unflinching patriotism never wavered.

After Dick's death in October 2002, I returned to the competitive bridge network for distraction and because none of the avid bridge players had any idea who I was or cared. It was a strange comfort to be with people who did not know me. And through the years, many of them became friendly acquaintances. It kept me from crying all the time because no one mentioned Dick and my loss. I did return to the agency and disgraced myself by bursting into tears when they showed me Dick's portrait in the office of Director George Tenet. But I think they understood.

I also had to sort through his papers before donating them to Georgetown University. It was not a simple process. Dick had left classified materials at the agency when he left, but there was still a mountain of paper, correspondence, and documents to be vetted. Dean Robert L. Galucci of the School of Foreign Service sponsored a symposium on Dick's years as director in April 2008, but, of course, they asked me to get the speakers! It was heartening to hear leading figures from the era, including former secretary of state Henry Kissinger, General Brent Scowcroft, and historian Michael Beschloss, give Dick his due as one of the major figures in the history of U.S. intelligence. George Tenet shared with me his thoughts on Dick's legacy. The passage of time has shed a great deal of light on, and given great insight into, Dick's behavior, and George says that Dick's legacy lives on in the agency's commitment to the importance of collecting data. Indeed, the Navy Seals could never have found and killed Osama bin Laden were it not for years of careful analysis and data collection by the CIA. And even though we live in a far more open era, George says there is still a need for secrecy for the same reasons Dick always cited: to protect the identities and safety of agency operatives and foreign nationals who help the United States.

Dick had never been particularly interested in children. He did not dislike children; they were just not part of his life. He was studiously neutral on the subject. But he came to love my young, and they loved him. It gave me great satisfaction to see him evolve into a happy family man and become a valued mentor to each one separately. It enriched his life as well as theirs. They enjoyed teasing him about his Depression-era foibles.

Some years ago, Dick inscribed a photograph to me with the words "To my dear beloved copperhead. Much love, my joy, the light of my life." It was a sweet and deeply personal inscription. I felt the same way about him. I look back over my life with few regrets. I still wish I had been able to end my first marriage without hurting my husband and children, but I know I did the right thing. I will never regret marrying Richard Helms. We had a joyous partnership.

Change now happens so quickly and is such an accepted part of modern life that I often wonder if people realize how the past century has profoundly transformed the lives and opportunities for girls and women in Western, developed countries. I grew up a protected girl on a farm with a Victorian-era ethos constraining even my thoughts and aspirations. Little girls were expected to grow up to be wives and mothers. Divorce was difficult. Women were second-class citizens. In my lifetime, I have seen one woman become prime minister of Great Britain and another run as a serious candidate for the presidency of the United States. Women have choices now, and sometimes, my grandchildren tell me, maybe too many choices.

My daughters had fulfilling professional lives in addition to their roles as wives and mothers. Today I have one grandchild who is the openly gay mother of twins and another who is the single mother of a biracial child. We communicate by e-mail and visit all the time. Would my own parents have understood their lifestyles? When I was told about my gay grandchild, I had only one question: Do I need to march? How fortunate we are to live in times when every girl and boy can live fully and freely.

I felt compelled to realize my own potential as best I could. I raised my children, took care of Dick, and also had my own life. For a woman of my era, I was lucky in my partner. Dick viewed and treated me as his equal. He allowed me to pursue my own interests. Young women today would cringe at the idea of needing permission from a husband, but for my generation, that was the best one could expect. The second half of my life allowed me to indulge my love of books, art, travel, and people. Had I focused more, I suspect I may have had more impact. I never changed the world. But I did enjoy life and still do. I still read several books every week. Every part of my house is covered with stacks of books, which my children have despaired of ever bringing under control. But those stacks of books are a manifestation of my interests and my curiosity and an insatiable appetite for knowledge.

I look back with great satisfaction on my role in enlightening American housewives about the toxins in everyday household goods at Concern. I supported important institutions to further beauty and art, like the Freer Gallery of Art, and I tried to show my appreciation of Washington by donating and helping my daughter Lindsay create two libraries in DC Prep charter schools. When they were in the planning stage, I was distressed to learn that there was not enough money for a library. To me, nothing is more important. We inscribed this saying in each library: "My hope is you will always be surrounded by good books. . . . My dream is you will learn to love them." A love of reading is one of the greatest gifts one can give to another. I work under the leadership of Mary Oakes Smith to bring Iraqi professors to American universities, such as Stanford and MIT, for a year. The Iraqi women who have participated in the program have all been memorable and remarkable in what they have overcome to get their education in Iraq. And I must note that I was particularly proud to campaign door-to-door in Pennsylvania, a key swing state, for Barack Obama, the first African American president, in 2008 when I was eighty-five years old. I wore a sweatshirt that read, "Old White Women for Obama."

In my life, I met presidents, senators, kings and queens, and some of the most interesting and accomplished people who populated public life and many other walks of life in the second half of the twentieth century. I lived through major moments in history: World War II, the extraordinary postwar baby boom, the Cold War, and Watergate and its aftermath. I lived long enough to see the baby boomers, my young, become "old" themselves, to see the Cold War end and a more insidious and challenging war against Islamic terrorism begin, and to witness remarkable cultural changes that will allow a little girl born in 2012 to achieve her dreams, whatever they may be. I come away from those experiences convinced that there is no substitute for good character and sound judgment in private and public life and certain of the folly of denying full rights and freedom to entire groups of people, whether they be women and girls or people of color or gay people or any other ethnic or religious minority.

I have a lifetime of memories. I remember dancing in the arms of Dick Helms, my one true love; the wordless joy at the birth of each child; the dazzling debates over this or that war, the merits of this or that public policy, and the motive of this or that politician during decades of dinner parties. Yet I do not live in the past. Arthritis forced me to hang up my tennis racket. Age does take its toll. But I still play championship bridge. I have outlived my beloved husband as well as many wonderful friends. I will always miss them, and living with those losses is part of my life and the inevitable side effect of longevity. But I have never lost my zest for life, my appetite for knowledge, and my enjoyment of new people and places. I can still lose myself with utter pleasure in the pages of a good book. My social life remains busy and active. My four children live within blocks of me. They and their spouses and children are in and out of my house at all hours. Every year I go over to the CIA headquarters in McLean, Virginia, and attend the briefing held for former directors and their spouses. When she comes to town, Sandra Day O'Connor still contacts me one as of her many friends in Washington, and she still endearingly bosses me around. What a great joy her friendship has been. She invited me to share the celebration of the thirtieth anniversary of her appointment to the Supreme Court, and I spent an hour and a half alone with her and the three other female justices—Ruth Bader Ginsburg, Sonia Sotomayor, and Elena Kagan—before the ceremony. What a privilege for me to be in the company of such talented, accomplished women. I inhale the newspapers in the morning and pay close attention to world events, often marveling at those who fail to learn from history. I love Washington, and it has been very kind to me. The little girl who grew up on a farm in Maldon looks back at almost nine decades of life and marvels at her good fortune and at her full and interesting life. It is what I always wanted: a life of my own, shared with those I love.

ACKNOWLEDGMENTS

This is the story of my life, and I drew upon my own memory, my personal papers, and other documents to confirm times, places, events, and other details. I tried to be accurate in every way, and any error is inadvertent. I do hope readers understand that this story is told from my point of view, and perception often varies with the individual. Not everyone will agree with my interpretation of events, but this is how I experienced them.

To refresh memories, I consulted with family members who were both supportive and hilariously funny in recalling moments from the past. I chose to keep some of those stories in the family! I thank each of them for convincing me to write this book and for their love and encouragement throughout the writing process. I would be remiss if I did not extend special thanks to my brother Leonard Ratcliff, who generously shared his memories of our family and childhood in Maldon.

I hope the reader comes away with a better understanding of Iran and its rich culture. David Ignatius, the *Washington Post* columnist and son of my dear friend Nan, persuaded me to write about Iran again. To make certain my account of the history of Iran and Islam was accurate, I consulted with Shaul Bakash, Marian and Henry Precht, and Golnaz Samii. Goli was particularly helpful in explaining the evolution of Iranian films. Bruce O'Brien, a noted medieval specialist, helped me with data on the history of my home-town of Maldon. Helen Romness found the photograph of the flood of the prefab housing in Rochester, Minnesota, at the time of my youngest child's birth. Gregory Craig kindly helped ensure the accuracy of my account of the government's legal case against my husband. Former director of central intelligence George Tenet was generous with his time and thoughts on Dick Helms's legacy in intelligence. David Robarge, the CIA's remarkable historian, helped me understand and reconstruct some old operations that have since been declassified. Joan Shorey succinctly summed up the role of Concern, and Richard Viets reminded me of the "good old days" of social Washington. Burton Gerber, a highly respected intelligence officer, has helped me in numerous ways. And finally, I thank Chris Black, an inspiring professional who was a great pleasure to work with. Each offered valuable insights. I deeply appreciate their help.

INDEX

ABOUT THE AUTHORS

Cynthia Helms is the widow of Richard Helms, former director of central intelligence for the United States. They were married for thirty-four years. She grew up on a farm in Maldon, England, and served as one of the original Boat Crew Wrens during World War II. She came to the United States after the war with her first husband, a physician. Throughout her life, she has been involved in many civic and charitable causes. She was the host of Radio Smithsonian and a founder of Concern, Inc., a groundbreaking environmental organization aimed at women, and served on the board of the World Resources Institute for fifteen years. She serves as an honorary trustee of the Freer Gallery of Art and Arthur M. Sackler Museum and the National Fund for the U.S. Diplomatic Garden, as well as on the boards of the Pamela Harriman Foreign Service Fellowships and the Iraq Women's Fellowship Foundation. She is the author of *An Ambassador's Wife in Iran* (1981) and *Favourite Stories from Persia* (1982).

Chris Black is a writer and communications consultant. She was a political reporter for more than thirty years and worked at the *Boston Globe* and as a White House and congressional correspondent for the Cable News Network (CNN). She is a native of Massachusetts and lives in Washington, DC, and Marion, Massachusetts, with her husband, B. Jay Cooper.